Infinite West

Infinite West

TRAVELS IN SOUTH DAKOTA

by Fraser Harrison

SOUTH DAKOTA STATE HISTORICAL SOCIETY

PRESS Pierre

This publication is funded, in part, by the
Great Plains Education Foundation, Inc., Aberdeen, S.Dak.

Library of Congress Cataloging-in-Publication Data
Harrison, Fraser.
Infinite West : travels in South Dakota / by Fraser Harrison.
p. cm.
Includes index.
ISBN 978-0-9846505-8-3
1. South Dakota—Description and travel. 2. Harrison, Fraser—Travel—
South Dakota. I. South Dakota State Historical Society Press. II. Title.
F651.H37 2012
917.83—dc23
2012021255

The paper in this book meets the guidelines for permanence and
durability of the committee on Production Guidelines for Book Longevity
of the Council on Library Resources.

Text and cover design by Rich Hendel

Please visit our website at www.sdshspress.com

Printed in the United States of America

16 15 14 13 12   1 2 3 4 5

To my dear friend Alvin Handelman

Contents

Acknowledgments

I am grateful to the Authors' Foundation who provided crucial financial assistance with my travel. I am also grateful to my mother, Kathleen Fraser Harrison, who generously contributed to my expenses.

I am grateful to the staff of the South Dakota State Historical Society Press, especially Nancy Tystad Koupal, who agreed to publish the book, and Martyn Beeny, who edited the text, enhancing it in the process.

My visit to Harrison, South Dakota, would not have been possible without the unstinting help of Steve Hayes, pastor of the town's two churches. Steve introduced me to the residents whose voices are heard in the chapter devoted to Harrison: Mabell De Jong, Aletha and Ted Maas, Cecelia Oakland, Char and Richard Uilenberg, and Stan Hoekman. I thank them for talking to me so willingly and openly. I am only sorry that Stan Hoekman did not live to see the publication of this book.

I am grateful to Peter Larson at the Black Hills Institute of Geological Research in Hill City, who took the time to show me his astounding collection of fossils.

Alvin Handelman, to whom this book is dedicated, has been my intrepid companion on several journeys into the infinite West; I thank him and his wife Carol Holly for their unfailing hospitality, which has made Northfield, Minnesota, my favorite American destination outside South Dakota. Another reason for visiting Northfield has been the friendship shown to me by Riki and Eric Nelson, Barbara and Jonathan Hill, and Ellen and Ray Cox. I also owe thanks to my friend Steve Polansky, who invited me to Northfield in the first place. And I thank Bonnie Blodgett for her invigorating company and encouragement.

My family and I would never have made our first, momentous expedition to South Dakota without the instigation of my remarkable wife, Sally; for that, and much else, I'm grateful. I offer this book as an affectionate souvenir of the trip to the other members of our party: Tilly and

Jack, their friend Jessica Widdows, and our friend, the celebrated motor-ist, Nigel Hamlin-Wright.

Finally, I would like to salute my splendid grandchildren, Douglas, Arlo, and Dilys, even if, as a travel writer, I cannot be grateful to them, because they always make me hurry home.

Infinite West

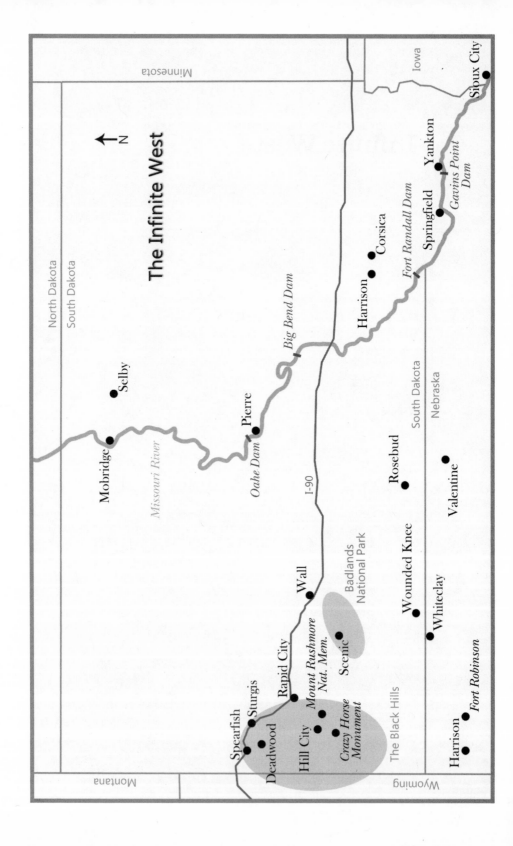

The Infinite West

Introduction

This book is an homage to South Dakota, which has been in my thoughts, on and off, since I made the first of many visits twenty years ago in 1992. Over the two decades, my preoccupation has roused a variety of feelings, from infatuation to occasional abhorrence, but I have never lost a kind of yearning for the place, and there has hardly been a month when I have not been laying plans for yet another return. I am beguiled by its intrinsic qualities—its history, landscape, character—but the hold it has over me also derives from a more mysterious source, located a great distance away: my childhood.

When I was a small boy, my conceptual map of the world was dotted with fabled places that belonged to no particular country. These included the White Man's Grave (a jungle in West Africa where my father had fought in World War II), the other jungle in Africa where Babar the Elephant ruled over his kingdom, Canada (quite a small, snow-bound place where my cousin Donald did his exploring), and Kashmir (where I mistakenly believed a school friend of my mother had been scalped by bandits). Like a medieval map, it depicted familiar places as far greater in size than little-known ones. Thus, Great Britain occupied a very large space, but it was in turn dominated by Liverpool, the world's premier city, and Stackpole, a village of fifty souls over which my grandfather ruled somewhat less benevolently than Babar ruled over his kingdom. Occupying almost as large a space as Great Britain was the United States (which I thought of as "America"). Geographically this was an interesting country, for it had no coasts and consisted entirely of the landscapes that made up the Wild West. (West of nothing, since there was nothing to its east.) According to my childhood projection, "America" was a continent bereft of cities and composed entirely of prairies, mountains, colored deserts, and mighty rivers; it was the topography of the buffalo, coyote, creaking covered wagon, cavalry patrols, and Indians on the warpath. My "America" was not so much a place as a story.

Most Americans, certainly those under the age of fifty, do not realize how deeply the myth of the West penetrated the imagination of the British child during the 1940s and 1950s. It is no exaggeration to say that every small boy, and not a few small girls, in the Britain of those years went through a cowboy phase. There wasn't a toyshop in the land that failed to stock cowboy hats and cap pistols; not a park or a playground where some kid wasn't filling another full of lead.

I can't remember a time when the West was not part of my imaginative landscape, and the fact that my father, in common with many Englishmen of *his* generation, was a great fan of westerns must have made the frontier familiar terrain even before I began to dream of it. One of the first children's programs to be broadcast by the British Broadcasting Corporation (BBC) in the early 1950s was *Hank the Cowboy*, a cartoon parody of the western movie, though that was not how I viewed it. Hank, a garrulous teller of tall tales with a droopy moustache, was forever in contention with Mexican Pete, who was so tough he shaved with a broken bottle and sang a song to underline his villainy: "I'm Mexican Pete zee bad bandeet." Hank's other perennial enemy was Dirty Face, the Indian chief, who also had a song: "Me Big Chief Dirty Face/Me always in disgrace." These appalling stereotypes seem hardly credible today, but they gave hundreds of thousands of small children in this country their introduction to the Wild West.

Later came the more orthodox adventures of Hopalong Cassidy, a character played by the grey-haired William Boyd dressed in a black cowboy costume. These were the days of black and white television, but "Hoppie" was a monochromatic character in other respects too, for he belonged to the generation of heroes whose virtues were never compromised. He was just plain good, and once you'd said that you'd said it all; he righted wrongs, protected the weak, stood up to bullies, and was as dull as ditchwater.

Much more thrilling was the Lone Ranger. Whoever devised the credit sequence with the Masked Man and Tonto as they raced along the trail to the strains of the William Tell overture was a genius. "Return with us now to those thrilling days of yesteryear," said a thrilling voice introducing every episode, "when from out of the west with the speed of light and a hearty 'Hi-yo Silver!' the Lone Ranger rides again!" Did anyone know why he wore his mask, which was more of a fashion accessory than a disguise since it hardly veiled him? Did anyone care? And why was he the *lone* Ranger? In truth, the excitement was pretty well over once the Tell overture and the credits had come to an end, for the Masked Man belonged to the same genus of worthy hero as Hopalong Cassidy, and you were never convinced, as you were with Sherlock Holmes or Robin Hood, that his powers were really greater than the villain's. The result of every shoot-out was a foregone conclusion; he couldn't lose because he was the hero. You knew that his triumph over evil was as ritualized as the penultimate line uttered at the end of every episode by some grateful but bewildered character: "Who was that masked man?"

When I was a child my grandmother took me to what she called "the pictures." She tolerated or perhaps shared my taste for bloodthirsty costume dramas, and it was probably with her that I saw my first western. But these movies and television shows only enriched and confirmed what we children already knew and seemed always to have known. The Wild West, its costumes, props, stock characters, basic plots, and, most vivid of all, its landscapes were part of the cultural heritage my friends and I had acquired at birth and, with the possible exception of Sherwood Forest, nothing rivaled it as an imaginary locale.

The theatre where I acted out my frontier fantasies was the back yard of our suburban house in Liverpool, which comprised a modest apron of mown grass surrounded on two sides by flower beds and bounded on the third side by a cinder path that marked the frontier between my mother's civilized horticulture and the wilderness of my father's vegetable patch. At the side of the house was a smaller lawn that was kept in continual shade by a lime tree and a high sandstone wall. I never took any interest in the garden and its plants, nor did my parents encourage me to do so. I never had my own little flower bed or vegetable patch, nor was I assigned any chores. My father never asked me to mow the lawn or rake leaves; my mother never showed me the flowers that were her passion or taught me their names. As a result the back yard was an open range for the imagination, unspoiled by any chore or responsibility, or any meaning rooted in the ordinary actuality of back yards.

I have a memory—one of those memories that must sum up in a single vignette a hundred repetitions of the same activity—of riding my trusty horse (Hi-yo Silver!) through the dank canyon beneath our lime tree and then pausing, as if on a bluff, to survey the lawn, now metamorphosed into prairie, that lay beneath me. I could see the sagebrush, the tumbleweeds, the cacti holding up their branches in surrender, the herds of numberless buffalo, and above it all white clouds rolling like wagons across a blue sky dotted with circling vultures. I could smell the dust; I could hear the cavalry's jingling harnesses; I could sense the Indians lurking treacherously just below the skyline. It was a moment of imaginative transubstantiation that only small children experience: the yard was the prairie; the prairie was the yard. Thus, the Wild West was as real to me as its alternative reality, the lawn on which my father labored with his manual mower.

Since I was an only child, the gang was an institution much to my liking, and both Robin Hood and cowboys and Indians had the great virtue of being games for gangs. Until my ninth summer I belonged to a long-established gang, whose members were three boys and a girl, exotically named Leonore. We were ordinary suburban children, and there was nothing about our games that could not be observed in thousands of middle-class yards all over the country. We chased around each other's lawns in rudimentary western costume, slapping our buttocks to indicate galloping at breakneck speed, and firing whatever weaponry we possessed. My mother would not allow us to bring firearms to the table, and, in the manner of a sheriff cleaning up a lawless town, she would disarm us at the dining room door, collecting a lethal heap of six-guns and rifles. For the purposes of our games, Leonore went under the feisty sobriquet of Cactus Kate (rather ploddingly, I called myself Buffalo Bill), and she seemed to enjoy our perpetual shoot-outs with their histrionic deaths and immediate resurrections. Sometimes, she allowed herself to be roped to a tree while we whooped round her. When her patience ran out, she would simply untie herself and, without apparent rancor, walk home.

As I grew older, I began to boost my knowledge of the West by reading comics, magazines, and books printed in western-style typefaces on spongy paper and illustrated with lurid pictures, whose colors ran as freely as the blood in the gun duels they depicted. I studied these books with a child's unquestioning, all-absorbing scholarship and accepted as truth everything I read. The biographies of Jesse James, Billy the Kid, Cochise, Sitting Bull, Custer, and Buffalo Bill were subjects in which I became a juvenile expert.

One of the peculiarities of my generation's schooling was that we were taught nothing about our own immediate past. I studied history for twelve years, and was well taught, but I came away knowing far more about the Roman testudo, rotten boroughs, and the dissolution of the monasteries than I did about the war in which my father had risked his life. I taught myself more about Geronimo than I learned at school about Hitler's generals, and I could not have told you the year of D-Day, though it was the year of my birth. The official silence of the curriculum over World War II was matched by the silence maintained by our fathers. This was only natural, I suppose. They wanted to close that grim chapter and move forward; they wanted to recover the normality that had prevailed during their pre-war childhood (a grail that forever eluded them). My father, who died in 2000, probably spoke more than most of his personal military experience, but he never talked about the war in general or explained its main strategies to me.

My father's attitude to the war and, indeed, all things military was always a puzzle to me. He played an honorable but hardly bloodstained role, in that he served in West Africa—the "White Man's Grave" of my map—where he contracted several tropical diseases and was lucky to escape with his life. He hated the army that had taken him away from his new bride and burgeoning career, while submitting him to all sorts of miseries and privations. And yet, ever after, he retained a paradoxical and schoolboyish delight in martial ceremony. The lobby of our small Liverpool house was hung with his collection of swords; and once he had retired, he amused himself by painting military uniforms. This unexpected side of him was also expressed in his taste for movies and TV shows; he loved westerns and would watch almost anything in the genre, especially if it starred John Wayne, his model of manliness, but his particular favorites were films showing the exploits of the United States cavalry—in other words, war films.

These puzzles did not concern me as a child. I enjoyed the fact that my fantasies and my father's overlapped, allowing me to slide without friction from my world to his. For the most part, his world was mysterious and unimaginable to me. What on earth did he do all day once he had caught the bus in his suit and bowler hat? What was an "office"? We enjoyed watching westerns together, but perhaps we were sharing more than a common taste. Perhaps the war film in its cowboy version provided a kind of therapy whereby our two generations, the ex-soldiers and their sons, could come to terms with the recent past. The bloodshed and sudden death that usually went unmentioned could be brought into our sitting room and contemplated with relative tranquility. We were able to witness battles that were safely removed to a distant time and place, fought between mythological enemies in a war that had become a storybook convention, as harmless (to us) as cops and robbers.

Apart from following the precedent set by my father, I don't know why the West took hold of my imagination in the way it did. In their civilian forms, so to speak, I disliked many of the elements that made up the classic western scenario. For example, I took no pleasure in riding horses even though, at the height of my cowboy mania, I was given the chance to ride ponies on my grandfather's farm. Unfortunately, it only taught me to fear horses, and, worse still, I felt foolish as I bobbed precariously in my saddle, wearing my cowboy hat, sheriff's star, and gun belt. Fantasy could not prevail over the ignominy of being led by the groom assigned to teach me, a kindly German who had been a prisoner of war on the farm and addressed me as "Frizzer." This was not how the Masked Man had thundered across the plains in those thrilling days of yesteryear.

Nor did I learn to love firearms. As part of our rehearsal for National Service, thankfully abandoned before I was called up, we were taught how to shoot air rifles at my prep school (grades three to seven). Although my cowboy games largely consisted of shooting Indians, or men in black hats, with ricocheting bullets—peeowang!—and biting the dust myself in theatrical death throes, I could never connect those epic encounters with lying on coconut matting and picking out the bull's-eye on a cardboard target with an air rifle.

At my prep school, a Dotheboys Hall in darkest Wales devoted to beating into its pupils the principles of Christianity and the Boy Scout movement, I learned to hate many things, among them camping and its attendant discomforts.[1] I hated blanket beds, leaking tents, burnt food in billycans, and jolly songs round the jolly campfire. The school's program of character-building had a contradictory effect on me. I did not dream of lying under the stars on my bedroll, my Stetson over my face; I aspired instead to be the kind of cowboy who occupied a feather bed in the town's hotel and had his back soaped by dancing girls. The dude ranch was made for me, but despite scorning the discomforts of life on the open range, I remained enthralled by the Wild West and the western movie for most of my childhood. In adolescence a still more powerful fantasy took me in its grip, that of becoming a writer, or rather literary sensation modeled on F. Scott Fitzgerald (hardly a frontier archetype), but in some essential corner of my being, I was always loyal to the childhood cowboy who had slapped his backside as he galloped hell-for-leather down the lonesome trail toward his father's greenhouse.

I suspect that my parents, like many of their generation, faced a crisis of values after the war. As middle-class Conservatives they held little sympathy for the dominant values system that emerged during the immediate post-war years of the Labour government. They did not share the socialist-inspired vision of a welfare state that was then under construction. My father, a Thatcherite before the term was invented, believed in a politics that put profit first, while my mother, more nostalgically inclined, looked back to what, for her, had been the elegant, affluent days of the 1930s.

Insofar as my parents brought me up to any definable set of values, it was to be polite, well-spoken, and nicely presented; in short, to be a "little gentleman." They urged me to be an exemplary representative

---

1. Dotheboys Hall featured in Charles Dickens's novel *The Life and Adventures of Nicholas Nickleby*. Its headmaster was the one-eyed Wackford Squeers, who starved and whipped his pupils.

of my class, a class that felt itself to be under siege. The class hierarchy that had prevailed until the war was breaking down under the pressure of new democratic forces, and my parents found the change disconcerting. They were not snobs, but rather people who clung to the familiar, and what they had known for most of their lives was a social hierarchy in which everyone's rank was clearly demarcated. They yearned for the bourgeois dream of a fixed social structure that made it possible for the economy to function smoothly, allowing the rich to stay rich, the ambitious and hard-working (my father) to do well for themselves, and the poor to remain uncomplainingly poor. They nursed a picture of normality that was essentially a postponed version of the 1930s without the depression and the threat of war, and, strange to say, I believe they found an embodiment of this fantasy in the western movie.

It is the measure of a rich mythology that it inspires all sorts of applications, many of them obscure. My mother was not a western fan—she tolerated the films for my father's sake—but whether she acknowledged it or not, the frontier town conjured up by Hollywood chimed with her vision of a decent society. The western had its radical side, but its presentation of small-town life was generally nostalgic and conservative, affirming many of my parents' dearest-held convictions. The men tipped their hats to ladies, addressed them as "Ma'am," opened doors for them, and understood that it was their duty to provide and protect. Boys did not need telling twice to wear clean shirts and polish their boots, and young men were trained to be respectful of their elders, calling them "Sir." These practices might have been enforced in a rough-and-ready fashion, but they symbolized the fragile civilization of picket fences and poke bonnets that was at risk when the lawless men in black hats rode into town. It is not surprising that, as a child, I instinctively felt at home in these pretend towns, for in their way they were a realization of my parents' ideal town—a dream of humdrum normality, which was only natural to a generation that had just emerged from the hideous abnormalities of war.

One great distinction lay between my parents' code and that of the frontier. In Dodge City, or wherever, the preacher was by and large a respected, if occasionally comic figure, and his church was an important feature of the community, but I doubt my parents knew the name of the vicar of their parish, and they certainly never set foot in his church. They were not atheists in any formal, intellectual sense; they were simply irreligious. Neither had been brought up in a family tradition of church-going or belief, and I don't recall that my parents or grandparents ever attended a church service that was not a christening, wedding, or funeral. In this respect, they were no different from many of their neighbors and friends. Yet despite their secular way of life, my parents were induced by the mores of their class to send me to a private boarding school, referred to above, which like most institutions of its kind offered an education that was faith-based. Distracted by the beauty of the school's location (a Victorian house set in its own extensive grounds complete with lake) and the rugged wholesomeness of its headmaster, my parents probably did not fully grasp the fervency with which the school's Christian regime was imposed on its luckless pupils.

Our headmaster led us in prayers every morning and evening, took matins and evensong every Sunday, and instructed us in Bible studies every Monday, but his efforts did not have the effect of bringing Christ into my heart; in fact, they had the contrary effect. I enjoyed listening to the Bible, but what I could not stomach was the way the prayers intoned by our headmaster, an Old Testament prophet in the flesh, continually obliged us to abase ourselves in front of God, our alleged Father, begging for his forgiveness. What crime had I committed? I was hungry, cold, and homesick; I was frightened of the masters and other boys; my life was grim enough without having to humble myself further to please a god in whom I could not bring myself to believe. If He was so merciful, why did He not take the nauseating lumps out of our morning porridge and why did He not stay the righteous right arm of his loyal servant, our headmaster, as he thrashed our skinny buttocks with a cane?

We were given an ethical education that was typical of its day and consisted of a melding of the Ten Commandments and the Sermon on the Mount. The latter must have been difficult to teach to cynical, literal-minded boys. In our eyes such ideas as loving thine enemy, turning the other cheek, plucking out the offending right eye, and taking no thought for the morrow were downright ridiculous. They were impracticable and extreme; they went against the grain of human nature. Nor, in the context of the school's regime, had asking produced much in the way of receiving. As for laying up treasures upon earth where moth and rust corrupted, most of us had fathers who were working like dogs to lay up a little treasure and voted Conservative to ensure they could hang on to it. What they feared was not moth and rust, but the Inland Revenue. And this was the treasure, by the way, that paid our school fees and kept our headmaster in the style to which he had become accustomed.

The model boy, in our headmaster's projection, was a clean-limbed lad in a Boy Scout's uniform, pure in thought, word, and deed, who carried a rugby ball under his arm, a fishing rod over his shoulder, and a Bible in his knapsack. To be fair to the man, his ideal boy would also have carried a novel by Dickens. Our headmaster's redeeming gift was for reading aloud, especially the works of Dickens, Wilkie Collins, and Arthur Conan Doyle, to which he brought a musical voice and a genius for characterization.

I could not respect the paragon of our headmaster's fantasies, but, laughable though it may sound, I did have available another model that I could respect, which was the cowboy. Nowadays, the cowboy—male, white, heterosexual, chauvinist, alcoholic, pugnacious, and racist— could hardly be less fashionable, but in our house he was regarded as a heroic figure, a role model my father himself seemed to admire. In my eyes he was heroic, not only by dint of his strength, courage, marksman-ship, and so forth, qualities which a villain might also possess, but be-cause he was honorable. He had true moral stature because he refused to disgrace his code, even when his life was at stake.

There was another element as well. In my moral book, no more de-spicable character was to be found in the West than the white man who dealt dishonorably with Indians: the soldier who broke the treaty, the trader who sold whiskey, the gun runner who set one tribe against an-other, and so forth, all stock figures in westerns. I never got as far as questioning the right of the white settlers to invade and dispossess, but I believed strongly in fair play and hated to see the game's rules flouted. This belief in turn led to an identification with the Indian cause, from which I learned a kind of liberalism that was not an explicit part of my formal education.

Despite World War II and its supposed crusade against the persecu-tory Nazis, my generation grew up in an atmosphere of casual racism and prejudice. I say *casual* because the middle classes represented by my parents did not cherish their hostilities with much vehemence, and they vehemently denied the accusation of prejudice when it was put to them. This petty bigotry was simply an unsavory part of the furniture that filled the collective mind. For some reason—and rightly or wrongly I attribute it to my reading about the history of the West—I developed a repugnance for the ambient racism of my day.

As I recall, my "histories" of the Wild West presented their Indians (the term American Indian had not yet been coined) in what was, at bottom, a spirit of romantic sentimentalism, mourning the decline of the brave and noble red man without protesting its necessity. But as a child, reading these books in isolation, I took them at face value. They aroused in me a strong affinity with the Apaches, Sioux, Comanches, and Cheyennes. With their tipis and powwows, feathers and war paint, their stealth and infallible arrows, they seemed to enjoy a way of life that was preferable to that of the cowboys, which apart from moments of high drama looked unenviably dull and strenuous. The Indians seemed to have turned their existence into a continual, exotic holiday. Yet they were also full of honor and clung to their code as defiantly as the cowboy to his. As a result of my admiration, I developed a corresponding contempt for anyone who treated Indians as racially inferior. This was, of course, an abstract matter, since my relations with Indian-haters and, for that matter, Indians was confined to the movies, but by extension I applied it to all subjects of racial prejudice, of whom Liverpool had plenty of examples. Such is the simple logic of artistic sympathy.

By the time I was nineteen my map of the world had greatly expanded, though without losing its emblematic quality. Its old locations were still marked, now in smaller letters, but a revised United States of America occupied a still more disproportionate space, for it embraced a score of new shrines, each inhabiting its own singular pocket of historical time. The eastern seaboard, for instance, was the site of Fitzgerald's West Egg, where the dateline was forever 1922, the summer when Nick Carraway rented a house next door to Jay Gatsby's gaudy mansion. Scattered a little imprecisely over the rest of the continent were Holden Caulfield's New York, Hemingway's Michigan and, not far away, his Key West, Al Capone's Chicago, Kid Ory's New Orleans, and that small town with its drug store and high school that was the classic setting of so many songs by Buddy Holly, Elvis Presley, the Everly Brothers, and Eddie Cochran. By then, the topography of my Wild West had shrunk considerably, but it had at least acquired a coastline in the shape of the eerily beautiful cliffs and beaches of Monterey, California, where Marlon Brando had shot parts of his western *One Eyed Jacks*. (For a while this turgid Oedipal drama was my favorite film, inspiring me to become Brando's English counterpart, not an easy task since at the same time I was also doubling for Marcello Mastroianni and Jean-Paul Belmondo.)[2]

Despite some European excursions, both actual and cinematic, the United States remained my imaginative heartland. Drawn with the cartography of dreams and hero-worship, the United States on my map not only loomed large, it throbbed with an irresistible magnetism. In the summer of 1963, between my leaving school and going to university, I was given the chance to stay in Philadelphia with some friends of my parents. I jumped at it. Philadelphia had not hitherto featured on my map, and it possessed no literary, cultural, mythological, or cinematic resonance, but though I regretted it was a long way from Tombstone, I was eager for an American adventure, wherever it took me.

When I arrived, having undertaken a flight that in those days required a refueling stop in Reykjavik, Iceland, I found myself in a household that was about to fall apart. Decorum was preserved for the sake of their children and their English guest, but when my parents' friends were obliged to confront each other at mealtimes across the chessboard of their gingham tablecloth, the clash of marital battle was audible even to my insensitive teenage ears. It was decided that it would be best for me to be transferred to another family, a doctor and his lawyer wife, who had a daughter, Melissa, of about my age—"a lovely girl." And so she was. Tall, auburn-haired, sun-tanned, and swinging a tennis racket, she was recognizable in retrospect as Brenda Patimkin, the heroine of Philip Roth's *Goodbye Columbus*. My blood jumped, as Roth puts it, but when I con-

---

2. I persuaded myself that I bore an uncanny resemblance to Mastroianni (*La Dolce Vita, 8½*) and Belmondo (*Breathless*) among several other glamorous European film stars of the era; this conviction was not impaired by the fact that they did not bear the slightest resemblance to each other.

fided in her that I had been educated at a single-sex school in England, she assumed I was covertly telling her that I was gay and shunned me for the remainder of the summer.

Fortunately, I had other plans. Like so many others, I took advantage of the Greyhound bus company's deal, whereby for $99 you could travel as far as you wished within the United States providing you returned to your point of departure. My grand tour took me west to Pittsburgh, Cleveland, Detroit, and Chicago, then south to Memphis and New Orleans, east to Miami, and finally north to Savannah, Charleston, and Philadelphia. I circumnavigated a third of the country, and although I was sorry not to have ventured into the Wild West, I felt proud of completing my journey, which had not been without its perilous moments, most of them provoked by my own stupidity. To my surprise, Melissa, still lovelier after six weeks' swimming and sun-bathing, was impressed by my traveler's tales, which concerned places she had never seen herself. While still suspicious of my sexual aspirations, she introduced me to her friends at the country club, showing me off as an exotic object of interest.

Towards the end of my stay, one of Melissa's poolside crowd offered me a place in a car that was driving to Washington, D.C., for the civil rights rally on 23 August, subsequently famous for being the occasion of Martin Luther King Jr.'s "I Have a Dream" speech. When it was all over, we drove out of the capital, slowly pushing our way through the legions of triumphant marchers. Somewhere in the suburbs, our driver asked if we would mind stopping for half an hour while he said hello to his parents. We were invited into the house, and I sat on a sofa next to our driver's father, who gave me a large vodka and tomato juice. We watched the news on television, which reported the march and King's astonishing performance. The father asked about race relations in Britain. Already excited by the day's events, I waxed eloquent, and spurred on by a second drink and the man's evident interest in my opinions, I explained to him exactly how the United States could solve its racial problems. When we finally left the house, one of our party asked me if I had any idea whom I had just been talking to, or rather lecturing. I didn't have a clue, though he seemed a nice enough chap. That, she informed me, was Dean Rusk (the then secretary of state).

A decade later I returned to the United States for a brief business trip, this time as a publisher visiting other publishers and agents in New York and Boston, and another two decades passed before I returned once again. In 1992, I had the opportunity to teach writing courses at St. Olaf College, a liberal arts college in Northfield, Minnesota, and, after a family conference, we decided that for the two semesters of my contract we would live there together—my wife Sally, my daughter Tilly (14), my son Jack (12), and myself.

I started work at the college in January of that year, and by the time spring break approached in March, we were all feeling in urgent need of a change of scene. Sally consulted the Chamber of Commerce and brought home a bundle of leaflets about the Black Hills and the Badlands. These places meant nothing to me, and since I was worried about the expense of an ambitious trip, I pooh-poohed her scheme. However, to humor her I borrowed a book about South Dakota from the college library and took it home. With no anticipation of pleasure, I started a chapter about mining in Deadwood and, as it were, panned a couple of pages. Alas, I have forgotten the title of this book, but I struck gold immediately. The story of Custer's gold-hunting expedition of 1874 in the Lakotas' sacred Black Hills, the gold rush to Deadwood in 1876, the inevitable war with the Sioux in the summer of the same year, their ill-fated victory at the Little Big Horn, and the surrender and punishment that followed—these events stimulated me more than anything I had read for a long time. I suddenly realized that the Wild West of my childhood was only around the corner, within my grasp. To Sally's amazement and annoyance, I became obsessed by Deadwood's history. My anxieties concerning expense suddenly seemed trivial, and I arranged a loan with my bank in Northfield to finance our adventure.

To anyone who knows about the history of Minnesota, my realization about the proximity of the Old West must seem idiotic, since it was not only round the corner, but on the very doorstep. Minnesota Territory was the site of an extremely bloody episode in 1862 when the Santee Sioux, frustrated by shortage of supplies and the corruption of white officials and traders, broke out of their reservation on the Minnesota River. Bands of Dakotas rampaged over the countryside, killing, raping, pillaging, and burning property. Farmers and their families fell by the score, "dispatched," according to historian Robert Utley, "with a savagery rarely equaled in the history of Indian uprisings."[3] When the situation was finally brought under control, the numbers of dead ran into the hundreds. Among those murdered was an agent notorious for saying, "If they are hungry let them eat grass or their own dung."[4] His mutilated corpse was found with blood-caked grass stuffed in his mouth. Two thousand prisoners were rounded up, and 303 were summarily tried and condemned to death, most of them on the thinnest evidence. President Abraham Lincoln demanded to see the court records and reduced the list of condemned men to 38. They were hanged in unison on 26 December 1862, at Mankato, a town a few miles southwest of Northfield, where two statues now commemorate these terrible events.

Still closer to home was the site of the abortive raid led by Jesse James in September 1876 on the First National Bank in Northfield itself. I confess to taking a gruesome pleasure in choosing this bank when I came to open an account, regretting that the original building where the James gang met its bloody fate had been converted into a museum. There was something typically Minnesotan—stubborn and principled— about the refusal of the bank's cashier to hand over the money when it was demanded at gunpoint. His brave gesture cost him his life, but the same spirit inspired the citizens of Northfield to fight the gangsters in the street and thwart their robbery. This triumph of civic resistance over criminal brutality has understandably become a prominent part of Northfield's folklore and is the subject of an annual re-enactment.

By overlooking the history that was under my nose, I was paying an unwitting testament to the power of landscape. For the most part southern Minnesota is composed of flat, monotonous farmland devoted to arable production, and it was a disappointment to us in that it seemed all too reminiscent of our local landscape in East Anglia, and it bore no resemblance to the landscape favored by the Hollywood western. The British countryside is remarkable for its variation and, in places, for its beauty—the Lake District, the Highlands of Scotland, the beaches and

---

3. Robert M. Utley, *The Indian Frontier of the American West, 1846–1890* (Albuquerque: University of New Mexico Press, 1984), p. 79.

4. Ibid., p. 76.

cliffs of Pembrokeshire, the Yorkshire moors, and so on—but by definition a small island such as ours cannot offer the vast scenic panoramas that John Ford, for example, made such a notable feature of his films, rendering Monument Valley almost a character in its own right. The western was defined by its landscape, and the epic struggle fought between the red man and the white man over the conquest of the West called for an objective correlative in the shape of an epic landscape. There was no sign of this heroic *mise en scène* in Minnesota.

Somewhere in the back of our minds, my generation (the generation of British post-war children that played cowboys and Indians) knows the dreadful truth concerning the Indians. And yet, despite what we know, I suspect we cannot rid ourselves of the romanticism that attaches to the West; we shamefully cling to our childhood dreams of adventure, unable to accept that our innocent garden game was a make-believe version of ethnic cleansing.

The western has not shirked from showing that the cowboy was capable of being rapacious or murderous, but as soon as he is revealed in his mythological posture, astride his horse, riding across the prairie, the romance of the West is restored. Regardless of the plot line, the landscape redeems the murderer, so powerful is the mythic vision that Hollywood projects onto its beauty, which is forever mystical and exalted. The movie landscape also prevents our remembering the truth about the subjugation of American Indians because it *ennobles* the Indian as he silhouettes himself on the horizon, imperious and invincible, looking down on the shambling wagon train or hapless platoon.

In March 1992, our westward party was six strong—three adults and three children—and instead of a prairie schooner, we traveled in an aging Volvo station wagon, with my son, then the smallest child, packed into the back like a last-minute piece of luggage. To look at our vehicle was to wince, because it had suffered a terrible blow to its offside fender, which had never received the benefit of cosmetic surgery, and the wound was still sore and rusting. The gouged indicator light had been replaced by a makeshift equivalent taken from a motorcycle and screwed into its crumpled flesh. In retrospect our expedition would have been an act of folly even if we had been driving a Cadillac, for the weather at that time of year can be savage and is always unpredictable.

However, we drove in blithe, foreigners' ignorance, not realizing that if we had been caught by a spring blizzard on the remote, seldom-used roads we had picked out on the map we might never have been rescued before freezing to death.

Leaving Northfield, we joined Interstate 90 and entered South Dakota just north of Sioux Falls. The scenery remained indistinguishable from the farmland we had crossed in Minnesota: level and featureless, with the interminable horizon interrupted only now and again by a barn and grain silo indicating the location of a lonely farm. But then everything changed as we crossed the Missouri River at Chamberlain. The river, which bisects the state, marks the boundary between the glaciation that flattened the land to the east and the Great Plains to the west, where the landscape begins to undulate and the unplowed grassland turns the tawny color of a lion's mane. Rocks broke the dry skin of the prairie; buttes appeared like castles on the horizon; the sky turned even more blue and seemed to expand; the white clouds rolled across the horizon like snowy freight trains. I knew where we were and I was thrilled; we had crossed the river into the Wild West of my childhood back yard.

When we got home (unscathed) from our trip to the Badlands and the Black Hills, I was determined to return as soon as possible and explore further. The opportunity came in June that same year after my family had left for the United Kingdom and my teaching responsibilities had ended. By then I had been lucky enough to make a friend of Alvin Handelman, a fellow writer married to a St. Olaf faculty member, who was also keen to discover what lay to the west of Northfield. Together we drove westwards along I-90 and more or less repeated the visit I had made only three months earlier, though this time we added the Crazy Horse Memorial in the Black Hills to the itinerary.

Back home again, I managed to persuade the BBC (radio) and *The Sunday Times*, the United Kingdom's largest broadsheet Sunday newspaper, that this extraordinary and disregarded part of the world was worth reporting on, and during the 1990s I made four more trips, expanding my range to include North Dakota, Montana, and Wyoming. In the course of these expeditions, I had the chance to interview General Custer (impersonated by a "living historian") on the Little Big Horn battlefield, both before and after his Last Stand—something of a coup.

I stood on the outstretched arm of the Crazy Horse Monument while "sculptors" with jackhammers packed explosives into the face of the great warrior before blasting tons of rock out of his eye socket. Accompanied once again by the intrepid Alvin, I followed (by car) the Lewis and Clark trail over the Continental Divide and, in imitation of one of the expedition's soldiers, stood with a foot on each bank of a little rivulet that downstream became the mighty Missouri. At the site of the Wounded Knee massacre, I was approached by a ragged American Indian man who told me he was sorry to hear about the "troubles" we were having in England ("What troubles?" I asked him. "With Charles and Di," he said). And in Texas, I witnessed the authentication of a diary that proved that Davy Crockett had not died a hero's death at the Alamo. These may not be credentials for writing this book, but they do, I hope, demonstrate a certain loyalty to my subject.

I completed my last American assignment in 1999 (the Lewis and Clark trip), and a year later gave up the puerile, if well rewarded, life of a freelance travel journalist to do other things. However, I was left with a powerful sense of longing for the West and for South Dakota in particular. In May 2011, I returned once again to start the journey that is the source of this book. Though brief, the trip was planned to take me to certain places that had become essential to my understanding of South Dakota, and they provide the subjects of these essays—my homage.

Harrison

When I worked as a journalist and regularly drove through the Midwest, one of my few regrets was that I never made the time to visit my namesake town, Harrison in Douglas County, South Dakota. On the strength of nothing more than the coincidence of our names, I had always been curious to visit the town and find out if it had any connections with England. All I knew about the place was that out of the twelve towns called Harrison in the United States (there are none in the United Kingdom), Harrison, South Dakota, was the smallest, with a population of forty-three.[1] And so, when planning the trip on which this book is based, I was determined to rectify my negligence.

While traveling I used to keep an eye open for the Harrison name, which I often found in the frontier graveyards scattered all over the West. For instance, buried in Mount Moriah Cemetery in Deadwood, South Dakota, with Wild Bill Hickok and Calamity Jane for neighbors, is a James Harrison and a John E. Harrison, apparently no relation to each other. In nearby Montana, I found the name of Corporal William H. Harrison of L Company, Seventh Cavalry, inscribed on the cenotaph commemorating the 268 white casualties who died at the Little Big Horn in June 1876.

On a trip to San Antonio, Texas, for a BBC radio program to inspect a diary kept by a Mexican officer that appeared to show that Davy Crockett had not died a hero's death but had been

---

1. New York, population 27,472; New Jersey, 13,620; Arkansas, 13,183; Ohio, 9,841; Tennessee, 7,769; Maine, 2,759; Michigan, 2,108; Georgia, 509; Nebraska, 279; Idaho, 267; Montana, 162; South Dakota, 43. *United States Census*, 2010.

been ignominiously shot after the siege, I discovered that two Harrisons had also died at the Alamo in 1836. One of them was Private Andrew Jackson Harrison, and the other was Captain William B. Harrison, who had formed a company known as the Tennessee Mounted Volunteers, which included Crockett himself.

A third Harrison, I. L. K., is sometimes included in lists of the heroic dead from the Alamo, though his place is debatable. A local historian once confided in me that this Harrison was rumored to have qualified as the only coward at the Alamo by sneaking out at night before the battle and saving his pragmatic skin. The word was that his shameful exit was later hushed up because he was related to the politically powerful Harrisons of Virginia. I take some pride in this scandalous legend, but I wouldn't boast about it to the formidable Daughters of the Republic of Texas who guard the Alamo shrine, especially since our program came to the conclusion that the diary was authentic and that Crockett may well have been executed as a prisoner.

I cannot claim a genetic connection with any of these historical Harrisons, either the illustrious or the scurrilous or the plain ordinary, and the frequency with which our shared name crops up proves nothing except that continuous emigration has made Harrison a common name in the United States, just as it is in England. And yet I do feel a connection with these men and women, a kind of fellow-feeling based on sentimentality, vanity, and coincidence, that makes me seek out our cognomen whenever I am looking at advertisements in local newspapers, or the names of stores lining some one-street town, or the markers in the graveyard outside a desolate fort on the prairies.

Harrison is said to be the thirty-seventh most common surname in England, but appears to be growing less common; in the census of 1881 it was ranked thirty-third. In the United States, Harrison is ranked between Ford and Morales at 122nd, with nearly 150,000 people using it as their last name. Thus, I share my name with thousands of others, and yet it seems singular to me and my family, an illusion enhanced by the fact that we are a small unit. My wife exchanged her maiden name for Harrison when she married, and we have two children, a son and a daughter, though the latter is no longer a Harrison, having taken her husband's name. The only other relative who bears our name is my mother, who of course acquired it by marriage (as did my first wife, who continued to use it after our divorce). Despite the name's statistical frequency, we are acquainted with only one other family of Harrisons in England. The local telephone directory brings up forty-one entries, and I recognize none of them, except my own father, now long since dead, who for some bizarre reason continues to be listed not once, but twice.

The name appears to derive from the medieval name Harry, the vernacular form of Henry, which in turn derives from the Germanic *haim*, or *heim* plus *ric* (home plus power). Like all names ending in -son it carries an obvious meaning, but that goes unregistered; when people hear the name they don't think, "Ah, the son of Harry!" As a word it's so nebulous, being all vowels and soft consonants, it's hardly a word at all. It's an exhalation, a barely audible whisper, a harmless puff of air, a draft sighing under the door. It's not funny, like Shufflebottom; it's not a pun like D'eath; it carries no smutty double meaning like Allcock; it doesn't indicate a trade like Cooper or Butcher. There have been distinguished and interesting Harrisons, but the name is not automatically synonymous with a famous person in the way that Kennedy is, or Presley, or Dickens. Nor do people immediately think of George when they hear our name as they think of John when they are introduced to a Lennon. We Harrisons are as good as anonymous.

A handful of Harrisons have, so to speak, made names for themselves, including the English regicide, Thomas Harrison, who was executed in 1660. Samuel Pepys witnessed this event and wrote in his diary, "I went to see Major General Harrison hanged, drawn, and quartered, he looking as cheerfully as any man could in that condition."[2] The name has more distinguished representatives in the United States than in Britain, thanks to a certain Benjamin Harrison who emigrated from England to Virginia in 1633 and founded what became a great slave-owning dynasty. The family seat, the Berkeley Plantation not far from Jamestown, in Charles City County, Virginia, was the site of some memorable historic events. The first official Thanksgiving was held here on 4 December 1619. There too an Episcopal priest by the name of George Thorpe distilled the first bourbon whiskey in 1621, and the first army bugle call

2. Pepys's diary entry is dated 13 Oct. 1660.

of "Taps" was played there in July 1862, the tune having been written at Harrison's Landing on the plantation by General Daniel Butterfield.

The Harrisons owned plantations in Virginia and produced numerous governors during the colonial era and later. Their most eminent member in the eighteenth century was a Benjamin Harrison, known as "the signer" because he put his name to the Declaration of Independence. In the nineteenth century the Harrisons were the political equivalent of the Kennedys, for the family produced two presidents: William Henry Harrison, the ninth president, elected in 1841, and his grandson, Benjamin Harrison, the twenty-third president, who held office between 1889 and 1893. The elder Harrison holds two records: he made the longest inaugural speech (two hours) and then enjoyed the shortest period in the job, dying after just thirty-two days.

I have never researched my Harrison ancestry further back than the nineteenth century, but as far as I know, my immediate family has no connection with any American Harrisons, whether presidents or soldiers or whatever the Deadwood Harrisons were (gold diggers? brothel keepers?). Behind me stand four generations of Harrison lawyers who practiced in Liverpool. They all worked close to the city's waterfront, which before the advent of air travel served as the gateway to the United States, and two of my great-great-grandfathers actually worked for the Mersey Docks and Harbour Board. However, there is no record that any of these men considered the idea of emigrating to the United States (they were doing nicely where they were), and I believe I can claim to be the first Harrison in my family to cross the Atlantic.

When planning my trip to South Dakota in 2011 I was determined to visit Harrison. With only a few clicks of a mouse, I was able to compile an astonishingly detailed portrait of the town based on information extrapolated from the 2000 United States Census (astonishing, that is, to a British citizen, because our national census does not gather anything like the same wealth of facts and statistics). In 2000, Harrison had fifty-one residents, of whom twenty-five were over the age of sixty-five. By 2007, the population had dropped to forty-five, and the 2010 census recorded a figure of forty-three. The residents of Harrison were not wealthy; in fact, the median household income in 1999 was below the state average at $25,500. Racially, the town was all-white, with the exception of a single person in the Asian category, and most people were of German, Dutch, and Irish ancestry. Other details testified that the town was the quintessence of a certain kind of old-fashioned Great Plains ordinariness: 86 percent married, 4 percent divorced, 4 percent graduates, no unemployed, no foreign born, no gay or lesbian households, and no sex offenders, with 79 percent voting for George W. Bush in 2004.

Harrison was evidently an old person's town, with nearly half its population over the age of sixty-five in 2000; it was a town, furthermore, that was itself aging in the sense that its population was dwindling. My guess was that the remaining people had neither the resources nor the inclination to flee their homes, even in winter; these were not "snowbirds." Harrison's residents were facing and dealing with their old age on the basis of their own resources in a small, more or less sequestered community, which therefore represented a sort of laboratory of old age—a subject that had become of increasing interest to me since I had retired and turned sixty-five myself in 2009.

Old age, in the developed world at least, represents a new and daunting challenge, both material and philosophical. According to recent surveys, in South Dakota a woman can expect to live until she is eighty and a man until he is seventy-five. For anyone who is sixty-five today, these numbers mean that she or he has at least another decade of existence, and medicine is continually advancing the finishing tape. In the United Kingdom, life expectancy is roughly the same—eighty-one for women, seventy-seven for men. My guess is that most people have not formulated a plan for using those additional years. We are only just at the end of the era when our vision of retirement at sixty-five was governed by the old biblical prediction of a life stretch of three score years and ten.

Take my own case. At the time of writing this, I am sixty-seven, but that hardly counts as old. On the other hand, my mother, at ninety-six next birthday, can certainly be defined as old, though she leads a more or less independent existence, living alone in her own house. She is somewhat hard of hearing but continues to look after herself, keep her house, do her own shopping, cook for herself, and generally subsist as well as the rest of us. Furthermore, she reads her newspaper (*The Daily Telegraph*) from cover to cover and listens to the television news (at deafening volume). If healthy longevity is to be envied, then she is lucky, but her situation puts my own "old age" in a special context. Assuming the genetic runes are reliable, I can anticipate living until my late eighties, perhaps my mid-nineties, which means I am facing another twenty-five or even thirty years. Three decades! What on earth am I going to do with all that time? What did they do with it in Harrison, South Dakota, I wondered as I studied the town's census statistics.

It cannot be sufficient simply to remain alive; that would be life without a life. We owe it to ourselves to fulfill the potential granted us, to put our years of grace to good use. And, for that matter, we have an obligation to the generations following us, who are bound to carry some of the burden of our support, if only by paying the taxes that fund our pensions. I grew up in a world where people considered retirement a kind of terminal vacation that the rest of the world was happy to provide for them because it was expected to be a brief, well-earned rest brought to an economic end by death. Times have changed, but my generation seems to be neither practically nor philosophically prepared for the additional years that lie ahead. We are in danger of turning longevity into a curse if we don't find satisfactory ways of filling what could be our *fourscore* and ten. How were Harrison's old people meeting these challenges?

Even though I had never visited Harrison, I was familiar with similar towns strung out along the minor roads of South Dakota, east of the Missouri River. I knew they were possessed of a special kind of loneliness, or so it seemed to an outsider. Like so much of the Great Plains, the landscape surrounding them was flat farmland, uninterrupted by anything vertical apart from silos, grain bins, barns, and stands of trees that protected farm houses from the unforgiving wind. Presumably, this landscape—not beautiful in the classic sense, but full of agricultural promise—had seemed inviting and familiar to the Germans, Dutch, Irish, and Norwegians who chose to make their homes here rather than push farther west to more exotic horizons. It was not a landscape for restless souls; its vast emptiness seems to have had the paradoxical effect of fixing people in their homesteads.

For all that, I was taken by surprise when at last I found myself in Harrison itself. I approached the town from the east, driving out of Corsica on County Highway 560, which runs east-west for ten miles and was as straight as the proverbial arrow. In the bewildering way of American roads that foreigners never quite grasp, it is also marked on maps as 273rd Street and, closer to the town, 8th Street. The landscape on either side was typical of farmland east of the Missouri: orderly fields looking green and fertile after the recent heavy rains, cottonwoods marking the line of creeks, small farms and their buildings, and Holstein cattle standing in yards, hay hanging out of their mouths, or knee-deep in muddy ponds.

After six miles, a sign appeared at the side of the road announcing, "Harrison, Centennial Community." I counted one, two, three turnings running due north—Le Cocq Avenue, Main Avenue, and Vanden Bos Avenue—and then Harrison was behind me, all 0.1 square miles of it. Having turned round, I drove along these three avenues, pausing to look up and down the lateral streets. Ten minutes later I had seen the sights and driven past most of the houses, including several that were deserted or derelict. The town was empty except for a gang of small children playing in a yard, a heartening refutation of the census that suggested the community had one foot in the grave. I took an unmerited pride in the fact that Harrison had turned out to be a pretty town of modest single-story houses shaded by trees and surrounded by well-kept yards, all comfortably dispersed among its wide streets. However, the feature that most surprised me was the complete absence of any commercial enterprises: no gas station, café, or store; no hotel or bed and breakfast; no agency or workshop. Harrison was no longer open for business. However, it was spiritually compensated for its lack of material outlets by not one, but two churches, both large and relatively old, whose white wooden spires poked above the treetops.

What I saw as I wandered around those innocuous, dormant streets was the fall-out from a catastrophe that had struck the town more than a century before, a devastating blow that had taken all these years to deliver its gradual but fatal effect.

Harrison was founded in 1882 by pioneers, most of them of Dutch descent, who were finding the price of land too high in northwest Iowa where many "Hollanders" had already settled. In October 1881, Dutchman Frank Le Cocq, Sr., held a meeting at his home in Orange City,

Iowa, to discuss the location for a new "Kolonie." It was the period of the "Great Dakota Boom" that followed the Black Hills Agreement of 1877, which effectively confined the Sioux to reservations and freed up huge tracts of land that hitherto had been part of the Great Sioux Reservation. Two men who had recently traveled in Dakota Territory attended the meeting and reported that they had seen "beautiful, undulating, and extensive prairies."[3] They had been in Dakota Territory in order to attend a sale of ponies confiscated from Sitting Bull, the Hunkpapa leader, who had been on the run in Canada since his victory at the Little Big Horn, but had recently recrossed the border and surrendered to the United States Army at Fort Buford in today's North Dakota.

A series of rainy years prior to 1881 made those attending the meeting in Orange City especially receptive to the agricultural promise of the prairies east of the Missouri River, and they decided to send a three-man "committee of locators" to investigate the area. The three men chosen, Leendert Vander Meer, Dirk Van den Bos, and Frank Le Cocq, Jr., are commemorated in Harrison's street names. Traveling by covered wagon, the men made the journey in mid-November, a sign in itself of their desperation and tough-mindedness and on their return reported favorably enough for the committee to dispatch a second expedition, which set off in January 1882 in two wagons. Writing in the third person, Frank Le Cocq, Jr., reported that "they moved westward over the boundless prairie, by compass, like ships on the ocean," reaching the Missouri River five days later.[4] At one point the smell of frying ham attracted hungry wolves to their camp, but they only came close without attacking. In another place a band of American Indians confronted them, angry because the thoughtless Dutchmen had emptied their clay pipes on the dry grass and started a small fire. Finally, the Dutch pioneers reached the western side of today's Douglas County, which they explored thoroughly. To mark their claim, they drove a surveyor's stake

---

3. *Harrison Centennial, Harrison, S.D., 1882–1892* (Stickney, S.Dak.: Harrison Booklet Committee, 1982), p. 5.

4. Henry Van der Pol, *On the Reservation Border—Hollanders in Douglas and Charles Mix Counties* (Stickney, S.Dak.: By the Author, 1969), p. 92.

into the ground, which according to local legend took the form of a plasterer's lath topped with an empty oyster can.

On 15 February, the expedition returned to Orange City and gave a detailed report of the land they had chosen and its potential. They were sufficiently persuasive for twenty families to form an advance party of colonizers. As soon as spring arrived and the weather improved, the families loaded their possessions on freight cars at Hull, Iowa, and on 6 April traveled to Plankinton, South Dakota, using a railway line that still exists today, although now it carries only freight. There they purchased lumber and provisions and immediately set forth for the area that would be their new home. Locating that home, however, was not easy, for the lath and oyster can proved elusive, but around noon the next day, they found the right place and by nightfall had raised a shelter for common use.

Frank Le Cocq, Sr., wasted no time in directing the survey of individual sections. The original locators were assigned as claimants to choice sites around the eighty-acre plat in Section 34, Township 100, Range 65 West. This plat had been set aside for the proposed village, to be called New Orange, and the homesteaders began the arduous business of plowing the land and building huts. By the following year, all available government land in the area had been taken, and the towns of New Orange, New Holland, and Joubert were beginning to expand and do business.

Within a couple of years, New Orange changed its name to Harrison in a gesture of deference to Benjamin Harrison, the president-to-be, who at that time was a senator from Indiana and a member of the committee on territories. (So much for the idea that the town might have had an English connection or a long-lost ancestor of mine among its founding fathers.) The change of name was made at the recommendation of Le Cocq, who, according to the town's centennial history, "had had a personal interview" with this influential politician. It would be interesting to know what was said, or hinted at, during this personal interview to make it worth renaming the fledgling town in the senator's honor, for neither history nor folk myth has preserved any record of Benjamin Harrison's returning the compliment paid to him. Robert Karolevitz, the author of the county's history, *Douglas County: "The Little Giant,"* sorrowfully observes that "if the founders of Harrison hoped to reap any benefits from their name choice, however, they apparently were disappointed."[5]

By 1886, the re-named town was thriving with a population of two hundred and a large number of businesses serving the needs of the town itself, as well as the outlying farming community. These businesses included a general store, post office, machinery shop, hardware store, shoe shop, wagon maker, building contractor, painter, mason, barber, milliner, saloon, blacksmith, harness maker, furniture store, creamery, hotel, loan and real estate office, sewing-machine shop, livery stable, drug store, and a newspaper office. Harrison had its professional class in the shape of a doctor and a lawyer, and a music studio provided a touch of culture.

The town's leaders had astutely chosen their site because it lay on a direct north-south line between Fort Randall on the Missouri (the nearby army post) and the new railway town of Plankinton, which made it a convenient overnight stopping place for officers on their way to the railroad station, as well as ordinary travelers and mail carriers. Visitors to the town could stay at Harrison House, a hotel sarcastically referred to as Harrison's Waldorf Astoria by a minister who reported that the crevices between its boards were large enough to serve as portholes.[6] Harrison was a cohesive, mutually supportive community, but these Dutchmen also brought to the new town some age-old religious divisions. The followers of the First Reformed church raised money for a church, which opened its doors on 28 June 1883 with a church roll listing forty-five members. A minister was employed by the members in September 1883 with a salary of $700 per annum plus a free parsonage. Soon after, followers of the Christian Reformed Church, who had originally met in an upper room of the still unfinished house of the Le Cocq family, built a rudimentary sod church with board floors on land donated by the Le Cocqs. This first effort burnt down, though the wooden fixtures were saved, and in due course, followers constructed a proper

5. Robert F. Karolevitz, *Douglas County: "The Little Giant"* (Armour, S.Dak.: Douglas County Historical Society, 1983), p. 33.

6. Van der Pol, *On the Reservation Border*, p. 101.

church building, which opened in 1884. Their first pastor was called in June 1885, by which time his congregation had built a parsonage. These two Harrison churches combined forces to start a school providing secondary education to prepare students for college. In 1900, the substantial sum of $2,000 was raised to pay for a two-story building designed to house the Harrison Classical Academy, its grand name indicating that the curriculum stressed literary and cultural subjects.

By 1884, Harrison had its own newspaper. In its first issue, the owner of the *Harrison Globe* reported that the town was "the strongest and most enterprising portion of the county."[7] It seems that no town could rival Harrison in its Fourth of July celebrations, which would begin with a hundred-gun salute at dawn that rang across the prairie. An amateur balloonist, who was later county sheriff, sometimes put on a display of balloon ascensions, involving acrobatics on a trapeze and a death-defying parachute drop. Local American Indians performed trick-riding shows and were paid with sides of beef. And, in the words of one historian, "Harrison's bands and parades and the special kinds of sports and contests still bring up chuckles. There'd be the fat man's foot race, bicycle races, sack races," and so on.[8]

Here was a community tough enough to survive episodes of appalling weather, whose history was summed up in *On the Reservation Border* by Henry Van der Pol as follows: "1883 and 1884, good years; 1885, first taste of crop failure; 1888, the great blizzard, no crops; 1889 and 1890, no crops; 1891—Bonanza Year! 1893, poor crops, low prices; 1894, no crops to speak of, real need; 1898, hail and floods; 1899, dust storms and cyclones."[9] Many of Harrison's families must have questioned the wisdom of continuing the struggle to farm under these pitiless conditions, and with each disaster, a few surrendered and moved on. Enough people stayed to keep the town in business, however, and around the turn of the century the hardy farmers were rewarded for their doggedness with a little prosperity. But then in 1905, Harrison suffered the disaster from which it never recovered.

7. *Harrison Centennial*, p. 12.
8. Van der Pol, *On the Reservation Border*, p. 112.
9. Ibid., p. 128.

The Chicago, Milwaukee and St. Paul Railroad company decided to extend its line with a spur from Armour, a town seventeen miles to the southeast, and Harrison understandably hoped that, as an established community, it would be on the route of the new line. The company kept its plans secret to the last minute. On 22 April, a train rolled into Armour pulling six freight cars of horses, seven cars of grading equipment, and two cars of grain. Fifty construction workers arrived at the same time. The contractor was tight-lipped and would not reveal the exact direction of the line he intended to survey. For the first four miles the prospective line angled northwest of Armour toward Harrison, but then to the horror of those with interests in Harrison the railroad changed course and took the spur due north to the site of a new town. It emerged that the railroad company had already invested in land six miles east of Harrison where the new town was to be built. For reasons that remain obscure, the railroad company named the new community Corsica.

Within a year, the opening of the Corsica line caused the population of Harrison to drop from about 275 people to just 125 people. The majority of its businesses moved to Corsica: homes, barns, and business premises were dismantled, loaded up, and carted down the road, with steam engines furnishing the pulling power. The Douglas County centennial publication noted, "It was almost as if a tornado struck the town."[10] During the next twelve months approximately seventy buildings made the six-mile trip to Corsica. Hotels, livery barns, five stores, various shops, as well as homes and barns trundled away, deserting the old town. The *Harrison Globe* transmuted into the *Corsica Globe* (still published), and Harrison relinquished its commercial primacy in the area to the new railroad town. Some businesses remained, of course, but once the automobile became commonplace, and the six miles between Harrison and the shops in Corsica ceased to be an obstacle, Harrison became a mostly residential town. Corsica has remained the dominant community ever since, as the 2010 population of 592 testifies.

To this day Railway Avenue runs north and south along the edge of Corsica, but the line itself has long since been closed and uprooted,

10. Douglas County History Committee, comp., *Douglas County History and Centennial Observances, 1961* (Stickney, S.Dak.: By the Compiler, 1961), pp. 147–50.

leaving the name alone to serve as the ghost of Harrison's nemesis. In the end, the railroad did not last a century. On 15 September 1972, the last freight train hauled its load out of Douglas County, only sixty-seven years after the first one rolled into Corsica and decided Harrison's fate.

In only one respect did Harrison retain some prestige and that was through its churches. Both congregations—First and Christian Reformed—remained loyal in sufficient numbers to maintain their separate theological identities and continue employing their own pastors for many years. Both managed to raise the money to keep their buildings in good condition, which cannot have been easy during the many periods of hardship that befell the area during the twentieth century. In due course, dwindling numbers forced them to share a single pastor and worship together, even while keeping their doctrinal differences. When I visited Harrison in 2011, the incumbent, Steve Hayes, occupied a house with his family next to the First Reformed Church, the so-called north church. He took services in both buildings, with the location alternating each Sunday. The two churches stand within a hundred yards of each other, and the rubric is, "Just go where the cars are."

Pastor Hayes kindly arranged for me to talk to half a dozen men and women over the age of seventy, all of them residents or one-time residents of Harrison as well as members of his congregation. He took me to the home of Cecelia Oakland on Fifth Street, where she gave us a cup of coffee in her kitchen. Her life story proved to be representative of all the old people I met. At seventy-three years of age, Oakland was the youngest of those I spoke to. She owned her house with her husband, who was unable to join us that morning. Her parents, who were Dutch in origin, had owned a farm a few miles north of Harrison, where she had been baptized. She knew the boy who became her husband because his family's farm was next door, right across the fence. She married at seventeen and had two children. She never went to high school, and so, in a way, her Bible studies, which she still maintained, were her education. When she married, she joined her husband on his family's farm, and she had expected to die there. It had been in her husband's family for 125 years, in other words since 1895, and now her grandson-in-law farmed the land. Her son also farmed nearby, so he was maintaining the tradition his parents, grandparents, and great-grandparents had followed. In this respect the Oaklands differed from the rest, because their children had mostly moved away from the area and taken up occupations other than farming. She was a grandmother thirteen times over and was expecting two more grandchildren. She even had thirteen great-grandchildren, the oldest of whom was thirteen, and they had all gathered recently for her husband's eightieth birthday party.

Oakland's verdict on Harrison was that it had been good to her, though it was, of course, all she had known. Her life had been satisfying, and if possible, she wanted to remain in Harrison for the duration of her old age, because she knew almost everyone in the town. She acknowledged that old age was hard. Her happiest times had probably been when her family had been around her. Neighbors were beginning to die, and that was painful because they were people she had known all her life. The community was changing; there had been a time when she and her family had known everyone that lived in Harrison, but unfamiliar people had moved in lately, and she didn't like having to lock her door at night.

Oakland had never been to Holland—her ancestral home—and, speaking frankly, she said she wasn't interested; besides, she didn't know the language as Dutch was no longer spoken in her family. Her traveling had been confined to the United States. She had no regrets on this score, and in any case her husband was no traveler—he was a homeboy.

Most of the people who spoke to me echoed these sentiments, though one or two were sorry they had not visited Europe. Despite this relative lack of interest in Holland itself, they continued to enjoy sharing the common identity created by their émigré origins. For example, Richard Uilenberg, eighty-five years old, who lived on Main Street with his wife, Char, and had once been the local postman, commented that they no longer knew their neighbors in the old way; there were even people living in Harrison whom they hadn't met. In the old days everybody went to one or other of the local churches, and you always knew which church someone attended, but things had changed. "We can't say they aren't good people," Uilenberg said, "they're just different. They're not Dutchmen. In the old days Harrison was a hundred per cent Dutch. The newcomers don't take care of their houses like the old Dutchmen did."

He used to speak Dutch on his mail round, but he did not want to go to Holland. Their relatives were welcome to visit them, but he would prefer to go to Germany or Guam, where he'd been stationed in World War II. As far as he was concerned, the connection with Holland had broken when his parents died. On the other hand, the common heritage with other Dutch descendents was still important as a reassuring badge of identity, a way of knowing who your neighbor was.

These were not college people; in many cases, they had not completed high school. Ted Maas, eighty-eight years old and living in retirement with his wife, Aletha, in the Leisure Living Apartments in Corsica, had been born on his father's farm, near Harrison. As a boy, Maas had walked a mile and a half to school, where there had been between fifteen and twenty-five pupils. His parents spoke Dutch at home, but it had not been taught at school, and he no longer spoke it. His father took him out of school when he reached the eighth grade because he expected him to help on the farm, as his brothers had done. Maas continued to work for his father until he married, when he became a farmer in his own right. Did he think being removed from school was fair? At first, yes, but then he realized he would have liked more education. He enjoyed working with young people, and might have been a high-school principal. He had taught Bible classes to young people, but with no more qualification than reading the Bible himself. Once again education was synonymous with Bible study.

In this context, it is worth recalling that in the Christian Reformed (Calvinist) tradition the authority of the Bible is absolute and beyond question. The website of Harrison's church makes this clear: "The beliefs and doctrine of the Christian Reformed Church are based on the Holy Bible, God's infallible written Word contained in the 66 books of the Old and New Testaments. We believe that it was uniquely, verbally, and fully inspired by the Holy Spirit and that it is the supreme and final authority in all matters on which it speaks." All the people I spoke to in Harrison not only attended church regularly, but had also continued with their Bible studies since leaving school. While not a church institution, the Leisure Living Apartments was run on Christian lines, which was one of its attractions to Mr. and Mrs. Maas. That morning, just as Pastor Hayes and I arrived, they had been taking part in a regular study class held in

33

the main sitting room of the apartments. It is no exaggeration to say that for many of Harrison's residents the Bible and its study corresponded to their higher education.

Harrison's residents' lifelong fidelity to the church and its teaching had provided them with certain convictions, which they all shared with equal confidence. On the question of the afterlife, there was unanimity, even if individual visions of its exact constitution varied. Mrs. Maas gave me the most explicit response in religious terms. "We believe," she said. "We have a savior. We have Jesus. The best is yet to come, but we don't know what we have to go through to get there. Our Lord has promised to be with us all the time and he will never leave us." Mr. and Mrs. Uilenberg had no doubt they were going to heaven and would meet again. "It's going to be better, we know that," she said. Mrs. Oakland concurred, "I'm ready. I know where I'm going. I know I'm going to heaven." She believed that she was going to meet people she had known in life, her parents and her brother, though she didn't know exactly what it would be like. "I don't think God intends us to know."

Stan Hoekman, once the town's storekeeper and postmaster and now a widower living alone in his house in Harrison, was sure there was an afterlife and was confident that his wife had gone to heaven. However, he was troubled by a theological conundrum no one had been able to solve for him: if he failed to get to heaven, she would be disappointed, but that was not possible because there was no disappointment in heaven. Pastor Hayes, who was with me while I talked to Mr. Hoekman, reassured him that he would be going to heaven but couldn't provide an answer to the puzzle of heavenly disappointment. Like the others, Mr. Hoekman was more hesitant when it came to the actual makeup of heaven and its population. He didn't believe his friends and children would be recognizable in their old human form; he thought they might know each other "as angels," though he wasn't sure about that either. (Sadly, Stan Hoekman has since died.)

On the subject of heaven, I had a longer conversation with Mrs. de Jong, aged ninety-nine and also a resident in the Living Leisure Apartments, who asked me nearly as many questions as I put to her. She confirmed that she truly believed that, "at death you go to heaven because Jesus Christ died to save you from your sins," but then asked me if I did not believe the same. At that point I confessed—if that's the word—my atheism. I told her that my understanding was that my body, in common with all organic creatures, would simply decompose when I died.

"Oh dear! Is that really what you think?"

"Yes," I said.

"Is that what you've been taught?"

"No, it's my own conclusion, having thought about these things."

"I don't know what to say back to you."

I tried to explain to her that the United Kingdom was essentially a secular society and that I was not exceptional in my lack of religious belief. By way of illustration, I said that our politicians, when discussing public morality, might invoke "traditional" or "old-fashioned" or "Victorian" or even "family" values but, unlike their American equivalents, would never associate themselves explicitly with Christian values. I cited the example of Tony Blair, probably our most religious prime minister in recent years, whose advisors had gone to great lengths to disguise the devoutness of their man. "We don't do God," his press secretary Alastair Campbell had famously said, fending off questions about Blair's faith because he feared they would be politically damaging. The British media had ridiculed Blair for supposedly praying with George W. Bush, and it was only after he resigned the leadership that Blair fully acknowledged his allegiance to Christianity. Mrs. de Jong listened to this catalogue of heathenism with polite but evident incredulity; I might have been telling her that we sacrificed burnt offerings to a golden calf.

"We have such a strong faith that our Lord died for us and rose again," she commented after I finished.

I told her that in Europe the situation was different, that the numbers of people going to church were declining, especially in France and the United Kingdom.

"Now that causes me sorrow, it really does," she said in her charming manner.

Still incredulous, she asked me again if I was serious about being an atheist; when I assured her I really was, she asked me how I kept Christmas.

We talked about her idea of heaven, which she hoped would be a beautiful place. She didn't dread the prospect of death. She found it hard to believe she would meet her husband in the afterlife, at least in his physical manifestation, but the thought of heaven gave her comfort. We talked about the Lord's Prayer, the visit of the Pope to the United Kingdom in September 2010, the way that a Harrison resident was identified by the church that he or she attended, and so on. As our conversation was winding up, she reverted to the question of my unbelief with touching concern for my spiritual void. I asked her if she had ever met an atheist before.

"No," she said, and then added, "Though sometimes you think you have."

These elderly people presented an unusual homogeneity, derived largely from their common history, which consisted of two strands: farming and religion. They all knew or knew of the others and knew their histories; they had been to the same schools, or similar small rural schools, prayed at the same churches, studied their Bibles in the same classes; they had married locally, worked locally, retired locally, and would likely die locally. They had long since given up working on the land or serving the local community, but they were still unified by the discipline and ideology of their church. Their faith provided a rhythm to their week, brought them together socially, but most influential of all, it supplied them with an all-embracing ideology, a way of seeing the world, which was mutually reinforcing and changeless.

However, they were also a moribund generation, the last of their type. The small-scale family farming on which they and their forefathers had depended was no longer commercially viable, and many of their children had been forced to look elsewhere for different kinds of employment. No one I spoke to expressed dissatisfaction with having been born in Harrison, South Dakota, but they all recognized that their era was about to close. With perhaps a few stragglers still to come among their children, they were the ones fated to close the period of Harrison's Dutch history, which had spanned just five generations.

Farming will no doubt continue in this part of South Dakota, and perhaps Harrison will be populated with newcomers, but small farming communities united by religion and ethnic origin are surely an extinct phenomenon, especially those that can trace their origins back to a particular homesteading expedition. Today's equivalent of the Dutchmen of the 1880s, eager for new opportunities, will not see farming as their destiny. The remoteness and isolation of Harrison (both cultural and geographical), an agricultural tradition that did not foster secondary and college education as a priority, and the self-discipline fostered by the Christian Reformed tradition are a combination of factors unlikely to be repeated, at least in South Dakota.

There is nothing unusual, at least in the developed world, in seeing small agricultural communities in retreat; the same thing can be observed among the hill farmers of Wales, to take one example from the United Kingdom. As it happens, I have lived in such a world for much of my married life. When we first moved to Stowlangtoft in Suffolk (population 200), my wife and I were just in time to carry the coffin, so to speak, of a social system that dated back to the eighteenth century. One family owned most of the village: the cottages and smaller houses that made up its two streets, all the surrounding fields, woods, and copses, as well as two sets of farm buildings, two substantial farmhouses, and a Victorian mansion complete with stable block, walled yard, lake, and parkland. In 1975, when we arrived, the family still employed several tractor drivers, a shepherd, three stockmen looking after pigs, a gamekeeper, and a gardener, and all these men and their families occupied cottages that were tied to their jobs, for which they paid minimal rents. Not so long ago such landlords had owned or financed the other facilities in their villages as well, including shops, pubs, and even schools and libraries. They appointed or played a large part in the appointment of the parish vicar, and as local magistrates, they dispensed justice to their tenants. In effect, the village was their fiefdom, over which they ruled benignly or otherwise according to temperament. This squirearchical system gave rural villages a cohesion quite as powerful as Harrison's, though its dynamic was of course quite different; the English village's structure was hierarchical, whereas Harrison's was egalitarian. And yet both communities shared one vital quality: everyone belonged.

As incomers to the village, my wife and I were harbingers of the future collapse of the old regime, for the house we rented had previously been the home of a tractor driver, who had just retired but was not being replaced. Agribusiness, rather than antiquated squires, was beginning to rule in the countryside. Farmers grubbed out hedges to expand the size of fields, and under a paradoxical law of capitalism, smaller and smaller work forces were required to drive bigger and bigger machines across larger and larger fields, which became known as East Anglian prairies. The old cohesion was fragmenting as the power of the landlord diminished in direct ratio to the size of the work force he needed to employ. Unlike our predecessors in the house, we were conventional tenants, paying rent at the market rate and owing nothing to the landlord apart from our monthly payment. We lived in the community, but we were not part of its historic system and had no interest in working on the land. We were the people who weren't "Dutch," so to speak; we were the cause of the old villagers locking their doors for the first time. Nor did we have to acquire the habit of deference in relation to the old land-owning class. We could afford to decide how we fitted into our new community; we were uncommitted to anything in the village except by private choice.

Fortunately, my wife Sally (unlike her benighted husband) is a natural communitarian; in other words, she is sociable and hospitable and has found her own ways of forming bonds within the various villages in which we have lived. In addition, our two children were born, brought up, and educated in this area, and there is nothing like the common experience of rearing children to bring people together—of both generations. However, these forces were spontaneous and voluntary, and if they had owed their energy to a church, it would only have been the result of coincidence, rather than a uniform belief throughout the community. We have a beautiful medieval church in this village, whose tower I can see from our kitchen window, but it is only attended on Sundays by a handful of people, albeit a large handful by English standards. My guess is that as professed atheists we are in a minority, but as villagers who never go to church, we are among the majority.

I would also guess that few of those who do go to our church, and call themselves Christians (not necessarily the same thing), would express the same serene confidence regarding heaven and the place waiting for them as Harrison's church-goers. As I understand it, there is more to this certitude than a simple belief in Christianity. Christian Reformed (Calvinist) doctrine teaches that the "elect" will go to heaven, not as a result of virtue or good works or devoutness, but as a result of God's arbitrary choice, which may even fall on someone who is sinful. Harrison's faithful believers are the beneficiaries, if that's the right word, of a particular kind of Protestantism imported directly from the sixteenth century that has wrapped a powerful insulation around their minds, allowing them to enjoy a rare spiritual ease.

I don't want to give the wrong impression. The residents of Harrison struck me as decent, reflective people, who were by no means complacent in their faith. Like many people of northern European extraction on the Great Plains, they were earnest, frugal, and neighborly farmers, whose families had survived extremely difficult times during the dust storms of the Great Depression, and whose faith had therefore been sorely tested. But I was perplexed by their religious certitude, which might have been enviable if it hadn't been the product of minds that were closed—or so it seemed to me. They had been taught by their church and their parents that the Bible contained answers to all the philosophical questions that might have otherwise disturbed them, and I felt I was confronting a mind-set that, for all its friendliness, had not changed since 1884, when the original settlers had founded their church.

To get a more informed impression of Harrison's formal religious life I attended a service led by Pastor Steve Hayes. On this particular Sunday, the "South Church" hosted evening service, as was immediately apparent from the number of cars in its parking lot; I counted fifteen vehicles and others were arriving as I walked through the door. The pastor had been unable to take his regular morning service, having driven more than a hundred miles west to the Rosebud Indian Reservation to preach in Lakeview, another town founded by homesteaders in the nineteenth century, but one that had fulfilled what may well be Harrison's destiny. Lakeview had gradually lost its population over the years and was by now a ghost town, accessible only by dirt road. Its homes and businesses had all been abandoned, and the church was the only building still in use, providing the last few scattered farming families in the area with a religious and social center. Pastor Hayes told me later that his service had been well attended by these ghosts.

Entering the church was a curious experience for me because I realized I had not attended a service other than a wedding, funeral, or children's carol service since my school days. Nor had I ever attended a service in a Christian Reformed church. I was immediately welcomed by a greeter, who naturally wanted to know what had brought me to Harrison. I told him I had come to hear the pastor preach, and since I wasn't local, he assumed I must have met Hayes at seminary college.

By then the congregation had swollen to twenty-seven people, enough to make any Church of England vicar envious. An organ, played in melancholy style, whiled away the minutes until the pastor made his appearance. The church was large and airy, and a set of beautiful wooden pews arranged unusually in a kind of crescent, faced the altar. They must have been designed by a charitable soul, for they were surprisingly comfortable.

Dressed in shirtsleeves, the pastor walked in and took up a position close to his congregation. He opened proceedings by telling us about his visit to Lakeview. He was able to report that Harrison was indeed the center of the universe because his morning congregation had been full of cousins and relatives of the folks back here in town, and he mentioned several names, all Dutch in origin. He set the tone for the rest of the service with a spirited reading from Psalm 148, which invited the sun, the moon, and the stars; the dragons, the stormy winds, and creeping things; young men and maidens, old men and children to praise the Lord, for he had commanded them to be created and had established them forever and ever. Hayes then reminded us that God had also created us, a broken people, in his image and that we should give him our praise and ask for forgiveness. We then intoned a hymn in the quietly dirgeful manner of people for whom singing in public does not come naturally.

The sermon, prompted by Pilate's examination of Christ, asked two questions: what is faith and what is the purpose of faith? Hayes spoke for twenty minutes, without flagging or losing intensity. The goal of our faith, he summarized at the end, is the salvation of our souls. Without faith we would find ourselves in outer darkness, but through the grace of Jesus Christ, we would find eternal life.

His preaching style was simple and free of hysteria, which would not have been to the liking of his phlegmatic congregation, even if he had been inclined to it. I was surprised by the non-English way in which he spoke directly and intimately to his listeners about the salvation of their souls, much as a concerned bank manager might speak to them about their overdrafts, or a builder about the state of their gutters. But then, the whole relationship between pastor and congregation was strange to someone brought up in the tradition of the Church of England. Here was a man in his early thirties, firmly exhorting an audience of men and women at least twice his age to attend to their spiritual health, and yet these same men and women were his employers, who paid his salary and expenses, and provided and maintained his house. Presumably, he would not have been offered the job in the first place if his theology as well as his personality had not been acceptable to the church elders, but having got the job, he was required to execute it with the authority invested in his office—a delicate interplay of power. Although this relationship was no doubt familiar to thousands of small rural communities and their pastors, it was quite different to the centralized arrangement operating in the Church of England, whereby the Church appointed, employed, and housed its vicars and asked the parish to make only a small contribution towards these expenses.

At the end of his sermon, Hayes asked us to pray. We were to pray especially for those who had not yet opened their hearts to God so that they might have eternal life. He then directed the deacons to collect the tithes and offerings. After the service the greeter asked me a bit more about myself. I told him about my curiosity concerning Harrison, the town with my name, which amused him. I also told him that I was a writer. "They say that writers and painters only get to be famous when they're dead," he said and jogged me with his elbow to show he was joking.

The next day I intended to leave Harrison, but before I departed I had lunch with Steve Hayes at the newly opened and grandly named Travel Plaza in Corsica. By now I counted him as a friend, and I felt able to ask him some difficult questions that had occurred to me during my brief acquaintance with Harrison's residents. For example, I mentioned the fact that the area north of the Black Hills on the western side of South Dakota, had proved to be one of the richest fields in the world for dinosaur remains. The most complete Tyrannosaurus Rex skeleton so far unearthed had been discovered not far from a little town poignantly called

Faith. How to reconcile these spectacular examples of evolutionary evidence with Genesis and the teaching of the Christian Reformed Church, which insisted that the Bible was "the final authority in all matters on which it speaks"? Typically, Hayes took a plain and homely line: in his eyes the question of evolution came down to a matter of choice between science and the literal word of the Bible, between the two theories that were, as he saw it, on offer. He admitted that he had not wrestled long with this problem but had settled for what he had been taught all his life. He did not like the idea of resorting to metaphors, as some theologians did, by interpreting evolutionary time in Biblical terms and saying that with God one day was like a thousand years, and a thousand years were like a day.[11] This approach struck him as dodging the issue. He understood that there was an irreconcilable contradiction between Genesis and the fossil record, but once he had made his choice, he was no longer troubled. This conclusion seemed to me an honorable acknowledgement of his position, and it also showed that the elders in Harrison had chosen the right man when they appointed him their pastor.

What had I learned about old age from Harrison? The people I had talked to suffered from all the usual debilities that attend old age, but even those too old and frail to live independently in their own homes seemed able to cope with their infirmities, contemplating the prospect of death with an enviable equanimity derived from their collective confidence of going to heaven. Though their state of mind was enviable, it was the product of a particular set of historical circumstances that was no longer available to South Dakotans, far less the rest of us. Nor did one have to be an atheist to see that their spiritual composure came at a steep price in terms of geographical and cultural isolation, which even other Christians might hesitate to pay.

After lunch I took some photographs of the gigantic silver grain elevators in Corsica that stood between the county highway and Railway Avenue and were the town's distinguishing landmark. They were not objects of beauty, but a local journalist had reprimanded me for saying so. "You should see this town when harvest is in full swing," she said.

---

11. He was referring to 2 Peter 3: "But, beloved, be not ignorant of this one thing, that one day is with the Lord as a thousand years, and a thousand years as one day."

"Trucks and tractors will be lined up along the highway. When we see that, we know there's a good harvest, and a good harvest is good for the farmers and good for businesses in Corsica."

I left town, taking the straight road west that led to Harrison, where trucks and tractors would never again line the highway. I had intended to pass the town, driving on to the Missouri River and the Great Plains that lay beyond it, but at the last moment I turned onto Vanden Bos Avenue, past Sixth, Fifth, Fourth, and Third streets until, half a mile later, I reached Harrison's cemetery. It was beautifully kept, and I was reminded of Mr. Uilenberg's remark about how well the old Dutchmen cared for their houses. The grass was mown and the gravel paths were raked. There must have been a hundred or more plots, many of them marked with ungainly, monolithic lumps of gray or red granite. Some had individual names and dates carved into them, but most simply bore the name of the family whose members lay beneath: Vanderpol, Mulder, Lefer, Brinks, Nieuwenhuis, Huizenga, Bult, Plooster, Vandenhock, Aardappel, Smits, DeBeer, Maas, Van Zenten.

There was no sign of a Harrison; nor, as yet, of a name that was not Dutch in derivation.

2 Lewis and Clark

"The Lewis and Clark expedition is one of the great adventure stories in American history," wrote historian Gary E. Moulton. "Everyone knows about the two captains' trek across the continent with their band of intrepid explorers. And who has not heard of Sacagawea, the young Shoshone girl who accompanied the party with her newborn baby strapped to her back?"[1]

The shameful answer to that question is—the British. We have not heard of Sacagawea; nor do we know about the captains and their great adventure. Moulton posed the question in 1988, but despite the publicity and celebrations that have since taken place to mark the centenary of the expedition in 2004, the answer will not have changed: the names of Lewis and Clark—the most famous explorers in American history—continue to ring no bells in the British head.

On the face of it, this failure to recognize these men seems strange because there are several American folk heroes whose names radiate charisma in the United Kingdom, Davy Crockett and Buffalo Bill, for example, even if our knowledge of their actual deeds is foggy. For obvious historical reasons, we are a nation that relishes tales of exploration, and though we may have a forgivable chauvinistic bias in favor of home-grown heroes such as Francis Drake, Captain Cook, and Dr. Livingstone, the legend of the American wilderness has had a powerful hold on the British imagination ever since the landing of the

1. Gary E. Moulton, "On Reading Lewis and Clark: The Last Twenty Years," in *Voyages of Discovery*, ed. James P. Ronda (Helena: Montana Historical Society Press, 1998), p. 281.

Mayflower. Why then should a narrative filled with the classic elements of frontier adventure, fights with bears, near-death struggles through snow and ice, clashes with Indians, and so forth, arouse so little interest in us?

Two explanations occur to me. It may be that the very success of the Lewis and Clark expedition and the exemplary character of its leaders (at least while on the trail) has proved uncongenial to a national temperament that likes its heroes to be flawed and their enterprises ill-fated. After all, the perennial British idea of an explorer-hero is Scott of the Antarctic, a man whose last expedition, for all the personal virtues of its leader and members, cannot be counted a success. In contrast with Lewis and Clark, who fulfilled the objects of their mission and brought home safely a corps of more than thirty personnel, Scott failed to reach the South Pole before Norwegian Roald Amundsen and led his four comrades to perish from exhaustion, starvation, and cold.[2] As a reward Scott was immediately sanctified as a national hero, and while there have been many revisionist attempts to recast him as a bungler, his place in any list of the greatest Britons in history seems to be assured. What chance have Lewis and Clark of claiming a place in our pantheon with competition like this?

My second reason is probably more to the point: the expedition has never been the subject of a popular feature film. Hollywood has taught the British all we know about the American West, and what Hollywood has chosen to ignore has remained a closed book to us. Literally so, for it would be hard to find a copy of the journals in a typical British bookshop. On the other hand, events such as the siege of the Alamo, the gunfight at the OK Corral, and the defeat of Custer at the Little Big Horn have each been turned into films several times. As a result these episodes are inscribed in the British version of western history.

As far as I know, the Lewis and Clark expedition, which appears to be ready-made for a film treatment, has only been translated to the big

2. Sergeant Charles Floyd died on 20 August 1804, probably of complications caused by appendicitis, which would then have been incurable under any circumstances. The final expeditionary corps that was recruited during the following winter at Fort Mandan all came home.

screen once, and that was in a movie called *The Far Horizons*, directed by the Polish-born Rudolph Maté in 1955. Clark, played by Charlton Heston, is depicted as an Indian-hater whose racist heart is melted by Sacagawea, the beautiful Indian maiden, a development that plunges the pair into "an immortal romance," according to the trailer. In 2011, *Time* magazine rated the film second in its top-ten list of historically misleading films, partly because it objected to the casting of the Caucasian Donna Reed as Sacagawea. Since the list also included *10,000 BC*, a film we took to our hearts, it cannot have been historical inaccuracy that prevented Maté's film from throwing the Lewis and Clark spell over the British.

Despite appearances, perhaps the Lewis and Clark story does not lend itself to the sort of treatment that has made western movies so popular because it lacks a villain and an enemy, both indispensable to the genre. The captains were never obliged to confront the equivalent of the black-clad gunfighter, whom western heroes are required to slay (Jack Palance in *Shane*, to give one classic example among hundreds); nor do the American Indians whom Lewis and Clark encountered qualify as traditional figures in feathers and war paint who lurk on the horizon, waiting their chance to slaughter the wagon train. The success of the western film is built on the romance of frontier landscape, which the Lewis and Clark story can provide in abundance, but it is also built on the elemental clash of good and evil, and this element seems to be missing and can only be recognized with historical hindsight. Although the captains may have been the agents of Manifest Destiny, and therefore in some sense villainous, they behaved honorably by their own lights and never deployed the military power at their disposal. Far from being hostile, or capable of being cast as "hostiles," most of the American Indians on their route offered the invading guests assistance and hospitality; harmonious exchanges do not make the stuff of classic western dramas.

But these are excuses; the fact is, for whatever reason, the British remain stubbornly unresponsive to the Lewis and Clark magic. I count myself fortunate that I am one of the few who has discovered, as it were, the great discoverers.

In 1998, *The Sunday Times* (London) commissioned me to follow the route taken by Lewis and Clark as they made their near fatal crossing of the Continental Divide for the first time. The Montana and Idaho offices of tourism organized a press trip for my benefit, and I requested the company of my old traveling companion, Alvin. Following the Lewis and Clark Trail, our itinerary took us from Great Falls, Montana, across the Rockies to Spalding, Idaho, a grueling section of the captains' journey that occupied them for eighteen weeks, between 13 June and 9 October 1805, during which they carried their equipment upstream on boats and over the mountains on pack horses. Conditions were so tough they were obliged to eat some of their horses. We, on the other hand, were whisked through by car in four hectic days, with pauses here and there to see the most important sights and sample local cuisine.

For those who have not experienced the quaint joys of a press trip, let me explain. As the guest of a tourist office, which does not want to see its money wasted, the intrepid journalist is generously mothered from one end of his expedition to the other. Meals and hotel beds are provided at every staging post, and guides stand by to point out the spectacles and marvels the journalist might otherwise overlook since he is presumed to be too drunk or stupid to notice them unaided. I was used to these arrangements, which if nothing else ensured that the journalist's limited time was put to efficient use, but Alvin, a dedicated individualist, chafed under the solicitude of our minders. He had a point.

It is true that we were shown some truly beautiful landscape, in particular the "the most remarkable clifts" that Lewis had ever seen, which, in a poetic moment on 19 July 1805, he aptly named the "gates of the rocky mountains."[3] Alvin was content to enjoy the boat tour that took us through the canyon, in what is now Holter Lake, with its perpendicular cliffs of black granite and its "towering and projecting rocks [that] in many places seem ready to tumble on us." Even so, I think he was a little ashamed that we were paying homage to the great explorers in such effete luxury.

Our trip pointed up a fundamental distinction between Alvin and

3. All quotations from the journals are taken from Gary E. Moulton, ed., *The Journals of the Lewis and Clark Expedition*, 13 vols. (Lincoln: University of Nebraska Press, 1983–2001). The complete text can also be accessed online at http://lewisandclarkjournals.unl.edu/.

myself: I was one of nature's tourists, and he was not. His instinct, constantly frustrated, was to leap out of the car, escape our minders, and climb the mountains alone; mine was to worry about our next meal. But, for all our differences, we both came away from the trip as devotees of Lewis and Clark, and our interest has not waned.

In my case, I had to satisfy myself with armchair exploration by reading about the Corps of Discovery, to use its official name, back in England. I was enthralled by the fact that, thanks to a sort of literary x-ray, it was easy to reveal the route of a journey into what had been wilderness through the skin of the most developed country in the world. Not many great journeys of exploration can be followed so exactly through terrain that has since been paved and ploughed and dammed. For example, the course of the Niger was correctly identified by Mungo Park in 1806, though the effort cost him his life, and it remains remote and inaccessible to this day. No "Mungo Park Trail" signs, campsites, and scenic overlooks mark the route he took through today's Guinea, Mali, and Nigeria. The great imperialist expeditions mounted by British explorers necessarily took them to far-flung (far, that is, if you were doing the flinging from London) parts of the earth, Africa, the Pacific Ocean, and so on, whereas Lewis and Clark were sent to explore the western parts of their own country that were as yet undiscovered by white Americans. The British love of the Wild West is partly explained by our fascination with a country that contained an internal frontier beyond which lay wilderness, something that has not been experienced in Britain since Roman soldiers shivered on Hadrian's Wall.

There are only a few parts of Lewis and Clark's route where today's topography would be both recognizable to them and unchanged since their time, mostly because so much of their river route has disappeared beneath the various lakes that now submerge the old course of the Missouri River. But thanks to the precision of their journals, it is possible to pinpoint their progress day by day, and on some occasions hour by hour. Though by no means literary men themselves, Lewis and Clark left behind the most bookish legacy of all explorers, and I feel sure that as many people have become fascinated by them through reading a book as by hiking or camping.

The historian Donald Jackson, famously called the captains the "writingest explorers of their time," adding, "they wrote constantly and abundantly, afloat and ashore, legibly and illegibly, and always with an urgent sense of purpose."[4] Most books of exploration are formal accounts, composed after the event and derived from raw notes made in the field, but the Lewis and Clark journals were never domesticated, so to speak; much of what we read is what was written on the spot, day by day, under conditions that were far from conducive to literature. The captains were not the only members of the party to keep journals, for Lewis encouraged the sergeants to make their own records. Two privates also wrote daily accounts, and it is thought that others may have been doing the same.[5] Although President Thomas Jefferson expected them to record information that would be of scientific, military, or ethnographic use, the explorers wrote so vividly and accurately that two centuries later we can not only locate them but hear their voices as they called out to each other; we can hear the splash of their paddles and the crack of their rifles; we can hear the rain as it fell interminably on their makeshift roof at Fort Clatsop; and we can hear the scratch, scratch, scratch of their pens.

For those interested in such things, it seems that the men used both quill pens and metal nibs. While in Philadelphia in 1803 preparing for the expedition, Lewis purchased "100 Quils," "4 Metal Pens," and "6 papers of ink powder." Clark almost certainly used quills, which varied his penmanship according to whether they were blunt or sharp. One expert even claimed to be able to tell from Clark's field notes when he paused to sharpen his quill pen. He was also rather careless with his ink: some of the sheets from his notes are badly blotched, and some bear clearly-delineated fingerprints.[6]

My interest in Lewis and Clark had the happy effect of amplifying my interest in South Dakota. On their outward journey, the corps of forty-five men traveled through today's South Dakota between 21 August and

4. Donald Jackson, ed., *The Letters of the Lewis and Clark Expedition with Related Documents*, 2nd ed., 2 vols. (Chicago: University of Illinois Press, 1978), 1:vii.

5. Moulton, *Journals*, 2:542–45.

6. Paul Russell Cutright, *A History of the Lewis and Clark Journals* (Norman: University of Oklahoma Press, 1976), pp. 8, 151, 157.

14 October 1804, a stretch of their long journey that brought them onto the northern Great Plains for the first time. (Sailing and paddling downstream on their return journey, the same distance took them just sixteen days, between 21 August and 5 September 1806.) On 4 September 1804 they passed the mouth of the Niobrara River and the next twenty days of their journey, when they traveled 263 miles according to Clark, have been identified by historian Paul Cutright as zoologically the most exciting and important of the whole trip, for they discovered no less than nine animals and eight plants new to science. This first period in South Dakota was also distinguished by their most challenging confrontation with American Indians, the Teton Sioux, or Lakotas, whom they met at the mouth of the Bad (Teton) River near today's Pierre.

Nowadays, the South Dakota stretch of the Missouri barely counts as a river, and the appearance of its present course through the state would be unrecognizable to the captains if they made a ghostly reappearance. Under the Pick-Sloan Plan, five dams were built in the 1950s and 1960s—the Garrison, Oahe, Big Bend, Fort Randall, and Gavins Point—the latter four in South Dakota, with the result that the Missouri is now less a river than a chain of lakes or reservoirs. In view of this radically changed topography, why bother to return to a site that lies beneath the water? By the same token, why bother to revisit the expedition's route at all, since few parts of even the wilder stretches have remained unchanged since the early nineteenth century? The answer, at least for someone like myself, who is more of a reader than a hiker, more bookworm than pioneer, is that the significance of a historical location is as much a matter of empathy as authenticity. Indeed, the search for authenticity is a false trail, to use an apt metaphor, because the past cannot be returned to us without some kind of mediation, and that always involves artifice.

But I think our interest lies elsewhere. Jefferson once observed with disapproval that few public figures took notes, adding that without them "history becomes fable instead of facts."[7] The history of the Lewis and Clark Expedition is so securely founded on the voluminous quantities of facts recorded in the journals that it has proved strong enough to sup-

7. Ibid., p. 5.

port a towering superstructure of commentary, to which this chapter adds yet another curlicue. If I had the resources of Charles Foster Kane, I would collect all the books ever published on the subject of the expedition, including those devoted to Seaman, the dog, who has his own bibliography.[8] And yet, there is nothing to compare with making a physical connection across time in order to create the kind of intimacy that confirms the experience we have been studying on paper. Although we learn nothing we could not have discovered from a biography when we visit the reconstructed study of a famous writer, those primitive spectacles with their wire frames and tiny lenses, the chewed end of a steel-nib pen holder, that scribbled note—these mundane bits and pieces, which, to be frank, could have belonged to anybody—possess a deeply touching quality because they exist in two time dimensions at once: ours and that of our hero.

And so, despite the reconstitution of the Missouri River, when I came to plan my own modest expedition through South Dakota, I still wanted to pick up the Lewis and Clark Trail wherever possible. Several opportunities presented themselves.

Before leaving home, I had read in Julie Fanselow's *Traveling the Lewis and Clark Trail* that two stretches of the Missouri between the Fort Randall Dam and Sioux City, Iowa, were the least changed from the days of Lewis and Clark. My *USA Rough Guide* told me that Yankton, which stands between these two points, was a "gem-like historic town," and so, on the strength of these prospects, I booked myself a room in Yankton for the first two nights of my trip.[9]

Perhaps, I should have paid more attention to my hotel's self-description on the internet, which boasted of its proximity to the town's prison. When I checked in, I was dismayed to find that my room bore a distinct resemblance to a cell, with bare brick walls and naked light bulbs; furthermore, it was a cell built on a marsh to judge by the green

8. Charles Foster Kane was the extravagantly wealthy protagonist of Orson Welles's 1941 film *Citizen Kane*.

9. Samantha Cook et al, *USA The Rough Guide* (London: Rough Guides, 2000), p. 714.

carpet and its moist, spongy texture. My heart sank, and I knew that I would have to find another hotel, but at the same time, I was shamed by the sorry contrast I made with Lewis and Clark and their men.

Their passage up the Missouri during those September days was relatively easy by the standards of their journey, since game was plentiful and the weather mild, though the men were troubled by mosquitoes and the river continually presented obstacles. Take, for example, 14 September 1804, during which they traveled nine miles with the southern part of today's Lyman County on their left side. The morning began, wrote Clark, with "Drizeley rain . . . cloudy and disagreeable," and the rain continued for the greater part of the day. Clark walked on the shore and killed what he called a "goat," but which was in fact a pronghorn. Private Shields shot a "hare," which Clark described as "clearly the mountain Hare of Europe," though it was later identified as a white-tailed jackrabbit. Meanwhile, on the river the men were wrestling with shallows and obstructive sandbars, which forced all hands to get into the water several times in order to drag the keelboat free. At the end of the day, the corps camped in a place that is now inundated by Lake Francis Case and made supper, presumably out of what the hunters had shot. The remaining animals were carefully skinned and stuffed with a view to sending them back for Jefferson to examine. Clark's final entry for the day reads, "Some heavy Showers of rain all wet, had the Goat and rabit Stufed rained all night." However, it did not rain hard enough to prevent him from writing up his journal for the day, which included an account of his activities, the weather, a reference to the local geology, and descriptive details of the game that had been shot, which were the first scientific descriptions of these creatures.

Mosquitoes, heavy rain showers, several drenchings in the river, a supper of jerked meat or roast goat washed down with muddy river water, then to bed in wet clothes to spend the night in continual rain—and I wanted to change hotels because I didn't like the light bulbs. At least the corps could enjoy the consolations of their equivalent of a minibar, until the whiskey rations ran out on 5 July 1805.

The next morning, fortified by breakfast in my new hotel, I drove west from Yankton, hoping to find a stretch of unreformed Missouri. I paused at Sand Creek, which was at the far, downstream end of the original river course that now flowed from the Fort Randall Dam into the Lewis and Clark Lake. I pulled the car onto a loop of track beneath some cottonwoods that overlooked the river and scrambled a few feet down a bank to the river's edge, where there was a little beach made of near-white sand.

It has to be said that the Missouri does not have a reputation as a beautiful river; some have called it "Old Misery" on account of the difficulty of navigating a boat through its snags, sawyers (submerged logs), sandbars, and whirlpools. No one denounced it more abusively than George Catlin, the famous artist, who called it "a filthy abyss," a "Hell of waters," and a "huge and terrible deformity of waters."[10] On the other hand, he also referred to the "beautiful shores of the Missouri," when recounting his own canoe voyage down the river in 1838: "From day to day we thus passed on, surveying the beautiful shores; the grass and rounded bluffs rising in groups, sometimes hundreds on hundreds, appearing in the distance as if green carpets of velvet were spread over them. . . . The sand-bars in the distance sometimes seemed as if they were covered with snow, from the quantities of pelicans and white swans that were grouped upon them."[11]

I had already seen the river from the road, but this was my first opportunity to get close enough to wet my hand in the water and feel the current. It was a warm afternoon; the sky was blue; and the river, despite its reputation for dragging huge quantities of mud and silt in its turbid depths, was blue too, a soft blue in which the sky and clouds seemed to have been mixed to produce a single color. The low bluffs downstream curved away in a long, open crescent, while the upstream bank had been eaten away, leaving a series of grassy beaches. The grass was green thanks to the recent rain, and the cottonwoods, though they had not yet come into leaf, appeared at a distance to be enveloped in a soft green mist, generated by buds about to burst. From what I could see through my binoculars, the bluffs on the opposite shore, a great distance away,

10. Quoted in Larry McMurtry, *Sacagawea's Nickname: Essays on the American West* (New York: New York Review of Books, 2001), p. 165.

11. George Catlin, *Life among the Indians* (London: Bracken Books, 1996), pp. 122–23.

formed a continuous unbroken wall some twenty or thirty feet high. All was tranquil and fresh, though I was surprised by the enormous quantity of vegetable matter—reeds and bushes—that was floating down the river, much of it collected in long trailing islands hundreds of feet long and densely packed, in which small shrubs appeared to have taken root.

I am always moved by the great, winding rivers that pursue their courses across the Great Plains, though I feel an instant sense of identification with most rivers of any size. Why? Perhaps because I was brought up in a suburb of Liverpool called Aigburth, famous for its cricket ground, where the River Mersey was our neighbor. For much of its length, a mere seventy miles, the Mersey is an insignificant trickle of a river, but suddenly, as it opens into its estuary, it dons its cape and cloak and becomes one of the world's super ports. Aigburth lies four miles upstream from Liverpool's cyclopean docks, now reduced to a tourist attraction, and the river mouth is nearly at its widest with a mile and a half of water between Aigburth and the opposite bank, which in the polluted days of my childhood was often rendered invisible by the yellowish fog that hovered over the water.

Not long after World War II, the Liverpool Corporation, in a moment of civic genius, commissioned a promenade—a broad ribbon of riverside walkway—that would run upriver from the Pier Head, symbol of the city's historic grandeur, to Aigburth. The first section to be built lay at the bottom of our road and took the form of a park with acres of lawn scored with sinuous paths of purple asphalt. Facing the river was a chain of little kiosks or pavilions where people could shelter from the rain. Despite these pleasurable features, it was impossible to forget the power of the river because the colossal walls on which the promenade stood were constructed with all the defensive might of a medieval castle to withstand the tidal force of the racing water that could rise by more than thirty feet in the spring.

During my early childhood my mother pushed me daily along the promenade in my stroller, convinced as all Liverpudlians were, that the pungent, faintly fecal, ozone-laden breezes that blew off the river were deeply beneficial to health. Later I roller-skated down the network of slalom paths that led to the promenade, where I swooped like a young Mercury, showing a sporting aptitude for the only time in my life (apart from wielding a deft ping-pong bat at my prep school and spinning webs of magic with a yo-yo). I dragged reluctant dogs up and down its breezy length, loitered there in teenage melancholy, lay hopefully on its grass with girls in summer dresses; but most of all, at every age, I leaned on its railings and stared into the water.

The Mersey, like the Missouri, was not fabled for its beauty, though it was an object of great pride to Liverpool's citizens, for it was the source of their city's fabulous prosperity in the nineteenth century and the symbol of its fading glory in the twentieth. I loved the river. I loved it for being so huge and indifferent, for being an industrial highway and not a pastoral dribble out of *Wind in the Willows*. I loved it for carrying the effluent and outpourings, the sewage and secretions of a great city that once ruled the seven seas. It was a formidable, uninviting river, and its traffic was strictly workmanlike and commercial: dredgers, strings of lighters carrying sand or gravel, police launches, freighters, tankers, and small cargo ships. You never saw a yacht or a rowing boat on its yellow waters. Only a lunatic would contemplate swimming in it. You never saw a cormorant diving into its oily depths because chemicals and filth had long ago choked the life out of its fish. Only the rankest gulls fed off the detritus left on its muddy shore when the tide dropped. I loved those oozy, silt beaches that stank on warm days and showed the bones of rusting bikes. I loved the breezes that blew off its greasy waves and carried the melancholy calling of fog horns into my bedroom at night. I loved it for being neither river nor sea, a leviathan that thrived on freshwater and salt alike, that flowed one way then the other as it chose, a monster that was forever changing itself.[12]

I could tell the story of my youth in rivers.

As a thirteen-year-old, I was sent to a school in Shrewsbury, a Tudor town that the River Severn almost encircles in a loop like a watery necklace. At 220 miles, the Severn is the longest river in the United Kingdom, though a mere brook by American standards: the Missouri is 2,341 miles in length, and its tributary, the James River, is 710. Nonetheless,

---

12. I have to confess that I have plagiarized myself here, for most of this paragraph is taken from my novel *Minotaur in Love* (Hexham: Flambard Press, 2008), pp. 134–35, whose hero loved the river as much as I did and with the same emotions.

the Severn makes an impressive sight in Shrewsbury, where it has cut its course out of a sheer, crescent-shaped cliff some 100 feet high, on top of which my school had taken up its commanding position, looking down on the town in more senses than one. On our free afternoons, we were allowed to leave the school campus, and we would walk to a suspension bridge built for pedestrians and cyclists that crossed the river and carried us from the school's austere regime into the relative decadence of a small, market town. (I am talking about the late 1950s and early 1960s; only someone incarcerated in an English public school, where girls were as rare as giraffes and edible food not much more frequent, could think that Shrewsbury's drab amenities represented decadence.) I seldom crossed this bridge without pausing to lean over its rail and stare, if only for a moment, into the water. There was nothing much to see there, certainly nothing I hadn't seen before, rowing boats, skiffs, the odd swan, but I liked to stare at the water, its movement, flow, patterns, gray-brown tones.

As an undergraduate at Cambridge, I spent many contented hours leaning dreamily on bridges over the River Cam, surely one of the most decorative stretches of urban river in England, to which I contributed by being decorative myself (my only scholastic achievement and a source of regret ever since). Later still, when I worked in London and could stand my office no longer, a frequent occurrence, I would walk to the Thames Embankment and take the ferry from the Tower of London to Greenwich for the sheer pleasure of going somewhere on the water in order to come back. This trip took an hour or more depending on tides and weather, and the fact of its being dependent on such primal forces gave my restorative outing the sense of a voyage. London is a handsome city, and these historic points of embarkation made the excursion all the more pleasurable, but once again it was the water that soothed and revived.

I am a dedicated dilettante of rivers, if such a thing can exist: I don't want to swim or fish in them, ski or drive speedboats on them, sail or row on them (though as a schoolboy I rowed in a four, the most arduous exercise I have ever taken); I don't want to track them to their source or study their ecology. I simply want to lean on a railing and look at them. The water acts as a narcotic, allowing the mind to drift with the current, or float on a seemingly motionless surface, or rise like mist in the morning light. I'm not asking the water to wash away my sins, but rather to float my anxieties away. I can only speak for myself, but streams, no matter how brilliant or exhilarating, do not fulfil this therapeutic function; it takes a large river, a mighty body of water, to induce this moment of release.

Flowing water has often been used as a metaphor for time. It is a metaphor that defies logic because flow can only be understood in relation to a stable point, the river bank for example, which the narrative of human experience does not permit; there is no bank on which we can sit as observers; we are all swept along in the flux. But there are other ways of seeing the flow of a great river in terms of time. Because of its nature—the inexhaustible passage of vast quantities of fluid—a river, as Wordsworth wrote, that "glideth at his own sweet will" is a continuum: what has passed, is passing, will pass again, will pass again, will pass again; water seems to flow through its own extra-temporal dimension, and the future glides by continually, rendering tenses meaningless. Time's seemingly inexorable advance is turned into a circular metaphor by the river, an eternal repetition that brings relief from the apprehension of aging and mortality. This illusion (what else?) is only created for me by large rivers such as are rarely found in a small island; the larger the river, the more persuasive the illusion.

Leaving Sand Creek, I drove a few miles down the road to Springfield (population 1,092), a name that *The Simpsons* has made impossible to take seriously, and made directly for Terrace Park, which is located on a bluff overlooking the river, protected by a large, business-like cannon that was apparently trained on the state of Nebraska on the opposite bank. A notice board offered the information that on 1 September 1804 the Corps of Discovery had camped nearby on Bon Homme Island. A journal entry for that day, written by Sergeant Ordway, gives a good idea of the country the corps had just passed through:

we Set off eairly . . . we proceeded on under an unsteady Breeze from S. W. passed a chalk Bluff on N. S. where we found pleanty of fine plumbs, little above is a white clift called the den of the White Bear, we See large holes in the clift which appeared to go Deep into

the clift; this clift is about 70 feet high on the top is ragged round
knobs & praries all praries on Boath Sides of the river, Some Timber
in the vallies, Cottonwood Elm oak &.C. & on the Islands which is
covered with Small Cottonwood Timber . . . G. Drewyer went out
hunting on N. S. he returned in a Short time had killed a fine Buck
Elk; it was all put on board the pearague, we then proceeded on
past Bottom praries to the lower point of a large & well Timbered
Island where we Camped on N. S. & jurked our Elk.

I could not see Bon Homme Island or any other island, though I
walked up and down the edge of the park with my binoculars searching
for it among the trailing platforms of reed that were all but clogging the
channel. Here again, many of the reed rafts were solid enough for trees
to sink their roots into them and bushes to grow in large clumps.

I decided to ask some teenage boys who were sitting in a couple of
cars facing away from the river. There were four of them, and they could
have stepped out of a small-town coming-of-age movie: a good-looking
one, a red-headed one in a T-shirt that showed off his muscles, an over-
weight one, and one with acne and a wild look in his eye. They were in-
discriminately discussing girls and cars.

"Yeah, she's hot," said one.

"Not worth spending money on," said another dismissively.

I approached, and asked them about the island. They were suspicious
but humored me. One of them thought he'd heard of Bon Homme but
couldn't say where it was. The red-headed boy told me that the reeds
were the result of silt from the Niobrara River, which had only recently
started to come downstream. I asked them if they knew that Lewis and
Clark had camped nearby. They shrugged. I asked if they had all gone
to school in Springfield. The good-looking one said, "Yeah, they taught
us all that stuff but I never listened." The heavy boy said, "They never
brought us down here." I said it was a pity since it was on their doorstep,
adding that I had come a long way to see it. They looked at me as if I was
mad but wished me good luck.

I drove into town and did a tour of its business district, a handful of
blocks with an elementary school at one end and a prison at the other.

I ate lunch in the Grill and More Café, which had a sign outside saying, "Jesus Saves—Ask How." The owner told me there had been a fire on Main Street recently that had burnt out a couple of businesses, leaving the buildings empty.

"They're just shells," she said, "no one's going to fix 'em up."

Back on Main Street, I noticed a sign reading "Springfield Historical Society Museum" on the outside of a large building. The place was clearly closed, but displayed in the window was a list of names and numbers to call if one wanted a tour, and another sign advertised various exhibits within, including a display of Lewis and Clark items. I have visited many small-town museums in the Midwest and have never been disappointed; the promise of Lewis and Clark memorabilia made this one irresistible.

I went to a food store on the other side of the street, asked to use the phone, and rang the name at the top of the list. After a long while, a voice answered, old and frail. Yes, he would open the place up for me; he'd be there in fifteen minutes. I told him not to come if it was at all inconvenient. He didn't seem to hear and put down the phone.

I asked the woman at the check-out if she had ever been in the museum. She hadn't. I said I was interested in Lewis and Clark and that I believed there were some items in the museum connected with the expedition. She looked blankly and shook her head. I asked her if she had been to school in town.

"Yeah, but I had my mind on other things in those days." She looked a little angry and repeated herself: "I had my mind on other things."

I bought an ice cream, went back to the museum building, and sat on a bench outside. The town was asleep in the afternoon sun. The lumber yard opposite was closed, as were several other businesses and shops up and down the street. I picked out the premises that had been burnt. No one visited the bank. A couple of kids drove by, but theirs was the only car on the move.

After ten minutes, I saw an electric wheel chair in the distance, moving slowly along the opposite sidewalk. Five minutes later its driver crossed the street, taking a long diagonal line, apparently confident that no cars would threaten his progress. He drew to a halt in front of me and without saying anything drew out a large bunch of keys. He was elderly. I introduced myself and thanked him for coming, but he didn't look up. He peered closely at the bunch, holding each key up to his eyes. Finally, he admitted defeat and handed them to me. I found the right one and we entered.

The huge room was full of the usual objects to be found in small-town museums. The connection to Lewis and Clark was close to the entrance; it proved to be a crude model of the river and the expedition's keelboat and canoes made by school children many years ago. I must have indicated my disappointment because by way of compensating me the old man drew my attention to a numerous collection of wrenches, all clean and oiled, displayed in a beautiful wooden case with a glass front. He told me the name of the donor, whom he had known personally. I studied them with care.

My docent followed me closely in his chair as I made my way round the rest of the collection, presumably to ensure that I didn't steal anything. I tried to engage him in conversation, but he was too weak to talk much, and in any case I suspect he had always been a man of few words. However, I did ask him about Lewis and Clark, and he told me that Bon Homme Island was now under water. As I should have realized, it had been submerged, along with many other similar small islands, when the Lewis and Clark Lake was created in front of the Gavins Point Dam.

After I'd looked at a buffalo-skin coat large enough to fit a giant, several cases of American Indian beadwork, a case of sea shells from "all over the world" (largest collection in the Midwest, apparently), a collection of dolls, a collection of military uniforms, an ancient version of a wheel chair, and various other cases full of athletic trophies, valedictorian bronze plaques, and a "complete" collection of senior class pictures, all of which I examined respectfully, I turned to thank my host, but he only motioned me towards a door at the back. "You ain't hardly begun," he said, and how right he was.

The next room had been subdivided into a "model" Main Street dating from the pre-war era, with a bank, store, barber's shop, post office, dentist's surgery complete with fearsome-looking pliers that would not have been out of place in the wrench collection, a jail cell, and a pioneer home "furnished as in 1900 era," which alone comprised six rooms. Nor were these exhibits scantily equipped; the pioneer home was virtually ready for new occupants, though the bed with ropes for springs did not look inviting.

Once again I turned to thank my host, but he only waved me onwards. In the next room stood a collection of agricultural machinery, as well as a horse-drawn buggy dating from 1905, a beautiful, elegant thing, and a 1926 Model T Ford. All these items I could have stolen because the room was approached by a steep ramp, which defeated my guide's vehicle. However, he waited for me at the door, peering suspiciously round the corner.

It seemed that at last I had come to the end. I thanked him, and he sweetly thanked me for "coming by." I helped him turn out the lights and lock up, and I watched him as he ground his way back up the still-empty street, presumably to his home.

My next contact with the Corps of Discovery's route was at Snake Creek, a few miles west of Harrison, on the banks of what is now Lake Francis Case, which is the long, narrow reservoir (107 miles) that lies behind Fort Randall Dam. When the dam was completed the lake engulfed the course of the river that Lewis and Clark traveled, but there was no need to allow the imagination to be drowned by killjoy facts. It was here, or somewhere nearby and now under water, that one of the more touching incidents of the expedition took place, and there was a scenic overlook and information board to prove it.

On 26 August 1804, George Shannon, the youngest member of the party at nineteen, was dispatched to search for the expedition's two pack horses, which had gone astray not far from today's Yankton, South Dakota, but by the evening he had not returned. During the following days, the anxious captains made several efforts to find him; their concern was made worse by the fact that Shannon was not "a first rate hunter," as Clark put it in what was probably an understatement. John Colter, the expedition's best tracker, was sent out to find him, but after nine days he returned without either the missing private or the precious horses. Not until 11 September, sixteen days after his disappearance, did the corps find the young man. In Clark's inimitable words:

here the man who left us with the horses 22 [NB: 16] days ago and has been a head ever Since joined, us nearly Starved to Death, he had been 12 days without any thing to eate but Grapes & one Rabit, which he Killed by shooting a piece of hard Stick in place of a ball—. This man Supposeing the boat to be a head pushed on as long as he Could, when he became weak and fiable deturmined to lay by and waite for a tradeing boat, which is expected Keeping one horse for the last resorse,—thus a man had like to have Starved to death in a land of Plenty for the want of Bulletes or Something to kill his meat.

For sixteen days Shannon had been hurrying to catch up with the rest of the expedition, without realizing that he was ahead of them, not behind. He finally lost heart and turned round, hoping to be rescued by another boat coming up or down the river. Exhausted and famished when he was found, he was riding on the surviving horse, which he was on the point of slaughtering in order to eat. The location at which this happy reunion took place is reckoned to be somewhere near Snake Creek and the Francis Case Memorial Bridge that crosses what is now the lake.

I drove over the bridge to the Gregory County side and parked my car close to a little path that led through some dunes to a cove with a sandy beach protected by a horn-shaped bluff. At that point the lake was far narrower, and it was possible to envisage it as a broad river; the day was balmy, the sky blue, and the water calm. A pair of cottonwoods grew in the cove, and I sat on a dismembered branch that had fallen onto the shale and sand, its dead leaves washed away by the current. Looking up at the bluff, I pretended I could see the despondent Shannon, listlessly astride his doomed nag, as he scanned the river for a boat to rescue him. Though Clark's phlegmatic style keeps emotion at bay, Shannon's loneliness and fear are easily imagined, as is his elation on glimpsing the keelboat and his comrades on their way upstream, a sight he had long since despaired of seeing.

I have great sympathy for this confused young man, because I suffer to a far greater extent from what might be called orientation failure; I am constantly lost. Actually, Shannon was never really lost; he just made what might easily have been a fatal miscalculation.[13] By contrast, I am forever bewildered and pointing the wrong way, an inadequacy with which my wife, who is gifted with an unusually acute sense of direction, has no patience. (She disdains maps, regarding them as a form of cheating.) Only a person seriously disabled in this way could get lost on the Great Plains, where all roads are straight and tend to run north or south, east or west; I am that person, and in order to protect myself from getting off-course, I was obliged to drive throughout my journey with a compass beside me on the passenger seat.

One did not have to be a father to feel a keen compassion for this lost nineteen-year-old. Under the avuncular eye of the captains, he probably relished the adventure of the expedition, suffering its hardships and deprivations with youthful resilience, but once on his own, starving and helpless in the wilderness, he must have become truly terrified. Hunger is dreadful at any age, but nobody feels it like a healthy young man, and we are told that this one had eaten nothing but grapes and a rabbit for twelve days.

Although I knew that the bluff on which I had chosen to project my fatherly solicitude for Shannon's ghost could not possibly be the literal place where he had collapsed in despair, I relished the sense, however self-deluded, of being close to the young man. It was for this experience that I had made my own journey from England to Snake Creek, South Dakota. I could learn about Shannon's ordeal at home in my study, reading different accounts of the incident in the books I have collected over the years; I could follow his twelve day sojourn on various maps;

---

13. George Shannon survived a second, shorter separation from the main party in 1805, but the mishap was probably not his fault, and he showed considerable initiative in his efforts to rejoin the expedition. In 1807, travelling with another expedition, he was involved in a clash with the Arikaras that left a ball lodged in his leg, which had to be amputated to save him from gangrene. He used a wooden leg for the rest of his life and earned the unoriginal nickname of "Peg-leg" Shannon. In 1810, he assisted with the compilation of the first edition of the history of the Lewis and Clark Expedition. He later went on to study law, which he practiced while also pursuing a career in politics, and eventually became a senator. He died in 1836, aged forty-nine, and was buried in the splendidly named town of Palmyra, Missouri.

and using the magic of Google, I could even conjure up a picture of the very place where I was now sitting. But none of this could compare with having the river at my feet, with being able to see the great sweep of its emptiness from bank to bank, upstream and down, with seeing the great emptiness of the plains rolling back from the bluffs at the river's edge towards a faraway horizon, with the feeling of isolation and belittlement induced by the colossal prairie sky and its schools of leviathan clouds.

I was in my fifties when I became interested in Lewis and Clark, and I am now in my late sixties. I like to think that my visit to South Dakota in 2011 will not be the last time I cross the path of the expedition; indeed, I nurse an ambition to retrace their entire route, filling in the sections I have not already covered. However, I must also recognize that constraints of health and finance mean that I may not be able to make many more trips. But while I am aging, a process that no amount of riverside rumination can arrest, Shannon and the rest of them remain ageless, preserved in the amber of the journals; he will be forever nineteen, lost, and starving.

Shannon, not Christopher, should be the patron saint of travelers, casting his protection over those whose difficulties are self-made. As I drove across the interminable miles and infinite spaces of South Dakota, I felt a paradoxical shrinking of my world. The bigger the sky, the vaster the prairie, the more I seemed to concentrate on the minutiae of my life inside the car. I became obsessed with being able to lay my hands immediately, while driving, on items whose loss would have ruined my trip, or so I convinced myself: my passport, camera, audio recorder, wallet, notebook, and, on a slightly lower tier of anxiety, my compass, binoculars, pen, sunglasses, spare glasses. Since these objects were scattered round the passenger seat and foot well, I was forever scrabbling with one hand to find what I imagined had got lost while holding the wheel with the other. Clearly, I was not going to survive if I carried on this way. The solution presented itself in the shape of a cigar box I found in an antiques shop outside Yankton. It was a splendid wooden box, nine inches by five, and two and a half inches deep, that had been used to contain a brand called Roi-Tan, which advertised itself as "the cigar that *breathes*." What innocent, ignorant days! It cost me $3, and for the rest of my journey it sat on the passenger seat, acting as a receptacle for all my precious possessions. Ah, what peace of mind! With one sideways glance, I could reassure myself that they were all present and correct. These are the stupidities of age; forty years ago, I wouldn't have given any of this a thought.

Toiling upriver, the Corps of Discovery took thirteen days to travel from Snake Creek to the Bad River opposite where Pierre, the capital of South Dakota, now stands, and it was there that I rejoined them, so to speak, having driven west and back again to visit the Badlands and the Black Hills.

Running parallel with the river for a few hundred yards in Pierre is a residential street called Island View Drive. Only a cycle track and a strip of grass dotted with cottonwoods separate it from the water, and every time I visit the city I make a point of walking its length. As its matter-of-fact name suggests, this street does not face the river proper, but rather an inlet formed by a long narrow island now called La Framboise Island, which is usually connected to the town by a causeway and serves as a park and nature reserve.[14] At the western end of the avenue an official Lewis and Clark Trail marker stands next to a twenty-miles-per-hour speed limit sign, a restriction that would have brought a wry smile to Clark's face, for his records show that the corps, paddling, poling, sailing, and hauling their boats against the current, were lucky if they could manage twenty miles in a day. (It was a different story when they were making their return trip, coming downstream. On 26 August 1806 they passed this same spot during a day in which they traveled sixty miles.)

On 24 September 1804, as they approached this area, the corps traveled thirteen-and-a-half miles by Clark's reckoning. Here is part of his journal entry for that day:

> passed a Island on the S. S. on which we Saw Several Elk, about 1½ miles long Called Good humered Islds. Came to about 1½ miles above off the mouth of a Small river about 70 yards wide . . . The Tribes of the Scouix Called the Teton, is Camped about 2 miles

14. The flood of 2011 washed away parts of the causeway. Rebuilding work was expected to be finalized by the summer of 2013.

up on the N W Side and we Shall Call the River after that nation, Teton This river is 70 yards wide at the mouth of water, and has a considerable Current we anchored off the mouth—

The river he referred to is the Bad River, which issues into the Missouri from the western side, where Fort Pierre now stands, immediately opposite the island.

Things did not go well the next day, which was to prove perhaps the most demanding moment in terms of diplomacy of the entire trip. Lewis was under strict orders from President Jefferson to deal with any Indians they met "in the most friendly and conciliatory manner which their own conduct will admit," and the president was particularly concerned that relations with the Teton Sioux (Lakotas) should be both harmonious and beneficial to the United States.[15] The Lakotas were famous for their warlike behavior and military strength, but they were also skilled beaver hunters, and Jefferson was conscious of the priceless commercial opportunity to be had if they could be persuaded to deal with American traders rather than the British.[16]

The expedition's encounter with the Lakotas, which lasted three days, could well have turned out disastrously. Writing about the incident later, Clark described the Lakotas as "the vilest miscreants of the savage race, and must ever remain the pirates of the Missouri."[17] This observation was hardly fair. A lack of interpreters rendered the situation far more difficult than it already was, leaving both sides largely ignorant of what the other was trying to communicate. Nor was it was wise of the captains to issue whiskey to their Lakota visitors when they first boarded the keelboat on 24 September. Of that meeting, Clark wrote:

we invited those Chiefs & a Soldier on board our boat, and Showed them many Curiossites, which they were much Surprised, we gave they ½ a wine glass of whiskey which they appeared to be

15. Bernard De Voto, ed., *The Journals of Lewis and Clark* (Boston: Houghton Mifflin, 1981), p. 484.

16. *See* James P. Ronda, *Lewis and Clark among the Indians* (Lincoln: University of Nebraska Press, 1988), pp. 27–41.

17. Ibid., p. 40.

exceedingly fond of they took up an empty bottle, Smelted it, and made maney Simple jestures and Soon began to be troublesom the 2d Chief effecting Drunkness as a Cloak for his vilenous intintions (as I found after wards,) realed or fell about the boat.

After the Indians had accepted the whiskey, Clark tried to get his guests back on shore, but in the scuffle that followed, one of the chiefs jostled Clark and made "insolent jestures." Clark responded by drawing his sword and signaling to Lewis, who by then was in another boat, to prepare for action. The Indians meanwhile had strung their bows and taken arrows out of their quivers. It was a standoff. Sergeant Ordway described in his journal how this stalemate was gradually defused. After an exchange of threats, one of the chiefs asked if his women and children might look at the keelboat and its "curiosities," a request easily granted that allowed a certain amount of face to be saved on both sides. A difficult day came to an end with Clark's agreeing to take Chief Black Buffalo and a couple of his warriors on board before the boats were taken upstream and anchored off the island, leaving some soldiers on shore to act as guards. His final comment in his journal that day sums up his mood: "I call this Island bad humered Island as we were in a bad humer."

The following day they sailed five miles to the north. Curious Indians lined the river bank. When the corps anchored, the chiefs made a request that their women and boys should be allowed to see the boat and, as Clark put it, "suffer them to Show us some friendship." The request was granted, and large numbers of women and children gathered on the bank to watch the proceedings and stare at the Americans and their marvelous equipment. These friendly overtures set the tone for the day, which culminated in a great feast laid on by the Lakotas. The visitors spent the next day in the village reinforcing these good relations, but an awkward incident the following morning meant that their departure from the mooring near the village was fraught with tension and mutual aggression once again.

The Bad River episode was prophetic of the future history of relations between the Americans and the Sioux. For all his efforts at diplomacy and his gathering of ethnographic information, Lewis was a soldier, and he saw the Sioux as an obstacle to be dealt with in mili-taristic terms. "Unless these people are reduced to order, by coercive measures," he wrote, "I am ready to pronounce that the citizens of the United States can never enjoy but partially the advantages which the Missouri presents."[18] He had written the future history of the region in a nutshell.

When I take my walks along Island View Drive, I like to study the houses that overlook the island, choosing the one that I would like to buy if I had the chance. The island, by the way, was given its current name to honor Joseph LaFramboise, who built a fort on its western bank, though it seems a pity that Clark's bilious re-naming was not pre-served. Most of these houses are set well back from the water with long yards between their back doors and the avenue, a necessary precaution against flooding. To make my home on the Lewis and Clark Trail would give me a thrill, though I don't suppose it would console me through every hour of the long winters—winters that would not only be long, but *lonely*, because dear Sally would not be joining me.

(Had I been in Pierre a couple of weeks later, I would not have been able to indulge in this fantasy house-hunting because Island View Drive was essentially under the river, submerged by catastrophic flooding. If the test of a good journalist is an instinct for being in the right place at the right time, I disqualified myself by choosing dates for my trip that ensured I was in the right place at exactly the wrong time; I arrived in South Dakota just after the first floods along the James River had begun to recede and left just before the Missouri's deluge inundated Pierre, thus neatly missing the big story. As a traveler I was grateful to be able to move around freely; as a writer I have kicked myself repeatedly for failing to witness The Great Flood of 2011 at first hand. Do not call me "Scoop.")

The words "home" and "travel" are opposites, and there will always be tension between them; the one cannot be reconciled with the other.

18. Elliot Coues, ed., *The History of the Expedition under the Command of Lewis and Clark Expedition, . . . by Order of the Government of the United States*, New ed., 4 vols. (New York: Francis P. Harper, 1893), 1:128.

In some way, however small, the impulse to travel always contains an element of dissatisfaction with home, and by the same token, it must be a rare journey that is undertaken without some degree of homesickness. Staring into the lit windows of the houses on Island View Drive as if I were a burglar checking out possessions worth stealing, I was conscious of my paradoxical position: I had left home and journeyed thousands of miles only to find myself on the bank of a river in a strange city brooding on the significance of "home" and speculating about the charms of an alternative one. But then travel, to some extent, is always a meditation on the theme of home.

Over the years I have learned to guard against foreign infatuations. When I was a teenager and my parents began to take holidays "on the continent," the breaking of my heart by foreign girls became an annual event. It happened first on a beach in Italy where my inamorata and I conducted our innocent courtship while encircled by a small tribe of owl-eyed younger siblings, and then on board a cruise ship where my romantic nemesis took the fragile form of a Dutch girl with whom I learned to chain-smoke cigarettes under the approving eye (squinting through the porthole of his monocle) of my cigar-smoking grandfather, and finally in various heartbreak hotels around Europe and the United States where as a student I was able to make my own tear-stained bookings.

In those days, foreign locations were a mere backdrop to my operatic follies, but when in the 1990s, as a respectable married man, I began traveling for a living, I discovered I had not lost my weakness for infatuation, though now I gave my heart not to girls but to the places themselves. For a few enraptured days, I would imagine myself a happy exile in a palm-frond hut overlooking the west coast of Martinique where artist Paul Gauguin had first discovered the magic of tropical sunshine, or an apartment in the Anfiteatro Romano, a ring of medieval houses surrounding a piazza in Lucca, Italy (birthplace of Giacomo Puccini), or a chalet on a sloping meadow in the mountainous Basque country of France where my wife worked as a chef, or—why not?—a cabin marooned among the tawny grasslands of South Dakota. These places and many more, for I was nothing if not promiscuous, were irresistibly seductive and I was easily besotted. Then, at the end of each assignment, I would pack my case and return home like a chastened philanderer to the forgiving bosom of Suffolk.

My wife and I have lived in this part of Suffolk for thirty-six years; it has been our marital home as well as the home where our children were born, brought up, and educated, the home they fled for London, and now, in my daughter's case, the home to which she has returned to start her own family. And yet, despite these indisputable roots, I still do not feel completely reconciled to being here; a part of me still protests that I am a refugee, unjustly plucked from the city streets where I belong and rusticated like Ovid in Tomis, and the effect produces a kind of lingering wanderlust, whose demands seem to grow only more insistent with age.[19] Home is of course the place where you hope to gather round you those most precious to you; it is the place where you keep and collect your precious things; but it is also the place where you study that most precious of all books—your atlas. We travel to come home; we come home to travel.

As a nation, we British are a restless lot, and for us travel means going abroad; indeed, I believe we are the most traveled nation on earth. (According to official statistics, between May 2010 and May 2011, Britons made 56 million visits overseas. By comparison the figure for international outbound air travel by Americans in 2010 was below 39 million.) Americans are still content to explore their own country—the spirit of Lewis and Clark lives on—and the tensions between home and the road have a different complexion. In an essay written to celebrate the bicentennial of the Lewis and Clark expedition, James P. Ronda pointed to the ambivalent nature of the country's experience of travel: "We all live and find meaning at the crossroads and in the crossfire between home and the road."[20] Perhaps that is the difference between an imperial heritage and one deriving from internal colonizing: travel to the American fron-

19. Emperor Augustus banished the Roman poet Ovid to Tomis, on the Black Sea, in AD 8.

20. James P. Ronda, "Journeys—The Shaping of America," in *Finding Lewis & Clark*, ed. James P. Ronda and Nancy Tystad Koupal (Pierre: South Dakota State Historical Society Press, 2004), p. 1.

tier promised wealth to the pioneer or the gold-digger, but it threatened loss to those back home; whereas travel to colonies overseas always promised more wealth for the metropolis—the "mother" country. The nabob came back to England in the end, but the pioneer stayed where his journey ended. The founding fathers of Harrison never returned to Iowa.

My final contact with the Lewis and Clark trail was at Mobridge, where I arrived on 20 May 2011, which was the day before the beginning of the end of the world, according to Harold Camping, the tele-evangelist and owner of the Family Radio network. In the event, the following day dawned brightly enough, but Camping had foretold that the Rapture would not take place until 6:00 P.M., whereupon the ground would quake, graves would open, and two hundred million of the "saved," both dead and alive, would float upwards to heaven. Those left behind (among whom I would certainly be numbered) would be doomed to endure fire, brimstone, and plagues for five months before God finally annihilated the earth on 21 October.

At breakfast in the Grand Oasis Restaurant opposite my hotel, I overheard a group of men at the next table as they planned their day's hunting. They were dressed in camouflage, and the younger ones were taking their instructions from an older man, solemnly nodding as he laid out tactics and discussed weaponry. I wondered what poor beast would fall prey to their marksmanship: antelope or elk perhaps. Returning to my hotel, I found the hunters in the parking lot where they were stacking equipment into the back of their pickup, which was already loaded with a substantial armory. I stopped and asked their leader what they were hoping to shoot.

"Prairie dogs," he said with the air of a man squaring up to a gruesome but necessary task. What did they use to kill prairie dogs? He pulled a metal case out of the pickup and showed me a rifle with a very long barrel. He attached a telescopic sight to it and held it to his shoulder, peering down the highway towards the river.

"This thing can pick out the little critters at 400 yards," he said. One of the young men held out a bullet in the palm of his hand for me to examine. Relative to the size of the target, it was the size of an anti-tank missile. They had been invited to hunt on a farm on the Standing Rock reservation where a prairie-dog city had got out of hand. How many did they expect to kill? Two hundred, maybe. And did they do it for fun? Oh, yes, for fun. "They look cute," the leader said, "but they can carry the bubonic plague."

On 7 September 1804 as Lewis and Clark were making their way up-river from the mouth of Niobrara River, they came across a "Village of Small animals that burrow in the groun (those animals are Called by the french Petite Chien)." Mindful of Jefferson's instructions to send samples of newly-found fauna back to Monticello for his inspection, they set out to catch one of these creatures. Private John Shields managed to kill one, which was cooked for the captains' dinner, but they hoped to capture a live sample. The "village" covered about four acres, but they had great difficulty in trapping the inhabitants, which "set erect make a Whisteling noise and whin allarmed Step into their hole." The men attempted to dig to the bottom of a burrow, but having reached a depth of six feet, they ran a pole down the tunnel and realized they were not yet half way. Next they resorted to flooding, but it took most of a day's work and five barrels of water poured into the tunnels to flush out a single victim. Four days later, on 11 September, Clark had better luck when he came across a "village" 970 yards long by 800 yards wide, where he succeeded in killing four prairie dogs with a view to having "their Skins Stufed." In June the following year Lewis decided to sample prairie-dog meat again, and he seemed to find it tasty: "I had the bur-rowing squirrels roasted by way of experiment and found the flesh well flavored and tender; some of them were very fat."

In his book *Undaunted Courage*, Stephen Ambrose wrote, "If ever there was a time in which the Lewis and Clark Expedition bore some resemblance to a bunch of guys out on a long camping trip, it was in the first part of October 1804," the period when they were moving up-stream from Pierre towards present-day Bismarck in North Dakota.[21] (The corps passed the mouth of the Grand River, close to present-day Mobridge, on 8 October 1804.) Ambrose described Lewis's prowess as a marksman, which was increased by his use of an espontoon, a kind

21. Stephen E. Ambrose, *Undaunted Courage* (New York: Simon & Schuster, 1996), p. 176.

of pike about six feet in length with a wooden shaft and a metal blade. In May 1805, Lewis killed a rattlesnake with this medieval implement and Clark killed a wolf, though it was described as "fat and extreemly gentle." The espontoon could also be used as a walking stick, but for Lewis its chief function was to serve as a rest for his rifle when taking aim. Since his rifle weighed more than eight pounds and had a barrel more than four feet in length, this extra support was invaluable. As Ambrose wrote, "If the target was within a hundred yards and bigger than a mouse, he usually got it."[22]

That morning I drove across Lake Oahe, which stretches some 231 miles from just north of Pierre to Bismarck in North Dakota, and turned southwest at the Grand River Casino. I drove for four miles or so, following signs to the bluff where the Sitting Bull Monument overlooked the lake. Not far away on the same site was an obelisk made of gray concrete, standing some thirty feet tall, a forbidding object whose purpose, one might guess, was to commemorate the battles of a particularly bloodthirsty general. In fact, it was erected in 1929 to honor Sacagawea, the Shoshone Indian woman who accompanied Lewis and Clark on their journey, and its cost had been defrayed by pennies collected from schoolchildren in the Mobridge area. It therefore antedated the Sitting Bull Monument, which was erected in 1953, by many years.

Set into one of the four sides of the plinth was a bronze plaque, the work of Mobridge artist Jack Shillingstad, which showed in bas relief the faces of a woman and her child within a roundel of feathers. Although suggestive of a Madonna and Christ—the boy's shawl even resembles a halo—the monument's joyless bulk was not relieved. The obelisk was enclosed by concrete posts, a pair at each corner, which once carried chains between them, but with a single exception, they had been removed.

Standing at a distance was an explanatory signboard made of metal, which among other things declared: "Sakakawea won her place in history as the indomitable guide of Lewis and Clark on their trip to the Pacific in 1805. . . . By her courage, endurance, and unerring instinct she guided the expedition over seemingly insuperable obstacles. The

22. Ibid., p. 177.

leaders frequently gave her credit for the success of the venture." There was no date attached to the board, and I assumed it had been erected at the same time as the obelisk itself. Befitting its subject, the nearby bust of Sitting Bull possessed a kind of dignity, which was enhanced by the panoramic view of the lake beyond the bluff that the great chief was supposed to be contemplating. But the grim conformation of Sacagawea's shrine seemed to have no connection with the woman herself, her personality or her culture, and I was sorry that the children's pennies, no doubt earnestly donated, had been so wastefully spent.

The text on the information board, authoritatively pressed out of metal, struck an old-fashioned and hyperbolic note by asserting that Sacagawea had played an indispensable part in guiding the expedition, something she could hardly have done since most of the territory they passed through was as strange to her as to the others. It must have dated from the period when Sacagawea was elevated to the status of a virtual saint, a status that prompted historian Bernard DeVoto to comment sarcastically that, Lewis and Clark were "privileged to assist in the Sacakawea expedition."[23] Nor was it fair to her memory to claim that the captains credited her with the success of the venture; on the contrary, Lewis barely mentioned her in his journal and was sometimes disparaging when he did so. However, at the end of the expedition he did pay tribute to her and gave a fair summary of her contribution and character, saying that she was "particularly useful among the Shoshonees. Indeed, she has borne with a patience truly admirable the fatigues of so long a route, encumbered with the charge of an infant, who is even now only 19 months old."[24]

Sacagawea first came to the attention of the captains when they camped for the winter of 1804–1805 in Fort Mandan near today's Bismarck, North Dakota. They were looking for interpreters who could speak Shoshone, the language of the people living near the headwaters of the Missouri, and they interviewed Toussaint Charbonneau, a French-Canadian trapper from Quebec, who revealed that he had two

23. Bernard DeVoto, *The Course of Empire* (Boston: Houghton Mifflin, 1952), p. 478.
24. Coues, *History of the Expedition*, 3:1184.

"wives," both of whom spoke Shoshone. In reality his wives were teen-age Shoshones kidnapped by Hidatsas during a raid. Charbonneau had subsequently purchased them, though legend insists that he won them in a card game. The captains immediately decided to recruit him but would only allow him to bring one of the young women and he chose Sacagawea, despite her being pregnant. The captains rightly foresaw the indispensable value of their linguistic resources, even though the chain of communication between them was extended and must have sorely tested their patience. Beside Shoshone, which Charbonneau did not understand, Sacagawea spoke a little Hidatsa picked up from her cap-tors, which she shared with her husband, but he spoke no English and had to communicate in French with another member of the party, who finally spoke in English to the captains.[25]

Sacagawea went into labor on 11 February 1805, but things did not go smoothly, as Lewis reported:

> about five oclock this evening one of the wives of Charbono was delivered of a fine boy. it is worthy of remark that this was the first child which this woman had boarn and as is common in such cases her labour was tedious and the pain violent; Mr. Jessome informed me that he had freequently adminstered a small portion of the rattle of the rattle-snake, which he assured me had never failed to produce the desired effect, that of hastening the birth of the child; having the rattle of a snake by me I gave it to him and he administered two rings of it to the woman broken in small pieces with the fingers and added to a small quantity of water. Whether this medicine was truly the cause or not I shall not undertake to determine, but I was informed that she had not taken it more than ten minutes before she brought forth perhaps this remedy may be worthy of future experiments, but I must confess that I want faith as to it's efficacy.—

The boy was named Jean Baptiste, but during the expedition he had the nickname Pompey or Pomp bestowed on him by Clark. When he was two months old, the Expedition left Fort Mandan (on 7 April

25. Ambrose, *Undaunted Courage*, p. 203.

1805), setting off for territory that would be unknown to every member. Having crossed the Rockies and endured a miserable and rain-sodden winter on the Pacific Coast, the expedition finally returned on 14 August 1806, by which time Pomp was eighteen months old. Sacagawea, a woman of fifteen or sixteen, had carried her baby across the continent and back again, bringing him home alive, healthy, and, as far as we know, unharmed by his odyssey—a remarkable feat, which she probably achieved more or less unassisted. The journals do not record what sort of mother she was—patient or short-tempered, playful or dour; nor do we know how the corps responded to having a mother and child in their midst. (Was there ever such a lopsided family: one child, one mother, one father, and thirty uncles?) We don't even know whether he was walking or talking by the end of the trip, how many teeth he had acquired, what color his hair was, whether it was straight or curly, or any of the other wondrous achievements that loom so large for those close to a small child.

Most members of the corps were young, and only two of them were married: Private John Shields, born in 1869 and the oldest among the soldiers, and Sergeant Nathaniel Pryor. The sergeant is reported to have married an Osage woman in later years, leaving history silent on the fate of his first wife, who waited for him while he was on his historic expedition. In his brief biographies of the soldiers, historian Gary Moulton does not say if either of these men had children.[26] Perhaps some of the other men had children without being married; if so, how did the fathers among them respond to the presence of a baby? How did they treat him? Did his babyish ways bring back memories of their own children? And what about those men who had younger brothers and sisters, or who perhaps were uncles—what effect did Sacagewea's child and mothering have on them? I cannot believe that some of these men did not feel a tug of nostalgic affection for the young children in their lives at home, which they transferred to baby Pomp.

Reading his journal account of Pomp's birth, it is hard not to sense that Lewis felt a certain avuncular pride in his contribution to the baby's delivery, but he hardly mentions the child in his journals, apart from a

26. Moulton, *Journals*, 2: app. A.

series of entries in May 1806 when Pomp became ill. Not only was he cutting a tooth, but the boy was suffering from a high fever, and his neck and throat were badly swollen. Lewis, who acted as doctor throughout the trip and successfully treated many patients, both American Indians and soldiers, gave him some tartar and sulfur and applied a poultice of boiled onions to his neck, as hot as he could bear it. A few days later the child was no better. On 24 May, Lewis wrote that the baby was "very wrestless last night; it's jaw and the back of it's neck are much more swolen . . . we gave it a doze of creem of tartar and applied a fresh poltice of onions." By 3 June 1806, Lewis was able to report that the child had nearly recovered and that the swelling on his neck had almost subsided, leaving a hard lump underneath his left ear, though the poor child was still enduring the application of the onion poultice.[27] And that is the last we hear of young Pomp until the end of the journey.

No reference is made by any of the journal keepers concerning Charbonneau as a father, though even level-headed estimates of Sacagawea's achievements generally overlook the fact that the father of her child was present throughout the entire journey. As a husband, however, Charbonneau does not appear to have impressed anyone. Elliot Coues, one of the editors of the expedition journals, described him scathingly as a "craven French apology for a male."[28] The only direct account of his behavior towards Sacagawea appears in Clark's journal for 14 August 1805: "I checked our interpreter for Striking his woman at their Dinner."

At the end of the expedition Charbonneau was paid off—$500 and 33 cents—but Sacagawea received nothing. The husband asked to be further employed, but Clark refused him, offering instead to adopt Jean Baptiste. On 17 August 1806 Clark wrote the following:

> we also took our leave of T. Chabono, his Snake Indian wife and
> their Son Child who had accompanied us on our rout to the pacific
> Ocean in the Capacity of interpreter and interpretes . . . I offered to
> take his little Son a butifull promising Child who is 19 months old

27. It has been variously suggested that the boy had mumps, tonsillitis, or an external abscess on the back of his neck. *See* Ambrose, *Undaunted Courage*, p. 364.

28. Coues, *History of the Expedition*, 1:311.

to which they both himself & wife wer willing provided the Child had been weened. they observed that in one year the boy would be Sufficiently old to leave his mother & he would then take him to me if I would be so freindly as to raise the Child for him in Such a manner as I thought proper, to which I agreeed &c.—

By the end of the journey, Clark had clearly developed a strong pater-nal affection for the "butifull" child, but perhaps he also felt a little guilty about Sacagawea, whom he had nicknamed "Janey," because three days later he wrote to Charbonneau:

Your woman who accompanied you that long dangerous and fatigueing rout to the Pacific Ocian and back diserved a great reward for her attention and services on the rout than we had in our power to give her at the Mandans. As to your little Son (my boy Pomp) you well know my fondness of him and my anxiety to take him and raise him as my own child. . .If you are desposed to accept either of my offers to you and will bring down you Son your famn [*femme, "woman"*] Janey had best come along with you to take care of the boy untill I get him. . . . . Wishing you and your family great success & with anxious expectations of seeing my little danceing boy Baptiest I shall remain your Friend, William Clark.[29]

In due course, when he was about six years old, Charbonneau and Sacagawea sent Jean Baptiste to join the Clark household in Saint Louis, where he continued to live until he was adult.[30] By then, Sacagawea had given birth to a daughter, Lizette, but she herself only had a little while left to live. Documents show that in 1811 Sacagawea was living with Charbonneau at the Fort Manuel Lisa trading post in North Dakota.

---

29. Jackson, *Letters*, 1:317.

30. Gary Moulton noted that, in 1823, Jean Baptiste attracted the notice of the traveling Prince Paul of Wurttemburg, who took him to Europe for six years. On his return to the United States, the young man became a mountain man and fur trader and later a guide for such explorers and soldiers as John C. Frémont, Philip St. George Cooke, W. H. Emory, and James Abert. He eventually settled in California and died in Oregon while traveling to Montana in 1866. Moulton, *Journals*, 3:291n1.

She became ill and "longed to revisit her native country." The following year a clerk working at the post recorded her death of "putrid fever;" he thought she was about twenty-five years old and commented that she left "a fine infant girl."[31]

Back in Mobridge I looked at my watch and noticed it was approaching 6:00 P.M., the Rapture moment. However, the fateful hour came and went with no sign of the predicted mass ascension, at least none that could be seen from my hotel window. The television news channels took a ribald attitude to these failed prophecies and had great fun reporting on the discomfort of the credulous. I regretted not having asked my elderly friends in Harrison about the Rapture, for they had been taught to count themselves among the elect, but they did not strike me as naïve enough to believe in Camping's numerology, especially since his sums had proved inaccurate not once but twice before, in 1988 and 1994.

Yet the more I thought about it, the cheaper this television mockery of Camping's followers looked. These people were, of course, a soft target, and their extreme gullibility had indeed produced comical results, but from an atheist's point of view, the only thing that made the Rapture seem crazier than ordinary Christian expectations of immortality and the second coming, which were probably shared by many of the newscasters, was its mathematical precision.

Yet, atheist though I was, I could not altogether dismiss these Rhapsodic forecasts. Not that I anticipated brimstone and plague, but I felt some sympathy with the idea of drawing a line in time, of picking a date beyond which everything would be different and salvation awaited. When I was a young man, I believed, contrary to evidence and repeated experience, that I could improve my character by bringing about a sudden metamorphosis that would change me into a non-smoker, for example, or a more disciplined writer, a fonder father, a more attentive husband, and so on. I think it was Aristotle who had the wisdom to teach that virtuous behavior was the hard-won product of habit, but I was impatient and wanted my transformation to be immediate. I was not an evolutionist in this respect, but a catastrophist. Essential to my belief

31. Jackson, *Letters*, 2:639.

was a magical timeline, a moment of rapturous mutation that would instantaneously turn me from a caterpillar into a butterfly; all that was required to effect this transubstantiation was faith and will power—and the selection of a plausible date.

Later in life, I succumbed once again to the chimera of sudden character change, always a lurking aspiration, when in the 1990s I began to work for a living (half a living) as a travel journalist. That title flatters me. In reality, I was writing vacation journalism and never voyaged to anywhere more challenging than the restaurants of Bruges, in Belgium, or a scandalously sybaritic spa outside Tucson, Arizona. But there is nothing like leaving home to conjure up the illusion that, under a foreign sky, liberated from the shackles of your day-to-day, humdrum self, you will see your problems clearly and refine your personality accordingly. As you board the train, you fondly think that the pure air of desert or mountain will drive this domestic fog from your mind and all will be lucidly perceived. The truth is that under a foreign sky you are unlikely to gain a clear view of anything but the nearest bar or swimming pool, yet it did not stop me from entertaining this fallacy every time I caught a cab to the airport. Was I any less naïve than Harold Camping's followers?

One of the joys of travel that never fades, perhaps because it is not dependent on the destination or the importance of the trip, is the sense of purpose invoked by the simple act of making a journey. The mere pursuit of an itinerary, whether traversing the Gobi Desert or driving a rental car from Harrison, South Dakota, to Harrison, Nebraska, promotes a heady feeling of significance; life's problems are left at a literal and metaphorical distance, melancholy is dispelled, anxiety diminished, and self-esteem wonderfully enhanced. Keep moving and you will keep well. No matter how factitious its motive (e.g., around Ireland with a fridge[32]), once the journey is under way your need for achievement is satisfied by moving forward; onwards is always upwards, progress is always progress.

Sally and I faced a crisis of purpose when our two children finally

32. Believe it or not, this was a real project and the title of the resulting book written by British comedian Tony Hawks, 1998.

grew up and left home. What was the point of us, we wondered? Of course, our children—the phrase never becomes obsolete—still needed us in various ways, material and emotional, but there is nothing so purposeful as a household devoted to the upbringing of children, and nothing so empty, we discovered, as a house with abandoned bedrooms. It is true that a kind of liberation attends this redundancy. Sally followed our children and flew the nest to work as a hotel chef in the French Pyrenees for several summers. For my part, I found substitute children to look after by helping detained asylum seekers, some of whom, shockingly enough, were actual children, but all of whom required protection and guidance as they made their way through the pitiless labyrinth of the British immigration system. In hindsight, these occupations look like diversions, a necessary marking of time while, without realizing it, we waited for our sense of purpose to be restored by being appointed grandparents.

A journey liberates, even if like most journeys it too represents a loop, from home to home in a circle. Once begun, a journey needs no justification other than itself; "proceeding on," to borrow Lewis and Clark's famous phrase, becomes the imperative, if only for the sake of survival. Traveling provides its own impulsion, and for those, like me, who suffer intermittently from crippling inertia, traveling is a wonderful tonic. In this respect the literary archetype is Oblomov, the hero—a misnomer if ever there was one—of Ivan Goncharov's novel of the same name, who is afflicted by a kind of compulsive recumbence. For a third of this long book, Oblomov is incapable of rising from his sofa, despite many pressing reasons for doing so. When the book was published in 1859, Oblomov became a byword for the laziness of the landowning classes in Russia. However, as someone who knows what it is like to be afflicted by lassitude, I can testify that it is not indolence, nor a dislike of work, so much as a kind of depression that disables us Oblomovs and keeps us from doing what we would dearly like to be doing. We are bound by invisible negative forces that are as effective as a disabling drug.

Oblomov is intended to be a figure of fun, but there is a serious passage in the book where, alone and restless, though still recumbent, he acknowledges his failures with agonized regret and tries to describe the obstructions that prevent him from "flinging himself into the arena of life."[33] He reaches for various metaphors—a dead weight hampers him, a huge stone has been thrown in his way, a thick jungle is growing over the path of his existence, the good that lay buried within him was like gold trapped in the depths of a mountain, and so on. "It was," he thinks, "as though some secret enemy had laid a heavy hand upon him at the beginning of his journey and thrown him far back from the right road."[34]

The idea of a secret enemy does not strike me as fanciful since I, too, have felt a heavy hand on my shoulder, a kind of depression that took the form of stupefying apathy. Fortunately, I was not permanently cursed with this Oblomovism; I could shake it off, even though, like a python, it was always waiting to wrap me in its paralyzing grip. A friend of ours was once asked why he was going to China; "To get out of the house," he replied, and when I started to work for *The Sunday Times*, I discovered how right he was. If you are prey to Oblomovism, it is no good imagining that will power alone will galvanize you; to get off your sofa you have to go to China—or South Dakota.

It seems that Meriwether Lewis fell victim to a form of depressive inertia once his great journey had been completed. As an expeditionary officer he had been superb, but as a civilian public servant—Jefferson had appointed him governor of Louisiana Territory in 1807—he was a disaster, for he proved incapable of fulfilling any of the responsibilities that faced him.

In September 1809, three years after their triumphant return from the West, Lewis spent a few days with Clark at his home in Saint Louis, where they attempted to get Lewis's disastrous financial affairs in some sort of order. Lewis then set off for Washington, D.C., with the intention, so he said, of preparing his journals for publication and delivering them to the press. On 10 October he stopped at a place called Grinder's Stand, near Nashville, and in the early morning of the next day, he shot himself in the head and chest and attacked himself with a razor. As he died, he said that he had killed himself to deprive his enemies of the pleasure and honor of doing it. Every suicide is horrible to read about,

33. Ivan Goncharov, *Oblomov* (London: Everyman, 1992), p. 106.
34. Ibid.

but the violence with which Lewis dispatched himself and the determination he showed throughout what turned into a prolonged ordeal are especially shocking. It seems characteristic of the man that he should do this dreadful thing while on a journey; he who had prosecuted the most difficult journey of his generation had embarked on another, no less difficult, enterprise.

Clark's response to the news was anguished but suggests that he thought Lewis capable of suicide: "I fear O! I fear the weight of his mind has overcome him." In his biographical sketch of his old protégé, Jefferson wrote that Lewis had been subject to "hypocondriac affections" all his life, which was a family trait, adding that he had observed "sensible depressions of mind" in him when Lewis had worked for him in the capital. And Jefferson was surely correct when he asserted that, "during his Western expedition the constant exertion which that required of all the faculties of body & mind, suspended these distressing affections," but after his return to sedentary occupations, "they returned upon him with redoubled vigour."[35]

Lewis suffered from paranoia, alcoholism, and depression, which at a certain moment produced a combination toxic enough to make self-destruction appear to offer the only release. Encircled by seemingly insoluble problems, he could not manage his responsibilities as governor. He had made powerful enemies in government; his debts had grown so large that he believed he was facing financial ruin; he had failed in his attempts to court a wife. Alcoholism and his addiction to a kind of "medicine" for malaria that contained opium made all these difficulties a hundred times worse. But worst of all, Lewis had disappointed his mentor Jefferson by failing to prepare his journals for publication, and their relationship, perhaps the most important in his life, had cooled. In 1806, soon after his return from the expedition, Lewis had released a prospectus announcing the forthcoming publication of *Lewis and Clark's Tour to the Pacific Ocean through the Interior of the Continent of North America* in three volumes, but by the time of his death, not a single line of manuscript had been written.

No doubt, none of these difficulties, taken by itself, would have been

35. Jackson, *Letters*, 2:575, 591–92.

insurmountable, and there were several people, notably Jefferson and Clark, who still had faith in him, even if it was frayed at the edges. But it seems that a precondition of suicide is the conviction that the circle of problems cannot be broken and is forever tightening its noose-like grip. The only answer is to put your head in the loop and kick away the chair. If only he could have gone on another expedition, he might have saved his sanity and his life.

Seeking some relief from these melancholy themes, I went back to the journals and looked at the entries for the days the captains spent in what is now South Dakota on their downstream homeward journey in August 1806. At that time, Lewis was recovering from a wound in the left buttock, the result of being accidentally shot while on a hunting expedition with a short-sighted soldier. On the day after the accident, 12 August, he confessed, "wrighting in my present situation is extreemly painfull to me I shall desist untill I recover and leave to my frind Capt. C. the continuation of our journal." In fact, it was the last entry he contributed, but despite his pain he did his duty by composing a four-hundred-word account of the day's events. And even after he had signed off, he could not resist adding a few lines of detailed botanical description: "however I must notice a singular Cherry which is found on the Missouri in the bottom lands . . . the stem is compound erect and subdivided or branching without any regular order it rises to the hight of eight or ten feet seldom puting up more than one stem from the same root not growing in cops as the Choke Cherry dose."[36]

This was the man at his best; a true hero.

By Friday, 29 August, the expedition had reached the mouth of the

---

36. The entry continues in great detail: "the bark is smooth and of a dark brown colour. the leaf is peteolate, oval accutely pointed at it's apex, from one and a ¼ to 1½ inches in length and from ½ to ¾ of an inch in width, finely or minutely serrate, pale green and free from bubessence. the fruit is a globular berry about the size of a buck-shot of a fine scarlet red; like the cherries cultivated in the U' States each is supported by a seperate celindric flexable branch peduncle which issue from the extremities of the boughs the peduncle of this cherry swells as it approahes the fruit being largest at the point of insertion. the pulp of this fruit is of an agreeable ascid flavour and is now ripe. the style and stigma are permanent. I have never seen it in blume." Moulton, *Journals*, 8:158.

White River in today's Lyman County, and Lewis was healing slowly. They were making excellent progress, and the end of the expedition was in sight, but some old problems still obsessed the captains. "A cloudy morning," the journal recorded. "I Sent out two men to the village of barking Squirels with direcitions to kill Some of them. they after 2 hours returned and informed me that not one of those Squirels were to be Seen out of their holes." These "barking squirels" were of course prairie dogs, the elusive creatures they had tried to capture two years earlier.

The rest of Clark's entry for that day has the magical quality that would make an immediate convert of anyone who opened the journals for the first time:

> Set out and proceeded on passed the white river at 12 oClock and halted below the enterance of Shannons Creek . . . I assended to the high Country and from an eminance, I had a view of the plains for a great distance. from this eminance I had a view of a greater number of buffalow than I had ever Seen before at one time. I must have Seen near 20,000 of those animals feeding on this plain. I have observed that in the country between the nations which are at war with each other the greatest numbers of wild animals are to be found—on my return to the river I killed 2 young deer. after Dinner we proceeded down the river about 3 mile to the Camp

At the end of my own day's exploration, I had dinner in the Grand Oasis Restaurant and ran into the hunters I had met at breakfast. They were looking disconsolate. How many prairie dogs had they shot? Only six.

Perhaps they should have used espontoons.

The Badlands

The Badlands. To anyone who has not seen them, they're indescribable; to anyone who has seen them, there's no more to say.

Well, perhaps there are one or two things left to be said.

I first saw the Badlands[1] in South Dakota during the family trip we made in March 1992, the six of us in our ramshackle Volvo. After a long day's driving on Interstate 90, we were all exhausted, and even our son Jack had long since ceased to appreciate the humor of Wall Drug's barrage of road signs: "Free Coffee for Missile Crews," "Six Foot Rabbit," "You're a Big Shot at Wall Drug," "You'll get Wall-eyed at Wall Drug," and so on. The prairie rolled towards remote horizons in a vast, undulating emptiness, while the interstate lay across it like a gray stripe secured with barbed-wire stitching. The homely, almost private messages we were used to reading into our Suffolk scenery would not suffice here. Meanings, if any were to be discerned in this one-dimensional landscape, had to be of epic significance, and we were too tired for imaginative flights.

Most wearying was the slow corrosion of hope. Every distant rise of the road seemed to promise relief from the monotony, but always disappointed. The next incline, once topped, only unfurled another. Somewhere out there in the rolling desert we

1. The term *badland* can be applied to any deeply eroded, barren area. North Dakota, for example, boasts its own spectacular version, now contained within the Theodore Roosevelt National Park. In the United States at least, the badland aspires to a condition of abstract expressionism, and it has been the photographer rather than the writer who has attempted to capture its seemingly unnatural, *outlandish* beauty.

passed through a time zone, rejuvenating ourselves by an ephemeral hour, but by then we did not care.

Despite our contempt for Wall Drug's merciless self-promotion, we could not resist investigating the place, so we postponed our view of the Badlands and turned into "America's favorite roadside attraction." It proved to be a theme mall designed to represent a western town, with a raised boardwalk, swinging saloon doors, and walls apparently made of hand-hewn logs. We parked our car beside a hitching post, and as we entered the mall we were greeted by a mechanical cowboy orchestra playing honky-tonk music. At the other end of the "street" a chuck-wagon quartet, also made of life-sized plaster models, every one a comical frontier character, competed for our musical appreciation. The kids, glad to be released from the imprisonment of the car, set off to explore Calamity Jane's Jewelry Emporium, The Buckboard Clothing Store, and the Big Bull Harness Shop, while some of us sought the comfort of the Silver Dollar Bar. Surrounded by a display of cattle brands attached to the walls, we ate burgers in booths resembling brass bedsteads, while a pair of cigar store Indians glowered at us—and who could blame them? This was not the Wild West of my childhood fantasies.

We planned to spend the night in Hot Springs on the southern edge of the Black Hills, so we decided to drive there via the minor roads that led through the Badlands. Though this broken land was one of the chief objects of our trip, we were still mystified as to its exact nature, having nothing to enlighten us except some improbably lurid photographs in the brochures. Hardened by three hundred miles of vacant prairie and Wall Drug's cowboy kitsch, we expected nothing but the usual disappointment as we made our slow ascent of a ridge eight miles south of Wall. It was to be our last moment of cynicism.

We rolled over the crest of the ridge and found we had strayed onto a plateau of the moon. Its skyline was a palisade of jagged ridges and pinnacles, an extended curtain of rock many miles long, from which the town of Wall derived its name. The floor of this lunar grassland was littered with the ruins of peaks that appeared to have fallen out of the wall, and the entire moonscape was composed of pink and cream rock piled in layers but scattered across the plain like the remnants of an exploded ice cream.

We reached a junction and turned onto a secondary, gravel road heading west. It was late afternoon, and our destination still lay some eighty or ninety miles distant in the Black Hills. The façade of rock to the north loomed like the profile of a futuristic megalopolis, mile after mile of towers, blocks, and crazy superstructures, all designed in sci-fi gothic and lit by a low, melting sun.

We got out of the car and wandered over a patch of this moon crust. Close to, we could see that the entire system was scored with cracks, clefts, and runnels created by the rain. Apart from patches of grass, nothing seemed to grow on these candy-striped rocks. The rock itself looked no more concrete than dried mud, which we could break off with our hands in chunks and crumble to dust. It seemed a miracle that the whole sandcastle of the Badlands had not been washed away in the last storm. Our English eyes had still not come to terms with the immensity of the country we had been crossing, but now we were staring at a landscape that was both epic and sportive at once. The Badlands was a geological playground where a prodigiously creative hand had been fooling around with the rock, molding it into dozens of shapes, and spraying it in delicious pastels. Less a landscape than a light-hearted experiment, it was a folly of nature that might be re-assembled tomorrow, or simply erased to make way for something more fanciful.

Back in the car we swung around a bend and confronted a completely fresh panorama: the rock had been shaped in receding terraces of rosy-colored cones, some as huge as the Great Pyramid, some no bigger than straw hats. They were composed of horizontal streaks and tiers of rock that were mostly pink and mauve, but were mixed with occasional bands of tan, umber, sulfur, and violet. In the middle of this surreal landscape stood a buffalo.

We stopped to inspect the beast, wondering if it was real and not another publicity stunt organized by Wall Drug. Though virtually immobile, it was indeed real. Its thick winter coat hung in scruffy strips from its back and flanks, and it was contentedly ripping up a scrappy patch of grass with its purple tongue. We were all moved by the sight of this bull, whose massiveness was made all the greater by its apparent willingness to be examined at close quarters. From the safety of the car, we could see the fibers of its tangled beard, the almost wooden texture of its shoulders where the winter wool had left bare patches, the sharpness of its curved horns.

History usually presents itself in the shape of artifacts, documents, ruins, or some other inanimate form, but here we were faced by a primary piece of history that was flesh and blood, genetically indistinguishable from the buffalo that had made possible the plains culture of the Sioux and been the target of white extermination in the 1870s. We were impressed by the creature's majestic indifference to us and its monumental stupidity, for it had evidently learned nothing concerning the fatal habits of human beings.

The buffalo appeared to be living in solitude among these mud-pie rocks. The iron winter dusk was empty of birds, and the road, now hardly more than a dirt track, was also deserted. We had not seen another vehicle since we had turned onto it. As we drove deeper into the desert, one of the children asked a little anxiously, "I don't think this car's got a spare tire. Has anyone seen it?"

None of us had.

The Badlands National Park lies between the Cheyenne River and the White River, and comprises some 244,000 acres of rock and mixed-grass prairie; indeed, it is the largest protected prairie of its type in the United States. The park is divided into three units: the North Unit, the Stronghold Unit, and the Palmer Creek Unit, of which the latter two are located in the Pine Ridge Indian Reservation and managed jointly by the National Park Service and the Oglala Sioux Tribe. Contained within the North Unit is 64,000 acres of designated wilderness area, which has been made accessible to the hiker and car driver by way of its many marked trails and the Badlands Loop Road with its scenic overlooks.

The rocks of the South Dakota Badlands are largely mudstones and siltstones, which have the properties of rock but are vulnerable to disintegration by water. More than 65 million years ago, the area had been a shallow, muddy inland sea, but then a period of upheaval, resulting in the formation of the Rocky Mountains, caused this sea to be drained, leaving the basin to be filled with sandy and muddy deposits, some of which turned black. The effect of sun, rain, and decaying vegetation over millions of years worked chemical changes in the rocks, producing bright yellow soils in some areas.

Near the start of the Oligocene epoch, some 35 million years ago, the rivers flowing from the Black Hills began to carry large quantities of sand and gravel, and as they meandered into their flood plains they filled the Badlands area with huge deposits. These are now known as the Chadron Formation, in which rocks tend to be gray or greenish-gray in color, and the Brule Formation, which followed and is characterized by horizontal bands of yellow-beige and pinkish-red rock. These two formations are sometimes separated by thin sheets of limestone, suggesting the presence of shallow pools. Irregular outcrops of sandstone occur in the Oligocene deposits, and the top of Oligocene beds are frequently layered with white ash, which was probably blown eastwards from ancient Yellowstone eruptions.

The result of these multiple deposits was a layering of mud, sand, gravel, and ash, as well as other types of rock, which tended to erode at different rates when exposed to water and wind, creating the fantastical shapes for which the Badlands are famous. This process has been going on for the last twenty or more million years, during which the rate of erosion has been greater than that of deposition, and the White, Cheyenne, and Bad rivers have reversed their function, carving through the rock rather than dragging in new layers.

The White River Badlands in the southern part of the national park is one of the richest Oligocene fossil beds in the world, and in the middle of the nineteenth century, collectors could pick fossils off the desert floor and carry them away by the cartload. The majority of animals who left their bones in the mud are now extinct species of mammals. The most common were oreodonts, a kind of pig that chewed the cud. Other remains include those of a horse with toes, a saber-toothed tiger, a small camel, an enormous turtle, three sorts of rhinocerous, a giant pig with a large head but small brain, and the protoceras, a bizarre species about the size of a sheep whose males had long, narrow heads embellished with copious knobs or horns growing at different angles.[2]

---

2. The Museum of Geology at the South Dakota School of Mines and Technology in Rapid City holds an impressive array of such fossils. For this account of Badlands' geology and paleontology, I have mostly relied on an excellent monograph published by the Badlands Natural History Association, which has been in print since

The animals that once roamed the Badlands are easily imagined, thanks to their relative similarity to living animals that we have seen in the flesh or on film. In any case, Hollywood has given us an almost intimate familiarity with extraordinary animals of the past, especially dinosaurs. But the temporal dimensions—Miocene, Oligocene, Late Cretaceous—are another matter. Intellectually, I understand the principles of geology, but I find the scale of geology's ages, epochs, and periods impossible to grasp imaginatively. Thirty-five million years to make a rock! Frankly, the number carries no more meaning than the 150 million kilometers that we are told separate us from the sun.

I take no pride in this chronometrical blind spot; indeed, I feel obliged to register it as a kind of disability. I confess that the Badlands only becomes intelligible to me when seen as a piece of land art, a kind of installation (in the gallery sense) that has been thrown together by the ponderous hand of Geology, whose methods are as powerful and mysterious as those of any other Designer.

This may be a trivializing response, but at least it makes the Badlands imaginatively manageable. In 1836, John Constable, the English painter famous for his pictures of the Suffolk countryside, said of the landscape, "We see nothing truly till we understand it," and I immediately feel chastened by his remark, which seems to imply the need for scientific knowledge, to say nothing of historical and economic knowledge, before a landscape can be truly "seen" or appreciated. But his remark was preceded with these words: "It is the soul that sees; the outward eyes Present the object, but the Mind descries."[3] By this, I think he meant that merely to look at something, however knowledgeably, was not sufficient for understanding in an aesthetic sense something that needed both emotional engagement and artistic discrimination. The eyes gather information, but the mind makes the necessary artistic

---

1969 and is still on sale at the newly opened Ben Reifel Center in the North Unit: Joy Keve Hauk, *Badlands: Its Life and Landscape* (Interior, S.Dak.: Badlands Natural History Assoc., 1969).

3. Quoted from John Constable's, "The History of Landscape Painting," Third Lecture, Royal Institution, London, 6 June 1836. *See* C. R. Leslie, *Memoirs of the Life of John Constable*, 2d ed. (London: Longman, Brown, Green, and Longmans, 1845).

decisions. Above all, the mind "descries" the significance of the landscape, which the painter may see as tragic, redemptive, revelatory, and so forth, but they are qualities that are not directly determined by science.

When I was traveling in Jordan for *The Sunday Times* I was lucky enough to be given a driver, who took me to some spectacular and beautiful places, among them Mount Nebo, where Moses was shown the promised land, Wadi Rhum, which is a kind of badland with sheer mountains towering above a desert floor made of red sand, and Petra, "The Rose City, Half as Old as Time." Wherever we stopped, my driver repeated the same hospitable invitation. "Take your time," he would say expansively as we parked in front of a Crusader castle, "you are a guest in our country." But then he would add, "Ten minutes?" It was more of an instruction than an enquiry.

I did my best to accommodate him, but he never liked me, and it was for one simple reason—I did not carry a camera. He could not understand it and, on behalf of his country, was offended by what he took to be my careless disrespect for the great sights he was unveiling. Instead of taking photographs as proper travel writers did, I scribbled in a notebook.

At the time I was going through a purist phase, denying myself the camera and confining myself to written notes. After all, I told myself, I was a writer, and my job was to translate what I saw into prose, not pictures; better to tackle the job on the spot than to defer it to when I sat at my desk, relying on memory. I wanted to achieve an immediacy of response that the camera seemed to obstruct; it demanded much more attention than paper and pencil—fitting the right lens, checking the light, paying attention to foreground and background, avoiding laughable features (the lamp post growing out of someone's head), and so on. Nor did I take pictures that were as good or useful as those taken by professionals.

I tried to impose on myself the discipline of simultaneously looking, writing, and thinking; not just looking, the camera's only function, but engaging all the senses while trying to record my experience. It was a kind of sketching. I cannot draw for toffee, as they say, but I take it that the process of sketching is more than mere note-taking and involves Constable's distinction between presenting and descrying.

Sketching is drawing and thinking at the same time, never an easy task, but one that is made much harder when the place in question, say the Bridge of Sighs in Venice, has been stared at by millions of people during four centuries; when the looking, so to speak, has been done for you by innumerable guidebooks. In this context, sketching is a radical activity. It is the means of achieving independence of mind by trying to find a match between the object and some part of one's individuality that is not subject to convention or precedent. Sketching is a means to cultural liberation. Put to this purpose, the pencil was mightier than the camera—in my hands at any rate.

In practice, my purist experiment did not yield results in terms of quality that matched its principles. My driver was right; there are details of landscape and architecture that a photograph captures, and therefore "remembers" on your behalf, that are difficult to record in words, especially if they require technical terms to describe exactly. And a photograph, even a snapshot, always collects more information than the photographer intends.

I was in Jordan in 1998, and perhaps not coincidently I gave up professional travel writing the following year. By the time I came to make my trip to South Dakota in 2011, different priorities had intervened. Thirteen years earlier I had a memory I could trust, but now I feared losing the material I gathered on my journey. Ideally, I would have traveled, as gentlemen did in the eighteenth century, with an amanuensis, to whom I could have dictated my impressions and sensations, but in lieu of this amenity I equipped myself with every mechanical medium of preservation: camera, notebook, and audio recorder. In addition, at every stop I loaded my car with books, guides, brochures, post cards, handbills, local newspapers, anything that would support my memory of the location and revive its particular spirit.

I now owned a digital camera, which not only simplified and speeded up the actual business of taking a photograph, but allowed me to recollect the places I had visited and the emotions they had inspired by viewing the day's pictures on my computer in the tranquility of my motel room. And if the pictures proved disappointing, I had my own spoken commentary retained on my recorder, also in digital form and also transferable to the computer. This recorder, an elegant piece of miniaturization, was my silent, undemanding, and ever-receptive companion while I drove, and if I did any sketching, in the sense I have tried to define above, it was confided to my recorder, whose memory was faultless. The disadvantage of the recorder is that the process of transcription is laborious and time consuming, whereas the beauty of a written note is its practical simplicity, both to write and read (always assuming you can read your own writing).

To have lost any one of these mechanical aids would have been catastrophic, but only because it would have represented the greater loss of the actual places or experiences that had been recorded. Or so I feared. Throughout my whole journey I lived in dread of just such a loss, which would have rendered the trip no more than a dream, vivid but forgotten beyond recall as soon as it was over.

To get to the Badlands on my 2011 trip I drove south from Wall on South Dakota Highway 240 in the early evening. I paid my $15 fee to enter the park and headed east on the Scenic Loop towards Cedar Pass Lodge, where I had booked a cabin. No sooner had I entered the park than I instinctively took my camera out of its case and readied it for action.

Around the first bend a sign announced the Pinnacles Overlook, though I could see nothing from the road, apart from unremarkable prairie, to indicate why a stop might be worthwhile. However, I pulled over, got out of my car and gasped. I gasped as I had done every other time I had seen the Badlands.

To the south and west was a panorama of scattered rocks that stretched without interruption for many miles towards a murky sunset. The gray-green prairie floor seemed to have been built over by a paranoid regime that feared invasion and had chosen to defend itself with a mad military complex of castle walls, solitary donjons, buttresses bracing nothing, turrets and battlements, pillboxes and barbicans, and as if to invoke magic as well as might to scare off the enemy, it had also thrown up a plethora of temples, ziggurats, pagodas, spires, and stupas, some dwarfish, some almost mountainous, and all colored in shades of rose pink, salmon, and maroon.

It had rained for the most of the day, and though it had now stopped, the light was poor. Undeterred, I snapped like a maniac in all directions. The loop offered nine more overlooks, each offering a fresh variation of rocky configuration, and I paused at every one, taking more and more pictures in the dwindling light. Finally, it was too dark to continue, and although I stopped at the last couple of overlooks, I didn't take any pictures.

On the last stretch of road before the Cedar Pass Lodge, I turned a corner and saw something in the grass beside the road. I stopped the car and found myself staring into the face of a cat-like creature, which stared thoughtfully back at me. It was a large animal, with dense fur and a short, bushy tail. I suspected it was a bobcat, probably still in its winter coat. Fearing I would scare it away, I lowered the window, but it didn't move. Without taking my eyes off it, I felt for my binoculars, raised them, and studied its magnified image. It remained unconcerned and continued to look at me in mutual curiosity. I took a hasty photograph and then another, which still did not disturb it. Finally it became bored, and at a leisurely pace, looking back once or twice, it wandered into deeper grass until it was out of sight.

Darkness had fallen when I reached Cedar Pass Lodge at the far eastern end of the loop. By then restaurant, gift shop, and office had closed, but I was relieved to see an envelope bearing my name inside a steel box attached to the office door. I had been designated Cabin 5, my home for the next two nights, and its key was inside the envelope. Another man drew up in his car, and we agreed this was a splendid place. We also agreed that it was a splendid system to leave our keys in the box outside the center after it had closed. He looked inside the box for his envelope, but couldn't find it. Naturally, he looked disconcerted. He riffled through the uncollected envelopes again, but no luck. He pulled his phone out of his pocket.

"It is the nineteenth, right?"

"No, it's the twelfth," I told him. He shook his head, got back in his car, and drove off without further explanation.

95

I found my cabin, which was just what I expected, having stayed there before in 1994; in fact, it did not appear to have changed in any way since then. I unlocked my door and turned on the heater, for it was 7:30 P.M. and getting cold. The machine blew cold air. I gave it a couple of minutes, and the air grew colder. It was clearly an air conditioner. I tried various settings with what I realized were ice crystal symbols, and the air only got colder still. Outside the temperature was in the low 40s and dropping.

I decided to ask advice and walked to the next-door cabin, where I found a couple lying on their beds, she reading, he using his laptop, which was an encouraging sign. Their cabin was deliciously warm, but it was equipped with a quite different apparatus. They introduced themselves as Dennis and June. Dennis obligingly said he would look at my heater, sprang from his bed, put on his boots, and walked back with me.

To my horror, I found my door was locked. Looking through the window, I could see my key on the bed, also my car key, my cell phone, and my glasses—my whole life, locked in. We tried the windows, but they were all firmly secured. We returned to his cabin, where Dennis obligingly attempted to ring the manager. No signal. We returned to my cabin, this time with June. She tried to open the door with a credit card, but no success. She too looked at the windows and, with a muscular shove, managed to slide open the bathroom window, exposing a narrow and perilous gap.

"If anyone's going in, it's got to be you, Dennis," she said, jovially. Apparently, it was obvious that I was not the man for the job.

After several efforts, Dennis contorted himself with Houdini-like rubberiness and squeezed through the frame. Once he opened the door and let us inside, June pointed to a second device, a heater next to the air conditioner, which I had simply not noticed. True, it was a primitive affair, but it was there and operative. I offered them a drink, a large drink, several large drinks for their pains, but they refused and returned to their cabin.

When I was finally installed in my cabin, I looked at the pictures I had taken from the various overlooks and was relieved to find they were not as bad as I had feared. My pictures of the animal on the verge were predictably obscure, but there was enough shape and color discernible in the gloom to confirm that it had indeed been a bobcat. Even in the muted light of a clouded dusk, the rocks retained their beauty; in fact, they seemed to possess an infinite menu of beauty, with a variation for every nuance of light.

The next morning was overcast and, despite promises of sunshine, remained dull throughout the day. However, it did not prevent me from admiring, not for the first time, the setting of Cedar Pass Lodge. It lay within an amphitheater of pink, pyramidal rocks that enclosed the restaurant and two rows of cabins, divided by a strip of grass, in a kind of crab's embrace. In a less austere place one might have assumed that the resort had commissioned its own badland rocks and employed a fancy designer to arrange them.

The cabins, twenty-two in all, could not have been simpler. The park brochure described them as "historic, humble-yet-cozy cabins. All without the distractions of in-room televisions and telephones so that you may best experience the solitude and spirit of the park." In fact, the decadent visitor could distract himself, for the lodge now had a good Wi-Fi connection, but in any case the park had made other concessions to modernity. By chance I had caught the last season when these historic and humble cabins were in use. Once the season ended, they were to be demolished and replaced by modernized versions, which no doubt would accommodate tourism's current demands.

I hoped that at least one of these cabins would be preserved as a kind of museum piece celebrating a certain kind of old-fashioned, morally improving tourism that would be difficult to sell today. Cedar Pass Lodge was the brainchild of Ben Millard, a local businessman, who first opened for business in 1928. Starting with a dance hall that attracted people from within a hundred-mile radius to listen and dance to Lawrence Welk and similar bands, he expanded the lodge to incorporate a dining room and a shop selling curios, and he built the cabins for tourists who would be sensitive to the spiritual benefits of the Badlands. To reinforce these values, he entertained visitors in the evenings with geology talks (a tradition that might well be revived). A year after his death in 1956 the National Park Service named the ridge rising above the Cedar Pass area Millard Ridge in his honor.

In the restaurant I looked out for my saviors, Dennis and June, and offered to buy their breakfast, but they diffidently refused, dismissing their efforts of the previous night as a trifle. Anyone would have done the same, they said.

I then set out to walk some of the shorter trails through the Badlands that are close to the Lodge—the Cliff Shelf, Window, and Door. I persisted with my photographic project and dutifully snapped away with every turn in the trail. As soon as I penetrated the rocky hinterland, I was joined by a turkey vulture, a solitary flyspeck on the gray surface of the sky, which was soon teamed with a couple of others, a gang of black body-snatchers that cruised the neighborhood until I returned to my car. Through my binoculars I could see their naked faces, red as raw beef. The occasional flash of sunshine brought out the Technicolor extravagance of the rock stripes. A pair of bluebirds, apparently supplied by a Disney artist, flitted across my path. Like all deserts this one appeared at first to be lifeless and sterile, a wilderness of damp, spongy rock that would turn to dusty wasteland as soon as the sun got to work on it, but there were signs of life. Meadowlarks, easily identified by their bright yellow chests, made no effort to hide themselves and kept up a whistling serenade. Invisible crickets produced continual static with their stridulation. All sorts of plants, unnamable by me, had claimed homes in the crevices. The unmistakable prickly pear had laid out its torturer's cushions on flatter rock surfaces while some even flourished on the tops of domes and pillars, sprawled over them like ill-fitting toupees.

Each of these walks had a different display of rocks to offer. Some lay in mounds and domes; some were steeply stacked in layers of beige and pink; some, textured like elephant skin, rose vertically, arranged in folds and fissures so that it was easy to see how vulnerable they were to rain, which seemed to have cut fresh wounds overnight in their crumbly flesh, chiseling out new runnels and flutes. In fact, it was hard to think of these structures as made of rock at all, because the weather had pummeled and kneaded them into shapes that suggested a baker or a toy maker at work: loaves, bosomy muffins, mushrooms, balls, ninepins, chess pieces. A Picasso of erosion had used this place as its studio: every form had been experimented with over and over again, sometimes on a truly Pharaonic scale, sometimes in miniature. The cracks in a rock the size of a cathedral were exactly mimicked in a pebble no bigger than a netsuke. The Badlands was nature on acid; this was geology as psyche-delia.

A monograph could be written on the subject of how writers have attempted to describe the ineffable when faced with these rocks. The most common method is to resort to architectural metaphors, as I have done, but that is, of course, to mistake the essential agency at work: the Badlands are not the product of *con*struction, as it is easy to assume when confronted with these complex profiles, but of *de*struction—they are sculpted by erosion, not built. They are slowly disintegrating, rendering art through collapse and downfall. The Badlands that my family and I first saw in 1992 no longer exists; indeed, the Badlands I saw on the first evening of my present visit no longer existed by the time I woke up the following morning. It had rained heavily in the night, cutting new furrows in the rock, knocking the points off pyramid tops, smoothing what had been corrugated, creasing what had been sleek.

Somewhere out on the Door Trail I found a pleasant spot to sit, which commanded a fine view of small pyramids displayed by the dozen on shelves of rock, as if for sale in a gift shop. A few hikers wandered about, like customers deciding on a purchase. I laid aside my camera, put my notebook on my knee, and attempted to give the whole of my mind to this landscape.

Meditation does not come easily to me—that is, meditation in its primary sense: the act of thinking about something deeply and with sufficient concentration to exclude distractions. Thinking demands that one idea follows another in some sort of coherent sequence, but as soon as I take my mind for a walk down a straight path, it slips the leash and runs off, sniffing at every bush and lamppost. This is not necessarily a sterile activity, but it does not make for serious thought.

I attempted to apply myself by thinking about the seemingly irresistible urge to project human feelings onto natural objects, which the nineteenth century English art critic John Ruskin called the "Pathetic Fallacy," but no sooner had I fixed on it than I flitted to thoughts of my grandchildren, which had become a kind of mental default mode. I focused again on the rocks in front of me and the similes they suggested—castles, biscuits, ice cream, and so on. I reminded myself that these were geological phenomena, the products of erosion, and was immediately returned to habitual themes of age and time, the preoccupations of every grandparent. Erosion is an uncomfortable trope for the elderly to brood on. I wondered how the old folk of Harrison would have responded to these crumbling metaphors.

Anyone who has reached a certain age is conscious of the erosion that the years have inflicted on both body and mind. Every morning Sal and I perform a ritual to make sure that Dr. Alzheimer does not come knocking at our door. We no longer converse at breakfast; we barely say good morning before I bark at her, "savage—eight letters" or "wet and dirty—ten letters." (Barbaric, bedraggled.) We read somewhere that crosswords, sudokus, and puzzles of all sorts keep the brain active, and so we tackle the so-called "quick" crossword printed in *The Guardian* (London), which is confined to anagrams and . . . .

An Alzheimer's moment has intervened.

What is the word for words that mean the same as other words? Simile? Aphorism? Ah, yes. Synonym!

These are not joking matters. Badland rocks, for all their beauty and the curiosity of their shapes, are no more than sandcastles. Suffering from the same impermanence, my own shape has altered under the erosion of age. Once upon a time my waist and inside leg measurement were the same, a dapper thirty-two inches, but over the years I have gradually slumped and swollen and shrunk, leaving me with an inflated waist of forty inches and an inside leg that has inexplicably shrunk to thirty-one inches. Meanwhile, as if to bear the increased load, my feet have spread by a whole shoe size. My hair, once curly and dark, now resembles porridge, if my elder grandson is to be believed. Exercising a poetic streak, the little whippersnapper was seeking an analogy for the whiteness of my hair and found it in his breakfast bowl.

I defy anyone to contemplate the corruption of the flesh with equanimity, but nor is it any excuse for self-pity. Youth is fleeting; beauty, such as it was in the first place, is destined to wither; the brain will slow; the joints will ache. I am slowly losing my teeth, another version of human erosion. Yes, but while we have the resilience to carry on, we must not mourn these losses. All is not gone. (No one knows this better than grandparents, who cannot believe their luck at being given a second sort of life.)

What is it to grow old? asked Matthew Arnold in his superb, but terrible, poem "Growing Old:"

Is it to feel our strength—
Not our bloom only, but our strength—decay?
Is it to feel each limb
Grow stiffer, every function less exact,
Each nerve more weakly strung?

His answer, given three verses later, could not be more depressing:

It is to suffer this,
And feel but half, and feebly, what we feel.
Deep in our hidden heart
Festers the dull remembrance of a change,
But no emotion—none.[4]

If I understand him correctly, he is saying that feeling is subject to the same atrophy as the body. The capacity for emotion will decay as surely as our physical strength. I don't know what mood or circumstance drove him to write this poem, though it must have been extremely black, but much as I admire it as poetry I cannot subscribe to its feeling, which, ironically, flies in the teeth of its own meaning by being expressed with great intensity. I recognize what he is proposing, having witnessed it in people close to us, though I would put it in different terms. Old age is not the death of emotion so much as the slow retreat into a different kind of prison where the feelings that prevail are boredom and irritation, an ever-shrinking circle of self-absorption, where the only thing that can breathe is an angry preoccupation with personal comfort and its enemies. Old age becomes a prison when the victim—there is no other word—allows himself to become isolated and, out of a mixture of laziness and weariness, to feel nothing but indignation over the way the world has neglected him.

Aging is a process of loss, and loss is what you sense all around you in the Badlands. In the long run—and in geological time the Badlands

4. Matthew Arnold, *The Poems of Matthew Arnold, 1840–1867* (New York: Oxford University Press, 1909), pp. 408–9.

clock is running faster than most—the entire formation will be washed downstream to the Missouri, to the Mississippi, and out to sea, the whole bag of tricks reduced to multi-colored sludge. In nature there is no loss, just a reconstitution of matter, but this fact offers no consolation to us, for whom loss of life is unavoidable and final in the sense that the self, at least in its earthly incarnation, is extinguished forever. The knowledge of our ultimate and unappealable fate presses more keenly on the elderly, though it does not necessarily induce more terror. On the other hand, loss, in all too many of its forms, is to be dreaded for fear it turns old age into a state of deepening grief—grief for a body that's still alive.

Now that I was separated from my grandsons for the first time in their short lives, my thoughts turned to what I was missing, to what, in effect, I would be losing during my brief absence. For example, during the days just before my departure from England, my younger grandson, Arlo, suddenly got the hang of walking, and the prospect of missing out on the sight of his first efforts at tottering around the garden—pot-bellied, big-bottomed, bow-legged—felt like a deprivation. I was also frightened that I would miss another great milestone, his leap from nonverbal communication to talking. When I left he was using a series of grunts and little exclamations to indicate what he wanted or felt. His only recognizable word was "car," which for some reason he tended to shout. Otherwise, he put the noise "ooh!" to a comprehensive range of expression, making it a virtual vocabulary on its own, suitable for all situations and needs. I feared that by the time I got back he would be speaking proper words, and I knew from experience that once the process had began it would accelerate quickly, and one word would soon became a hundred.

But in what sense would my missing this moment be a loss? One of the joys of being in the company of a young child day after day, a privilege Sal and I are lucky enough to enjoy, lies in observing the changes, large and small, that comprise the child's development. The pleasure this affords is at the essence of our nature, because we are witnessing a biological success as our grandchild graduates from one stage to the next while remaining healthy. He is fulfilling his biological destiny, which is to cease to be a child, so that he can mature and produce children of his own. That natural imperative drives growth, and we have the satisfaction of knowing we played a part in assisting its consummation.

A child loses his childhood selves all the time; he sheds them, and good riddance, because he is moving on to the next phase of his maturity. But for us these losses have their painful side. Part of me would like to hold on to the little child that first walks and first talks, because he is so lovable and yet exists so fleetingly. I want our grandsons to grow up—it would be perverted to want anything else—but I'm also aware that Sal and I are not marching in step with them; their gain is our loss; the older they get, the older we get. Their maturity is our loss of youthfulness, or what's left of it.

Despite the barren surroundings of the Door Trail, I associated these thoughts with apple blossom. In our back yard we have a venerable apple tree, which defies its age by remaining exceedingly fecund, producing huge numbers of apples each year. Not long before my departure it had come into flower, glowing deep pink, but suddenly the pink blossom had been replaced with white, thrown over the whole tree like a bridal veil. This graphic transformation had taken a week, perhaps ten days, and it had coincided with the time it took Arlo to proceed from taking his first crumbling steps to perfecting his current and singular style of chimpanzee walking.

To witness fleeting moments of change in nature can be a source of consolation, of feeling better about the tyranny of time, because they are repeated season by season: next year there will be another costume change from pink to white, another avalanche of apples in the fall to box, give away, and turn into pies. But children throw these moments away as casually as they throw toys out of a stroller, and they are not repeated until the next generation. Arlo himself would not walk in just that way ever again, and whatever I missed while in South Dakota I would lose forever.

The next morning I left Cedar Pass and drove west on South Dakota Highway 44 through the Badlands National Park in the direction of the Black Hills. After thirty-four miles, having seen nothing but outcrops of striped rock and open grassland, I reached Scenic, a town named for its badland views, rather than its own appearance. Rapid City lay another forty-three miles to the northwest, with nothing in between to interrupt the isolation.

Several large buildings stood on either side of Main Street. Most conspicuous was the Longhorn Saloon, a single-story timber structure with a ramshackle canopy over its doorway supported by five poles. Nailed to an oversized false front were three rows of white cattle skulls, about sixty in all. Below this bizarre display, painted in faded letters, was the legend,

Old Longhorn Saloon
1906 Scenic SO Dakota Scenic 1906
Wiskey-Beer-Soda-Wine Tobacco-Lunch-Dancing
Indians Allowed

Nearby was an equally broken-down building that had been the town's general store, but was now closed and padlocked, and further down the road was a large whitewashed, clapboard structure that might once have been a barn, or even a church, but now bore a sign saying, Tatanka Trading Post. It too was closed. The only facility not locked up was a shed with rusting bars facing the street, no doubt the town's one-time jail.

In its tattered Wild West costume, the place had the air of a destination that had long ago resigned itself to being ignored by tourists. There was no sign of either visitors or inhabitants. Not a single car drove by as I walked around. The last census recorded a population of ten in Scenic, but only one house appeared to be occupied, and no one stirred within or without. I had been here before, on my trip with Alvin in 1992, and nothing seemed to have changed, except the buildings looked even more dilapidated. There was one difference. At that time, beneath a crude slap of whitewash designed to efface it, you could clearly see the word "No" in front of the hospitable message "Indians Allowed."

Scenic was evidently a ghost town in the making, another of many victims of railway line closure, in this case the branch line between Kadoka and Rapid City owned by the Chicago, Milwaukee, St. Paul, and Pacific Railroad, which closed in 1980. South Dakota is well populated, if that's the expression, with ghost towns, which in their ghoulish way tell a story of loss and failure among the state's chief enterprises, farming and mining. (Is there a more poignant monument to loss than a ghost town?) A website devoted to ghost towns in Pennington County, alone, lists more than sixty sites; admittedly, some were no more than camps for miners with a few shacks or a post office and a saloon, but some were more substantial communities.

Take, for instance, the gold-rush town of Rochford, in the central Black Hills, located twenty miles south of Lead. The town was founded in 1877 and within a year had more than five hundred residents, who enjoyed access to such civic facilities as a variety theatre, a hotel, two restaurants, and several saloons (but no church). It stood in a beautiful, mountainous position beside Rapid Creek, a stream fed from innumerable small gulches whose names told their own Black Hills story: Irish, Bearcat, Middle Nugget, Moonshine, Blood, Poverty, and Skull. But by 1900, the gold had been exhausted and its population had dropped to forty-eight, even though it had become a depot on the railway route that linked Deadwood and Custer. Nowadays its population is negligible, and Rochford has been reduced to a handful of houses, a museum, and a bar—the Moonshine Gulch Saloon, which is full of memorabilia and curios. In a last flickering burst of enterprise, the town has turned its ghostliness into a tourist attraction by becoming a sort of museum of itself. You might say it has resorted to exhibiting its dying breaths, though tourism may yet perform a miracle and resurrect it.

The majority of ghost towns in the state are genuine, in the sense that they are the sites of communities that gradually shrank in number and finally deserted their few remaining buildings, leaving them to rot back into the prairie or mountain where they had briefly stood. Such was the fate of Lakeview, the town on the Rosebud reservation where Harrison's pastor had preached. However, tourism, in its ingenious way, has conjured up a variation by inventing what might be called the professional ghost town. The "Original 1880 Town" near Murdo provides a good example.

Here, according to its website, you can "walk down Main Street of this 1880 town and explore more than 30 buildings authentically furnished with thousands of relics." The origins of this "original town" are instructive. In the 1970s, local businessman Richard Hullinger and his son acquired a movie set of an 1880s main street that had been built nearby and then abandoned by the film company. They moved the set to its present position and constructed their own 1880s town. But they were far from satisfied, and they began to collect both artifacts to equip their town and buildings to expand it. They bought the Dakota Hotel and moved it from Draper in Jones County, where presumably it had gone out of business. Built in 1910, it still carried scars made by cowboys' spurs on the staircase. They also bought a barn (from Draper), a church (from Dixon, Gregory County) complete with stained glass and chiming bell, a railroad depot, town hall, schoolhouse, and a homestead with its own outhouse.

These buildings were inhabited by their own ghosts, but instead of enjoying an afterlife of undisturbed haunting, they found they had been recruited to join the great congregation of ghosts that now thronged the Original 1880 Town, a town which, unlike many of its moribund neighbors, had an expanding population as the Hullinger family continued to add to its collection. Thus, the layers of "originality" were laid down in a complex pattern: some of the buildings were original in the sense that they were old, even if they did not date from 1880, while some were the handiwork of skillful set-makers made to look as if they dated from 1880, but in no sense could the town itself be called *original*, except perhaps in that it represented a unique, inimitable gathering of elements.

Yet one more permutation of this spectral shape-shifting may be observed from Interstate 90 near the border with Minnesota. A faded billboard advertises a ghost town that boasts all the usual features, saloon, jail, bank, and even rest rooms, but this attraction has acquired an unwanted authenticity. It has closed for business and its broken-down buildings have been left to decay. Its ghosts are now haunted by the ghosts of departed tourists. In the world of tourism, shadows cast shadows of their own.

What I did not realize as I wandered around Scenic, where it looked as though the ghosts were preparing to move in, was that I could have bought the place. Most of the land and buildings were in the possession of a single owner, who had decided to sell her property, in effect the entire town, and by the summer of 2011 the price had fallen from $3 million to a trifling $799,000. In my village this sum would buy you a comfortable four-bedroom house; in Scenic it would allow you to, "Own the town of legends!" Your money, according to the realtor's website, would buy you the following: "Longhorn Fuel & Food Convenience Store, World Famous Longhorn Saloon, Very Large Dance Hall with basketball court, Large Museum with knotty pine interiors, Bunkhouse sleeps 8–10, 2 freestanding Retail Stores, Historic Train Depot, One Working Jail, One Abandoned Historic Jail, Many Out-Buildings, Residence Home, Residence Modular Home."

I missed my chance. Shortly after I returned home, Scenic was sold to a most unexpected buyer, the Iglesia ni Cristo Church. Based in Quezon City, Philippines, and said to have nearly two million members, it was founded in 1914 by former Catholic Felix Manalo and is now led by his grandson. It is hard to imagine what this church would want to do with a ghost town in the Badlands. So far, plans for Scenic have not been disclosed, though it has been reported that some of the buildings on Main Street will be preserved. If the Old Longhorn Saloon is among them, I hope that its store sign will not be preserved. There are some losses that are to be welcomed.

4 Mount Rushmore

If you are planning a trip to Mount Rushmore, let me recommend approaching it from the north, driving along U.S. Highway 16A. Try to make your visit in the afternoon on a sunny day. Keep glancing up to the skyline on your left, and in due course you will catch sight of one of the oddest spectacles in the United States. The road runs beneath a sheer granite cliff bristling with trees that have somehow found a foothold among the crevices and fissures, and as you begin to circle the mountain-sized clump of rock in which Gutzon Borglum carved his presidents, there's a moment when the head of George Washington, nicely framed by pines, looms into view, alone and in profile, with his chin propped on the jagged summit of the mountain.

It is difficult to resist the impulse to stop, if only to confirm that the head in the sky is not a hallucination. The authorities have bowed to the inevitable by opening up a parking bay where people can pause in safety to stare at the first president or take a photograph of his noble features, which on a clear day are brilliantly illuminated by the mid-afternoon sun. From here Washington's expression looks pensive and melancholy, seeming to reflect his bizarre position, for his disembodied, neckless head appears to be in danger of rolling over the precipice and smashing on the rocks below. Every other comparably close view of the monument is visible only from the visitor center; this is the head that got away, the only one of Borglum's four presidents that can be viewed gratis.

On previous visits, I was struck by the reverential mood that overcame American tourists as they confronted the Shrine of Democracy; I saw people in tears, and more than once I saw people on their knees. To an outsider, such behavior might seem absurd, certainly puzzling, but no one who belongs to the nation that suc- cumbed en masse to hysterical outpourings of grief over the death of a divorced princess can afford to mock.[1] My guess is that these visitors, who were drawn from every state in the Union, as the license plates in the parking lot testified, regarded the presidents' heads more as a patri- otic monument than a celebration of democracy as such. Their emo- tion was not ideologically inspired, but rather a version of the sublime, the result of feeling overwhelmed by the sheer hugeness of the project. Which of them, under less sensational circumstances, would weep over Theodore Roosevelt?

However, on the occasion of my most recent visit, the place was full of Japanese tourists, who were by no means overawed, still less tearful. In their respectful way, the older ones took the monument seriously, but the younger ones were fooling about. One young woman stood on the viewing parapet and for the benefit of her boyfriend struck a pose more suitable for the Cannes film festival than the Shrine of Democracy.

Japanese tourists are an easy butt of humor, with their cameras, their seemingly sheep-like group discipline, their earnest if slightly puzzled attention to the sight pointed out by their guide, but I rather admire them. I admire their seriousness and their willingness to travel so far and go to such expense to look at what the world claims to be its great cultural objects. Seeing these Japanese tourists, I was suddenly struck by my own liking for being a tourist, that despised species. Unlike my dear friend Alvin, I'm a natural tourist: I like labels, and explanatory signs, and visitor trails, and all the other nannying devices employed by tourist spots that he hates. I quite like crowds, too, and often feel there is some- thing missing if I'm looking at a great attraction on my own. I especially like gift shops and have to force myself to see the sight before entering its souvenir shop. If I do make the mistake of going into the gift shop first, I sometimes wonder if it's worth looking at the actual object that all these calendars and brochures and key rings and mugs and fridge mag- nets are designed to remind me of. For one thing, it's unlikely to look as

---

1. I refer, of course, to Diana, Princess of Wales, and the unprecedented grief that followed her death in 1997.

good as it did when the photographer took the classic picture of it now reproduced on a million post cards.

From the beginning, tourism had posed a dilemma for Gutzon Borglum. On the one hand, the ever-increasing numbers of visitors that drove into the state to look at his work in progress (300,000 in 1939) provided him with an argument for demanding more funds. On the other, these people and the local businesses that catered to their needs brought with them the danger of vulgarizing his shrine through commerce, and he wrote to Governor Harlan Bushfield that he was glad that he had carved the monument "against the Heavens" where it was "out of the mob's reach."[2] The locals needed to be guided and the tourists protected in order that the monument (and by extension his own prestige) was perceived in a properly respectful light. As the years went by, he made a few reluctant concessions to tourism by permitting the sale of post cards, for which he chose the photographs, and miniature reproductions of the faces, whose design he supervised. However, he drew the line at hot dogs. According to Mount Rushmore historian John Taliaferro, the sculptor complained that while he was laboring to complete "the greatest monument that civilization had ever undertaken," the "nickel-chasers" in Rapid City were conspiring to degrade his creation and "cover [the hills] with hot dog stands."[3]

Nonetheless, Mount Rushmore was in fact the child of tourism, and despite Borglum's ambitions for its iconic status, it has never completely shaken off its appeal as a stupendous stunt. The idea of carving a mountain in South Dakota originally came in 1924 from Doane Robinson, State Historian for South Dakota, who was eager to promote tourism in the state, but believed that the landscape alone was not enough to lure visitors. His first plan was to invite a sculptor to make carvings out of the Needles, an area of granite pillars in the Black Hills. In a letter to Lorado Taft, a leading sculptor of the day, he wrote that in his imagination he could see, "all the heroes of the old west peering out from them," including Lewis and Clark, Sakagawea, Red Cloud, Buffalo Bill on his horse,

2. John Taliaferro, *Great White Fathers: The Story of the Obsessive Quest to Create Mount Rushmore* (New York: Public Affairs, 2002), p. 311.

3. Ibid., p. 261.

and the overland mail.[4] Quite a challenge for a sculptor, but by the following year Robinson's imagination was moving at full gallop. He told a correspondent he could envision "Custer and his gold-discovering cavalcade winding its way through the Needles, with Red Cloud and a band of Sioux scouts, resentful and suspicious, spying on it through rifts in the pinnacles of the opposite wall, while above, a great mountain buck, wary but unafraid, inspects the pageant with curiosity."[5]

This proposal was surprising in more ways than one; apart from its gloriously impractical vision, it showed a callous disregard for American Indian interests, which was unexpected in someone who was the author of the then-definitive history of the Sioux and well aware of the Sioux's hatred of Custer and his gold-hunting invasion of the Black Hills.[6] Borglum saw things differently. He jumped at the chance of working in the Black Hills, and after his first visit to the Harney Peak area, he declared that, although he knew the West, he knew of no rock formation "so near the center of our country that is so available to the nation or so suitable for colossal sculpture."[7] Historian Rex Alan Smith believes he was eager to create a work that would give him artistic immortality, as well as a large fee (something he always disputed), and immediately conceived of a sculpture that would have national, and not merely local, significance.[8] Borglum thought in terms of "a great Northern National Memorial" that would celebrate the "principle of an unbreakable union."[9] More astute in these matters than Robinson, he understood that to win federal support and generate public interest they would have to choose a subject for the sculpture that would have universal resonance. "If

4. Quoted in Rex Alan Smith, *The Carving of Mount Rushmore* (New York: Abbeville Press, 1985), p. 26.

5. Quoted ibid., p. 27.

6. Doane Robinson, "A History of the Dakota or Sioux Indians: From their earliest traditions and first contact with white men to the final settlement of the last of them upon reservations and consequent abandonment of the old tribal life," *South Dakota Historical Collections* 2, pt. 2 (1904): 1–508. The title tells its own melancholy story.

7. Quoted in Taliaferro, *Great White Fathers*, p. 57.

8. Smith, *Carving*, p. 128.

9. Quoted in Taliaferro, *Great White Fathers*, p. 199.

we pitch the note high enough," he told Robinson, "we will arouse the nation."[10]

Borglum also knew that the project would never get under way if it was not seen as more than the creation of two or three huge statues. He quickly jettisoned Robinson's idea of carving the Needles—"totem poles" was his dismissive description of this rejected idea—in favor of a whole mountaintop carved into a memorial that would be an unprecedented sculptural wonder. The selection of the final quartet of presidents' heads was not made at once, but a guiding principle soon became clear. Washington was a natural choice because he had been the Union's most prominent founder, and Abraham Lincoln made a natural pairing because he had been its foremost preserver; their two figures would represent a monument to the foundation and preservation of the United States. According to Smith there is no clear record of how the further inclusion of Thomas Jefferson came about, though it appears to have been Borglum's idea, which he justified by explaining that Jefferson had not only been the author of the Declaration of Independence but had also negotiated the Louisiana Purchase, which more than doubled the territory of the United States. In any case, Borglum was always pushing to make the Memorial as massive as possible. The sculptor told the project's executive committee that the incorporation of Theodore Roosevelt was justified on the grounds that, by opening up the Panama Canal, Roosevelt had "completed the dream of Columbus, opened the way to the East, joined the waters of the great East and West seas."[11]

Once these four empire builders and heroes of the Union had been chosen, Rushmore's theme could be fully articulated: the monument was, Borglum wrote, "in commemoration of the foundation, preservation, and continental expansion of the United States."[12] Nothing less than a mountain-sized sculpture would encompass the story of the nation—and, incidentally, its creator's ego. As Taliaferro put it, "Borglum's determination to meld American art and patriotism into a mountain-

10. Smith, *Carving*, p. 129.
11. Ibid., p. 131.
12. Ibid.

sized monument—Great Men carved by a Great Man—is the sum of every second and cell of his existence."[13]

To a foreign visitor, less sensitive to the symbolism contained in the presidents' heads, the quality that most impresses is the scale of the enterprise, which simply by virtue of being big seems essentially American. Borglum worked in an age that thought big: for example, the Empire State Building was completed in 1931, the year after the dedication of Washington's head on Rushmore, and since the destruction of the World Trade Center, it is once again the tallest building in New York City. Two years after its completion, King Kong, the greatest ape of them all, clung to the top of the building while fighting his fatal duel with biplanes. But not even moviemakers thought bigger than Borglum. The Stone Mountain monument that he designed in 1914, though did not finish, depicts three Confederate generals on horseback riding across *three acres* of carved rock, making it the largest bas relief sculpture in the world to this day. It also attracts four million visitors each year, compared with Rushmore's nearly three million. Before tackling Rushmore, Borglum also sculpted what was then the world's biggest bronze monument, the war memorial in Newark, New Jersey, known as *Wars of America*, which incorporated no less than forty-two life-size soldiers and two spirited horses. But even in the United States, bigger is not automatically better. In Rushmore's case, the scale of the monument gives rise to the following paradox: a political system that in theory enfranchises everyone, even the poorest and least significant, has been represented in the shape of four gigantically rendered leaders, who are all male and white.

It is true that presidential democracy focuses greater attention than other forms on the leader of the winning party, who becomes both head of state and head of government. Yet, despite all the power and prestige the president enjoys while in office, he (so far) is subject to dismissal by the electorate like any other officeholder. The essence of democracy is that the individual, no matter how remarkable, can never be more powerful than the system that installed him. This principle was reinforced by the Twenty-second Amendment, adopted in 1951, ensuring

13. Taliaferro, *Great White Fathers*, p. 210.

that presidents may only serve (the mot juste) for two terms. To identify the idea of democracy with particular presidents, even if they were political titans, seems therefore the opposite of democracy's spirit.

The title "Shrine of Democracy" was not a title that Borglum himself introduced, though it has become virtually synonymous with Rushmore and is trumpeted in every piece of publicity associated with the monument.[14] If you knew nothing about Borglum and his monument, you might easily guess that it dated from the period in the twentieth century when the strong leader was a more acceptable political ideal than he is today. Borglum appears to have believed in a kind of democracy— "We are reaching deep into the soul of mankind and through *democracy* building better than has ever been built before," he once said in his inimitable style—but his politics contained a distinctly undemocratic dimension.[15] Not to put too fine a point on it, he was an anti-Semite and a white supremacist.

It would be interesting to know if Doane Robinson, when he invited Borglum to the Black Hills, was aware of the famous sculptor's relations with the Ku Klux Klan. Borglum probably became affiliated with the Klan in order to consolidate its support for his work on the Confederate Memorial on Stone Mountain, but his involvement became more than pragmatic in 1923 when he was chosen to be a member of the Imperial Kloncilium (the quaintly named Klan national cabinet). It is true that his commitment to Klan affairs soon declined, but Robinson can hardly have been ignorant of the connection. On the other hand, Borglum was probably careful to disguise the full intensity of his racial prejudices from his sponsors in South Dakota, though he did confide them to his friend "Steve" Stephenson, the Grand Dragon of the Northern Realm, whose charisma temporarily dazzled him.[16]

14. According to Rex Alan Smith, the title was established by 1934.

15. Quoted in Simon Schama, *Landscape and Memory* (London: HarperCollins, 1995), p. 394.

16. In 1925, Stephenson was tried for the abduction, forced intoxication, and rape of a woman, which led to her suicide attempt and eventual death. He was found guilty of second degree murder. Among other atrocities, Stephenson had bitten his victim so many times that one man who saw her described her condition as having

On 4 September 1923, Borglum wrote to this "dear friend" saying that he had just written an essay on "the evils of alien races." A brief extract will give a flavor of this credo:

[The Nordic races] have been and continue today the pioneers of the world. . . . America has been peopled by these free, independent thinking races. . . . The Nordic has ever been a camp maker; the Mediterranean . . . a camp follower. The one establishes, creates, builds, the other attaches, feeds upon, corrupts . . . while Anglo-Saxons have themselves sinned grievously against the principle of pure nationalism by illicit slave and alien servant traffic, it has been the character of the cargo that has eaten into the moral fiber of our race character, rather than the moral depravity of Anglo-Saxon traders . . . [in southern Europe] no student of ethnology, or history or government or political economy need look for other cause of three thousand years of rape and rapine . . . than the mongrel blood that has destroyed original race purity.[17]

Is it fair to think less of a work of art because its creator held unsavory political opinions or because his personality was obnoxious? Should the artist, whether saint or sinner, be excluded as a distraction when the quality of the art is being judged? Or is it nonsense to imagine that art can be considered in aesthetic isolation from its historical or biographical context? As I write this, an exhibition of ballet paintings by Edgar Degas is on display at the Royal Academy in London, where it has received many admiring notices, adding yet further confirmation of the painter's standing as a great and much-loved Impressionist. Yet it is no secret that Degas held reactionary and anti-Semitic opinions, which hardened as he grew older and caused him to break with his Jewish friends when the Dreyfus affair divided France in the late 1890s, the period from which many of these highly praised pictures date.[18]

---

been "chewed by a cannibal." He continued a one-sided correspondence with Borglum during his long imprisonment.

17. Quoted in Jesse Larner, *Mount Rushmore: An Icon Reconsidered* (New York: Thunder's Mouth/Nation Books, 2002), pp. 219–20.

18. The Dreyfus affair split French society in the 1890s and early 1900s after Cap-

In Borglum's case, it is difficult to see his heads in aesthetic isolation, as a piece of sculpture that just happens to be very big, rather than a national symbol or political statement. For one thing, the immediate context makes such an effort impossible; from the moment you set foot on the monument's site, your way of seeing the sculpture on the mountain is directed and manipulated by the architecture that surrounds its viewing point.

Since 1998, visitors have been confronted by a new complex of stone and glass structures, built on a grandiose scale, through which they must pass in order to obtain a clear sight of the presidential heads. Facing them as they approach the shrine is a vast colonnade constructed from gray granite blocks that opens into an atrium where a bust of Borglum, carved by his son and surprisingly modest in scale, stands in a niche set into the blank face of a granite wall. Beyond the concession building, a vast affair, lies the Avenue of Flags, an arcade of rectangular granite pillars bearing the flags of the fifty-six states and territories that make up the Union. This thoroughfare leads towards another colonnade, also made of granite blocks and rectangular pillars but curved to form a great concave backdrop to the Grand View Terrace, from which, as its name suggests, the finest view of the presidents, many feet above the humbled tourist's own head, is available.

The design of this entire construction is uniform: the only materials used are glass and granite; the shapes are all hard-edged and right-angled; and the scale is huge. (South Dakota loyalists were not pleased that some of the granite for the new buildings had to be imported from Minnesota.) The result is a colossal setting that threatens to belittle the jewel in its clasp. The concession building is broader than the four presidents, and from some positions along the Avenue of Flags, they are either effaced or forced to peer ignominiously over the pillars.

The style of these buildings is reminiscent of the monumental classicism beloved of dictators in the 1930s. Look, for example, at the rectangular pillars supporting the reception hall of the Berlin Templehof

---

tain Alfred Dreyfus, a French artillery officer of Jewish descent, was wrongly imprisoned for treason. After spending almost five years in jail, his conviction was overturned, and he rejoined the army.

Airport, which was commissioned by Albert Speer in 1934 as part of the gateway to Hitler's new world capital, Germania; or look at the sequence of pillars forming the façade of the courthouse in Bolzana in Italy, which the fascist architect Marcello Piacentini designed in 1939. These brutalist erections are the wicked uncles in the family tree to which Rushmore's tourist facility belongs.

I am not suggesting that the architect who designed Rushmore's granite colonnades and fittings nursed fascistic longings. These mighty ornaments, with their solemn overtones of ancient grandeur, were no doubt intended to complement Borglum's carvings and put visitors in a suitable frame of mind for approaching the national shrine of democracy. However, apart from sounding an unwanted echo of Borglum's supremacist ideology, this style of architecture runs the risk of diminishing not only the monument itself but its visitors, who would be justified in feeling overwhelmed. Kneeling may be a suitable posture for the veneration of a religious shrine, but it is surely unsuitable for a shrine devoted to democracy, whose essence is that people are not overpowered by authority since they are, ultimately, the ones with the power.

At all events, having arrived at the wall of the Grand View Terrace, you are at last in a position to view Borglum's creation in all its glory. Speaking for myself, whenever I have visited Mount Rushmore my first reaction has always been, "You have to hand it to the old boy—this is an extraordinary achievement!"

Borglum undoubtedly knew what he was doing, and in the teeth of considerable odds, both practical and financial, he created a truly spectacular piece of work. Sixty feet high each and five hundred feet above the terrace, his four faces seem to thrust their way out of the mountain rock in defiance of the actual process that created them. Your eye is drawn first to Washington's head, partly because it enjoys the most conspicuous position with its domed forehead framed by open sky and it is carved to a greater depth of rock than the others, making it appear the largest of the quartet. It also comes closest to Borglum's original conception, which was to portray not just heads but torsos as well. All that remains of his ambition is Washington's coat collar and cravat. By contrast, the heads of Jefferson and Roosevelt are somewhat crammed, sans necks, into the fissure that separates Washington from Lincoln.

Jefferson's head was to have stood in a much more prominent position to Washington's right, but the rock proved unsatisfactory, and the first carvings had to be effaced, an accident that explains the area of smooth rock beside and below the Washington head and further adds to its pre-eminence.

Each of the four heads is a separate portrait, but we have seen them depicted as a group so often that it is impossible not to perceive them as a single unit. This familiarity makes us forget how unnaturally they are positioned, intimately bunched together like schoolboys in a team photograph, an effect made all the more incongruous by the spacious-ness of the surrounding landscape. Their exact disposition was dictated by the shape of the mountain in the first place and the quality of the rock, which contained variations and weaknesses that could only be discovered as the sculpting—detonation, drilling, and smoothing—proceeded, but despite these natural constrictions, the decision to dis-play the presidents in the form of a four-headed bust was Borglum's not the mountain's.

As a piece of public art celebrating a national hero, the head of Wash-ington is the most successful in that it achieves the appropriate air of nobility (and superiority); it is less a head than an emblem in the sense of being at once human and symbolic, like the Queen's features on British coins. However, in terms of character, Lincoln's head is the best developed. Borglum was a fervent admirer of Lincoln and in 1907 had exhaustively studied the many photographs and portraits made of Lin-coln before carving a marble head, which now resides in the Capitol Rotunda in Washington, D.C. On the strength of this success, the city of Newark, New Jersey, commissioned Borglum to sculpt a bronze figure of the president, which is now known as *Seated Lincoln* because its hag-gard subject, only one-and-a-half-times life size, is sitting on a bench where it appears to offer the passerby a bronze hand to hold. Borglum liked to think that Lincoln belonged to him, and in a sculpture whose scale did not permit much expressive subtlety, he managed to invest his Rushmore Lincoln with a sense of feeling.[19]

The head of Roosevelt, the last to be installed, suffers from seeming

19. Taliaferro, *Great White Fathers*, p. 107.

to be squeezed into its niche, forcing the great man to peep out from behind the others. On the other hand, it is probably the most ingenious from a technical point of view since it is easy to persuade yourself that he is wearing pince-nez lenses, an illusion created by the stone clip carved on the bridge of his nose, which leaves your eye to fill in the rest.

Jefferson's head presented Borglum with several difficulties, and it is the least satisfactory of the four. The area of rock chosen in the second instance for his face also proved friable, and Borglum was forced to make radical adjustments to the angle at which it emerged from the mountain. He hoped to portray Jefferson as he was at thirty-three, the age at which he composed the Declaration of Independence, but no portraits were done at that time, and there was no likeness of him that had acquired the kind of clichéd immortality (Lincoln's lantern jaw, Washington's nose, Roosevelt's moustache) that made the others immediately recognizable. Borglum struggled, resorting in the end to artistic license, but without creating a wholly persuasive result; in fact, some early visitors mistook the face nearest Washington's for his wife Martha. On the other hand, high claims have been made for the characterization of his sculpting. John Taliaferro, no sentimentalist, claims to be able to discern a twinkle in Jefferson's eye and describes his mouth as the most expressive bit of carving on the mountain. "We can actually see the muscles in Jefferson's face, flexing subtly, creating that momentary purse of his lips. Like the best Renaissance figures, Borglum's Jefferson is both sensual and psychological . . . his head seems to hold the most complex thought."[20] High praise indeed, though I fear my binoculars must be less powerful than his.

However, more than achieving likenesses, or expressing ideology, Borglum was obsessed with ensuring the immortality of his work, and by immortality, he did not mean anything as frivolous as centuries or even millennia. In 1936, while still at work on the sculpture, he wrote, "This colossus is our mark. Cut in the backbone of this western world, high in the heavens, fearless we have carved it, defying the elements . . . confident that [it] shall endure eons after civilizations have come, read, pondered, wondered, and passed away. I am assured that these

20. Ibid., p. 257.

carvings will endure as long as the Rocky Mountains endure; their message will outlast Egypt's entombed mortality, Greece's gift of grace and loveliness."[21] Referring to other great aspirants to immortality, he said, "None . . . have been so conceived, so located, and so designed that they became a definite messenger to a posterity ten thousand, one hundred thousand, or, if the material survives the elements, a million years hence."[22] A million years! The great progenitor of the faces had not made his clay out of mountains for nothing; when he cast his mind into the future, he thought in units of geology, not history.

You wouldn't have to know about Borglum's delirious longings for immortality to see that these heads were constructed to survive through eons, a need that seems to have taken precedence over all others. Most artists seem to feel a natural urge to make things, whatever their subject matter, that will last, or at any rate outlast their own lives. Franz Kafka's instruction that his work should be destroyed on his death was extremely rare (and it was not respected anyway). Much more common was the example of Marcel Proust, who had completed three unpublished volumes of his great novel at the time of his death and clearly intended them to be printed posthumously in order to complete his vast scheme.[23] Yet every work of art contains within it a conundrum; one that most leave unquestioned, but nonetheless remains implicit. The conundrum is that whereas human experience, the subject of art, is necessarily transitory, most artistic media—stone, canvas, print—are capable of great longevity, at least by human standards. And for this reason, it is works of art, whether composed yesterday or two thousand years ago, that attempt to convey the tragic brevity of life, the frailty of human endeavor, which move us most deeply. Borglum's craving for permanence has infected his presidents, whose durability, so vividly expressed through their adamantine, dazzling whiteness, seems to be at the expense of their humanity.

According to author Jesse Larner, Borglum extended Washington's

21. Quoted ibid., p. 1.

22. Quoted ibid., p. 124.

23. These three volumes form part of Proust's novel *A la recherche du temps perdu*, which is known in English as, *In Search of Lost Time*.

nose by a foot more than scale required as a way of extending its life prospects for an extra hundred thousand years. More modest in its ambitions for the monument, the National Park Services has recently completely renovations designed to preserve the work for a trifling twenty thousand years. But size comes at a price, for the larger a piece of sculpture, the further away the spectator must stand in order to get the full impact of the work. At a certain distance, the law of diminishing returns kicks in, and the loss of detail can only be repaired with the use of binoculars. This effect can be seen by comparing the nearby Crazy Horse Memorial with Mount Rushmore. The former is far larger—its owners claim that all four presidential heads could fit into the head of Crazy Horse—but the work's gigantic proportions have placed the spectator at such a distance from the work that only its basic outline is visible with the naked eye. (The humble post card is indispensable.) Borglum set the precedent in the Black Hills, and though he correctly assessed the proportions so that the spectator can see plenty of detail from the Rushmore viewing terrace, there can be no question that for him the attraction of size was less aesthetic than temporal: big things stood a better chance of surviving.

There is a celebrated riposte to this kind of thinking: Shelley's poem, "Ozymandias."[24] Published in 1818, it is said to have been inspired by the arrival in the British Museum of a massive figure of Ramases II carved in blue and white granite and dating from about 2000 BC. The poem is worth quoting in full.

I met a traveler from an antique land
Who said: "Two vast and trunkless legs of stone
Stand in the desert. Near them on the sand,
Half sunk, a shattered visage lies, whose frown
And wrinkled lip and sneer of cold command
Tell that its sculptor well those passions read
Which yet survive, stamped on these lifeless things,
The hand that mocked them and the heart that fed.

24. Percy Bysshe Shelley (1792–1822) was an English Romantic poet. His second wife was the novelist Mary Shelley.

And on the pedestal these words appear:
"My name is Ozymandias, King of Kings:
Look on my works, ye mighty, and despair!"
Nothing beside remains. Round the decay
Of that colossal wreck, boundless and bare,
The lone and level sands stretch far away."

It is true that Borglum's bid for perpetuity looks good at the moment, geology permitting, and it seems unlikely that a future traveler from the antique land of South Dakota will come across the half-sunk, shattered visages of the presidents. But then, as Shelley's poem tells us, history has no sympathy with hubris. Those who raised the statues of the Buddha in Bamiyam Valley, Afghanistan, in the sixth century probably imagined they had established something eternal and indestructible, but they did not anticipate the Taliban. Having no experience of the necessary kind of demolition, the Taliban first attacked the statues with rockets and tank shells, a method more symbolic than practical. When this failed, they resorted to dynamite, as Borglum might well have recommended to them. The statues were immediately reduced to rubble. (There is talk of attempting to reconstruct them from the debris, but there is probably talk among the Taliban of bringing them down again. The future holds its tongue.)

The old Soviet Union is littered with scrap metal deriving from titanic statues of Lenin and Stalin that were jubilantly toppled and dismantled when the Communist rule came to end. The Iraqis wasted no time in toppling Saddam Hussein's statue when their country was invaded in 2003, and as I write this, the Libyans are busy destroying statues of Muammar Gaddafi, who only a few months ago informed the world that his people loved him.

Is there a parallel between these statues of tyrants and Borglum's fathers of democracy? Only that they were all erected in a spirit of absolute certitude. When President Franklin Roosevelt dedicated the head of Jefferson in 1936, he celebrated the Shrine of Democracy as a great work of "permanent beauty and importance," and in doing so showed his allegiance to Borglum's fantasy of sculpting for eternity. Rushmore was accepted as a symbol of a nation and its institutions that had apparently reached such a state of perfection that they deserved to be commemorated for as long as there was human history.[25]

But no idea will stand being fixed forever; if it has any worth, it will be capable of adaptation and evolution. After all, what is the process of amending the Constitution if not an admission that democracy and its instruments are living things, capable of improvement or alteration as the needs of the people dictate? And who knows what sort of constitution will seem ideal to the country's descendants in a thousand years, never mind a million? Whatever it is, we can be reasonably sure that a certain mountain in the middle of the continent will still be presenting the face, or rather four faces, of an antiquated concept of perfection, which may by then be long-forgotten, discarded, or even disgraced. Consider Athenian democracy, which for all its pioneering virtues excluded women, slaves, and non-citizens from its franchise.

Part of Borglum's original conception for the monument had been an entablature, which, reminiscent of Darius the Great's two-and-a-half-thousand-year-old inscription on a mountainside near Bisotun in Iran,[26] would provide a record of American accomplishments and explain the carving to visitors in the unimaginable future when, in Borglum's words, "every other government on earth has melted into fine clay and blown away."[27] It was to be a vast panel carved into the mountain beside the four faces bearing five hundred words in letters three feet high. In 1930, the famously laconic Calvin Coolidge was invited to compose the text for the entablature, but when the presidential words were delivered, Borglum could not resist taking his editor's chisel to them and making minor revisions. Coolidge was furious and withdrew from the scheme, effectively wrecking it. The Act of Congress authorizing the entablature had specified that the text should be "indited" by

---

25. Quoted in Smith, *Carving*, p. 314.

26. Darius I (550–486 BC) was the third king of the Archaemenid Empire, which included modern-day Egypt, Kurdistan, and parts of Greece. His inscription at Besotun is a UNESCO World Heritage Site. The approximately twelve hundred lines of text form a biography of sorts, detailing the conquests and exploits of Darius I between 521 and 520 BC.

27. Quoted in Taliaferro, *Great White Fathers*, p. 241.

Coolidge. Coolidge's reaction was a catastrophe for Borglum; he feared that his work would be doomed to the same fate as Stonehenge, or the Nazca lines drawn on the Peruvian plains, or, most terrifying to him, the statues on Easter Island that stare out to sea, inscrutable and unintelligible, their meaning lost forever, leaving only the husks of a monumentalism made fatuous by time.

By 1939, Borglum had developed an even more colossal plan for ensuring that his work would be possessed with both immortality and meaning: the Hall of Records. Just behind and above the heads was a narrow canyon, which the sculptor dreamed of converting into a repository of information concerning, in his words, "the nine great steps the Anglo-Saxon has made pursuing the star of empire," from the Declaration of Independence to the Panama Canal.[28] Once hollowed out, the hall would be approached by a stairway flanking Lincoln's left side, built out of granite blocks from the site, eight hundred feet long and thirty feet wide, for which the only precedent would be the steps leading from the Acropolis to the Parthenon, or so Franklin Roosevelt was assured by the man who liked to think of himself as the modern-day Phidias.[29] According to Rex Alan Smith, "The entrance [would] be a polished stone panel forty feet high, inlaid with gold and lapis lazuli mosaics and surmounted by a bas-relief American eagle with a thirty-nine foot wingspread."[30] The hall itself would be eighty feet wide and a hundred feet long and would house bronze and glass cabinets containing the records of the "West World" typed upon aluminum sheets and rolled in tubes, which would remain sealed unless Congress decreed otherwise.

It was not to be. The authorities made it clear to Borglum that they were unwilling to fund this folly, and he was obliged to stop his men drilling into the canyon, although by then he had decided that not one chamber, but six would be required to do justice to his vision of the true

28. Quoted ibid., p. 296.

29. Phidias (480–430 BC) was a sculptor, painter, and architect. He is commonly regarded as one of the greatest of ancient sculptors, and his statue of Zeus at Olympia was one of the seven wonders of the ancient world.

30. Smith, *Carving*, p. 354.

Shrine of Democracy. His workers left behind a rectangular hole, which John Taliaferro, a little cruelly, described as "a shelter big enough for mountain goats, but hardly the Temple of Kor."[31]

So we are left with the four heads, four glittering white heads, Borglum's Siamese quadruplets, the fruit of the rock once the skin is peeled off, a nugget of white gold for the tourist industry, a cameo brooch pinned to the mountain, a sculpted wound in a sacred rock that will never heal, a license plate come to life, a great paperweight in the sky— what exactly are we looking at?

If, as Borglum intended, Rushmore is a symbol of territorial expansion, it must be said that not every American heart swells with pride at the sight of the four faces as they stare across the Black Hills. In 1970, John Lame Deer, a Sioux medicine man, joined the occupation of Mount Rushmore organized by the American Indian Movement, and from a position on top of Roosevelt's pate, he recorded his feelings about the monument. "What we object to," he said, "is the white man's arrogance and self-love, his disregard for nature which makes him desecrate one of our holy mountains with these oversized pale faces. . . . And a million or more tourists every year look up at those faces, and feel good, real good, because they make them feel big and powerful, because their own kind of people made these faces and the tourists are thinking: 'We are white, and we made this, what we want we get, and nothing can stop us.' . . . They could just as well have carved this mountain into a huge cavalry boot standing on a dead Indian."[32]

American Indians considered Borglum's defacement of Mount Rushmore an insult and, although he never hesitated to blast his faces into their sacred mountain, it is to his credit that he was sufficiently shocked by conditions on the Pine Ridge Indian Reservation during the winter of 1931 to write to President Herbert Hoover. He informed the president that the residents were not only starving but had been "corrupted, beggared, and crushed" by civilization—the very civilization to which he was busy paying homage. He publicly supported the reforms to Indian

31. Taliaferro, *Great White Fathers*, p. 297.

32. John (Fire) Lame Deer & Richard Erdoes, *Lame Deer, Seeker of Visions: The Life of a Sioux Medicine Man* (New York: Touchstone Books, 1972), p. 93.

policy proposed by the Roosevelt government in 1934, endorsing them in a radio speech in February that year, which, however, also included a very Borglumesque announcement. He believed, he said, that the Indians appreciated his sculpture because he had promised them that if they chose one of their great chiefs he would carve that person's face in the mountains as well, where it would stand "forever with the great White Chiefs." (What greater honor could he bestow on a crushed nation?) He added that they knew he had never spoken to them with "a split tongue."[33] It was the last the Lakotas heard of his promise.

Borglum hacked his heads out of the mountain side with drill and dynamite, and whatever his own ambitions for their significance, they stand as a symbol of power—power over nature. His presidents have become the icons of the nation's subjugation of its continent, and their masterful expressions browbeat the surrounding hills and, by extension, the prairies, rivers, mountains, and coastlines that lie between sea and shining sea. When people contemplate them, they are impressed first by their sheer prodigiousness and then by their evident supremacy over the rude rocks from which they emerge; the mountain has been made to look puny by man, a gesture of conquest that would never be permitted in our time. Rushmore was quintessentially a project of the West. The conquistadores of North America were farmers, miners, and railroad builders, and Borglum's fathers of democracy also symbolize their nation's industrial triumph over its natural heritage. Borglum put miner's skills to work on the mountain, and though he extracted a strange kind of precious metal, he still treated his raw materials as a miner would by dumping an avalanche of irremovable spoil below his sculpture—a kind of communal beard shared by the four granite chins.

What does Rushmore's whiteness signify? John Taliaferro wittily likened Borglum to Herman Melville's Ahab, obsessively pursuing his own white leviathan. Ishmael, the narrator of *Moby Dick*, does not share his captain's obsession and has many reasons to be terrified of the whale. He confesses that "It was the whiteness of the whale that above all things appalled me," though he cannot fathom the explanation. In a chapter devoted to uncovering one, he provides a lengthy list of the many phe-

33. Quoted in Taliaferro, *Great White Fathers*, p. 322–23.

nomena to be found in nature, mythology, and history whose whiteness has been "the intensifying agent" to their horrifying quality (polar bears, dungeons of the White Tower of London, etc.). However, he finds that the power of whiteness to appall is still a mystery, and he concludes with a brief meditation on light, "the mystical cosmetic" that produces every one of nature's colors (sunsets, butterflies, cheeks of young girls) but is forever white or colorless in itself. "Pondering all this," he writes with a final spasm of horror, "the palsied universe lies before us like a leper."[34]

Rushmore's whiteness probably does not rouse in our bosom the same vague and nameless horror that overwhelmed Ishmael, but we may be disturbed that it provides a symbol of what Melville ironically calls the white man's "ideal mastership over every dusky tribe," a symbol that John Lame Deer and many other American Indians before and after him, contemplated with no sense of irony. Of course, Borglum had no choice, for it was simply an unavoidable fact of nature that when he scrubbed the face of the mountain he exposed a white skin; the innocent and natural property of granite. But while granite may lose only a tenth of an inch every thousand years, history moves much faster, and the uncompromising whiteness of the presidents Borglum chose to depict may no longer furnish a welcome symbol of democracy for a nation whose people are by no means uniformly white. The rocks will remain, but as the white share of the population drops, an interesting question for the National Park Service to contemplate is whether Rushmore will continue to be regarded as their shrine of democracy by non-white Americans. Imagine a United States in which Mount Rushmore was just a quaint, slightly embarrassing curio, forgotten by tourists: "Two vast and trunkless legs of stone."

Take heart! For the time being, Mount Rushmore shows no sign of losing its popularity. Whatever conclusions you reach concerning Borglum's character or the quality of his work, the fact remains that Mount Rushmore's faces have become the face of South Dakota. They are, in that overworked and usually misused word, iconic, a status confirmed by Hitchcock's use of them for the final chase in his film *North by Northwest*. Mount Rushmore is probably the one thing belonging to the state

34. Several lepers in the Old Testament are described as being "white as snow."

that people who cannot place South Dakota on the map (including Americans) would instantly recognize. The monument has served South Dakota well, drawing many millions of tourists into the state, just as Doane Robinson intended all those years ago when he envisaged Buffalo Bill and Red Cloud among the Needles. It is the Black Hills gold mine that so far has not failed. Great Faces indeed![35]

On the day of my most recent visit, I walked the Presidential Trail, which is part of the new visitors' construction dating from 1998 and allows you to visit Borglum's studio and several well-placed observation points. It is a walk well worth taking because it has been beautifully designed and is quite free of the bombast that mars the Grand View Terrace. A series of boardwalks and wooden staircases takes you on a twisting route up and down paths leading through the pine trees and rocks that lie immediately beneath the monument. From here you get a less dignified view of the presidents because you tend to look up their noses, but there is something agreeable about meeting them on these homelier, more pastoral terms. For a moment, Borglum's giants seem humanized.

As I turned a corner, I suddenly came upon a shaggy snow-white creature that was blocking the path. Was it yet another incarnation of that horrific whiteness which had so appalled Herman Melville? No, it was a mountain goat, tame as a dog, contentedly cropping the grass, and quite indifferent to both the public and its exalted location.

35. "Great Faces, Great Places" is the slogan adopted by the South Dakota Department of Tourism to help boost that industry in the state.

Deadwood

As I said in my introduction, I became obsessed in 1992 with Deadwood and its history, and I encouraged my family to think that our visit to the gold-rush city would be the climax of our trip to South Dakota during that spring break. I looked forward to taking up a pedagogic role with my new-found expertise.

The adults in our party were Sal, myself, and our friend Nigel Hamlin-Wright, who had joined us from England. For some reason Nigel had equipped himself with a waxed mackintosh cut in the style of a riding coat with long skirts and a deep split in the back, which he wore with a desperado's swagger. As far as I know, he had never been on the back of a horse, but this was the costume in which he chose to explore the frontier, and I have to say that the farther west we traveled the more authentic he appeared. I was in no position, incidentally, to mock other people's clothes, since I was to be seen in a shapeless tweed overcoat woven in shades of dung and handed down to me by my father-in-law, who in his turn had inherited it from his father.

Our children had been joined by their lifelong friend Jessica Widdows, who at thirteen years old was a year younger than Tilly and a year older than Jack. She added incident to our journey by continually losing essential bits of herself: her contact lens, her watch, a ring from her newly pierced ears, and, most sensationally, her orthodontic brace, an item that had cost her parents a fortune and which she managed to drop irretrievably down a drain in Hot Springs.

This was the gang (including what was left of Jessica) that strode down Deadwood's Main Street on a sunny March morning.

I don't know what any of us expected, but I believe we were all surprised by our first impression of Deadwood, for the place was rather charming. To our left and right, we could see the steep cliffs bearded with pine trees that formed the canyon that enclosed Deadwood's handful of streets. Main Street itself was rather grandly divided into three sections: Upper, Historic, and Lower, each comprising a couple of blocks. A series of little residential streets built in terraces panted up the hill on the west side. I knew from my reading that in 1879 a fire had destroyed most of the wooden structures that had been thrown up during the gold rush. I also knew that a great program of construction had taken place in the following years, but I had not appreciated that so many buildings from that period had survived. What we confronted, as we stood outside the Franklin Hotel at the southern end of Main Street, was a more or less Victorian town of two- and three-story buildings designed in an exuberant mixture of styles. The charm of these old buildings was augmented by their colors: some had painted fronts and woodwork in shades of turquoise, maroon, green, and blue, and they were intermixed with buildings made of rusticated stones of rose and cream, while others made of brick had a mellow pink tone. It was a face of the West we had not anticipated, and we were beguiled.[1]

We strolled the length of Main Street, and though our pleasure in the architecture was undiminished, we became increasingly puzzled. We seemed to have strayed into a bizarre and unnatural place, a kind of madhouse; there were plenty of people going in and out of the build-

1. There is an excellent website devoted to the buildings on Main Street, each one illustrated with a contemporary photograph: http://archive.cyark.org/deadwood-intro. From the list compiled on the site, I counted no less than thirty-six buildings that had been erected between 1879 and 1899, and twelve more dated from between 1900 and 1915. Among the architectural styles adopted by the builders of these banks, stores, saloons, hotels, and so on were Richardsonian Romanesque, Second Empire, and Queen Anne, but it would take a more knowledgeable eye than mine to point them out. One of the few later additions, at 630 Main Street, is the splendidly curved, smooth white edifice of the Black Hills Motors building, which used to be a Dodge and Plymouth showroom and Texaco Station; it dates from 1939 and is a rare example of streamlined art deco in Deadwood.

ings, the windows were lit, music was playing, but we could not find a single shop, to use our English word. It slowly dawned on us that every business on the street was a gambling hall. We could not believe it. They had all been redesigned to look like gold-rush saloons and had been given names to evoke those rambunctious days: Gold Dust, Midnight Star, Calamity Jane's, Mother Lode Lounge, Silverado, Miss Kitty's, and so on. There did not appear to be a single place where you could buy a carton of milk. Even the drug store, the souvenir shops, and cafés, places that appeared conventional enough, turned out to have their own slot machines.

Deadwood's true identity came as a humiliating shock to me. I was exposed as an ignoramus, unaware of the city's most salient characteristic. Despite my extensive reading, I had not understood that Deadwood had turned itself into a town-sized casino, a cowboy Vegas. The explanation was all too simple: the books I had been reading were all published before 1989, the year Deadwood acquired a license to run legalized gambling and struck gold for the second time. So much for pedagogy.

From the moment the first bet had been placed in November 1989, the city had enjoyed a new gold rush, which two and a half years later was showing no signs of petering out; on the contrary, Deadwood's new gold was being dug up in prodigious quantities. Once we understood what we were looking at, we could see the benefits of this strike all round us. Most conspicuous was Main Street itself, which was being repaved from end to end and had been furnished with new lighting: beautiful clusters of white globes suspended from green, cast-iron lamp posts.

Having grasped the nature of Deadwood's single industry, we were disappointed to see that its gambling halls were not peopled with cardsharps in fancy waistcoats and bootlace ties. True, it was ten in the morning, an hour when any self-respecting poker player would have been in bed, sleeping off the previous night's exertions, but instead of card tables with glamorous croupiers, most of the gambling halls were filled with slot machines—or fruit machines, as we British quaintly call them. Music blasted from every doorway, but we found that even on the street we were never out of earshot of the "hot slots"; we could hear their electronic whining as they begged insatiably for coins, a noise occasionally broken by a shuddering spasm as they threw up some lucky gambler's winnings. The Hills were alive with the sound of money.

The kids were tremendously excited, suddenly willing to blow their entire vacation budgets on the turn of a tumbler. Their annoyance was therefore keen and vocal when they discovered their age forbade them to play. A reprieve seemed to be promised by a sign in a gambling hall saying "Kids' Corner," but it only took them to a small amusement arcade fitted with a few games to keep kids quiet while the adults hit the slots. "Deadwood," snorted Tilly in her journal, "the highlight of Dad's trip. A complete gamboling [*sic*] city. You're not even allowed to touch the machines until you're 21."

We walked back to the Franklin Hotel, a grandiose building with a handsome portico supported by eight white pillars and a veranda offering a pair of rocking chairs. Opened in 1903, its rooms were lit with electric light and half of its eighty bedrooms equipped with baths, a remarkable luxury for its day. Even in 1992, the lobby made an impressive spectacle, for it was furnished with an elaborate mosaic floor, an antique desk, a massive fireplace, and a positively regal staircase rising above a gigantic wooden lintel designed in neo-classical style; above them all hung an ornate tin ceiling. Filling the length of one wall was a mahogany glass cabinet in which photographs of eminent guests were displayed. They included Theodore Roosevelt, William Taft, Babe Ruth, Buffalo Bill, John Wayne, and Kevin Costner. However, the dignity of this handsome space was quite destroyed by slot machines. No attempt had been made to position them discreetly, allowing them to blend with the "historic" atmosphere; discretion was not Deadwood's way. To reach the desk, you had to pick your way round half a dozen flashing slots, the hope being, I suppose, that even before you checked in you would chance a couple of quarters, just to limber up your betting muscles.

We were not yet too jaundiced to try our own luck, and so we went downstairs to Durty (*sic*) Nelly's, the hotel's casino where a traditional vingt-et-un (blackjack) table was available. We proved to be the only gamblers, though the slots upstairs were well attended. Approaching the green baize, I felt nervous, despite the hospitable welcome from our dealer, Thomasina, known to all as Tommy, who was probably glad of some company. My anxiety derived not from the prospect of losing my money, an inevitable outcome I assumed, but from not knowing the protocol, from not knowing *how* to lose my money. The shaming truth was that I had never played before, and nor had either of my companions.

I needn't have worried. Sal suffered from none of these inhibitions, and in any case our charming croupier, who had identified us as beginners the moment we walked in, explained the rules and coached our play. Nigel proceeded to win $10 with the cool aplomb of one who shared his nationality with James Bond. Sal also won $10, though she shrieked with joy as if she were a millionaire, and the kids danced in triumph behind her. She gave me her winnings, and I took my place at the baize table. Tommy dealt me a hand and told me, "If you want another card, you gotta say 'Hit me.'" She only had to hit me twice before I was busted. The kids drifted away, not wanting to be associated with a loser. Holding my nerve, I staked another $10 and won $7. I went upstairs to the cage to cash in my winnings, but the teller easily persuaded me to buy a set of souvenir chips and a pack of used cards bearing the hotel's logo—total with tax: a couple of dollars more than I'd won. For no charge and, as far as I could see, with no hint of irony, she threw in a sticker that said, "I won in Deadwood." One of the chips sits on my desk as I write this.

Back on the street we walked a couple of blocks to the Adams Museum, a curious building put up in 1930 that appeared to have been cast from a jelly mold. Locally known as Deadwood's attic, it was a haven of relief from the incessant begging and jingle of the slots. One of the curators, a most respectable-looking lady, told us that, speaking for herself, she was grateful to the casinos for saving the city. Before gambling had been legalized, the place had been on its knees, but now they had new sewers and sidewalks and the potholes had all been mended. The gambling syndicates had renovated all the buildings on Main, but they weren't allowed to put up anything that wasn't "historic," a restriction of which she approved. Had there been any increase in "nastiness," Sal inquired. Yes, the crime rate had gone up, but only in driving offences and that sort of thing.

"This is a family town," the curator insisted with pride, "and we're going to keep it that way."

With these wholesome sentiments ringing in our ears, we turned to look at the exhibits. In pride of place at the front of the hall was a large, old-fashioned glass cabinet display case, and on its top shelf we were able to study the very noose used to hang a certain Charles Brown, "the negro," a label informed us, "who killed Mrs. E. F. Stone." Brown was executed on Wednesday, 17 July 1897, and a photograph showed him holding a cross and a bible and wearing a second cross round his neck. His victim had run a boarding house and was rumored to keep her cash under her pillow. Brown, intent on stealing her money, woke her dog, panicked, and hit her over the head with his cleaver. He then killed the dog the same way. The cleaver was also on display.

Next to these items, a second group was devoted to another victim of hanging, a Lakota called Two Sticks. A card read as follows, "You are invited to the legal execution of Cha Nopa Uhah, alias Two Sticks, at Laurence County Jail, in Deadwood SD, December 28, 1894 at 10 o'clock am. US Marshal. Admit One. Not transferable." Beside it lay a red pipe-stone pipe that had belonged to Two Sticks but had been given, according to the label, to William A. Remer, sheriff, on the morning he had been hanged. Beside these exhibits were various padlocks, handcuffs, and so forth, tools of the sheriff's trade. They included a strap used by Remer at these hangings. A photograph of Two Sticks was on display: he was holding his pipe and standing in what appeared to be a cart. There was far more to the Adams Museum, but this cabinet, which greeted the visitor at the door, left a taste that took a while to be washed away by other, less unsavory exhibits.

The museum possessed a fine collection of historic mining equipment, and many other items relating to the earliest days of the city. However, we were drawn to the more bizarre exhibits, among them a stuffed and mounted two-headed calf (a great favorite with children, according to our curator) and a set of 107 carved wooden figures, all about six inches high and all in the shape—the chaste and neutered shape—of naked women in various gymnastic poses. The only exception to this array of nudity was a male figure on a podium, his gender discreetly masked by a pair of jockey briefs, also carved. The creator of this extraordinary work was R. J. Poe, a resident of Lead, who had whittled every single figure with a jackknife. Striking a note of pride, the label added that Poe had never received any instruction in carving, the inference being, I suppose, that lessons would have corrupted the frontier purity of his vision with academic decadence.

We returned once more to Main Street, where we passed a gaming saloon under construction. Surrounded by dust and undisturbed by the men in their hard hats was a pair of gamblers pushing quarters into a slot machine still in its packing material. One of the axioms of gambling is that your luck will improve if the machine is "fresh" in some way. A brand new machine therefore offered an irresistible virginal promise. One of the staff at the Bullock Hotel, the Franklin's chief rival, later told me that guests liked to come down early in the morning in order to be the first to use the machines that day, as if the slots had been purified overnight. The myth of perpetual renewal is at the heart of gambling.

For the most part, the gamblers we encountered were retired couples who wandered like zombies from casino to casino bearing their shiny quarters in little plastic buckets. As Tommy put it, "the people who come here are either newlyweds or nearly deads." Gone were the grizzled prospectors of '76, the prostitutes, and gun-slinging cardsharps—the cast of HBO's *Deadwood*—and in their place were these innocuous old-sters, some of whom wore gloves to protect their slot-feeding hands. There was a laughable and touching discrepancy between Deadwood's actual customers and the blood-curdling atmosphere conjured up by the gambling halls, which flaunted the six-gun, the gold nugget, the whore's garter, and the hangman's noose at every turn. "Relive those lawless days," urged a brochure we picked up, adding with superb dis-ingenuousness, "Deadwood is the perfect place for all the family."

I took my family to the Dakota Territory Saloon, where we found our-selves sitting in a booth beneath the boots of an effigy hanging from a gallows. Behind us a tableau depicted a "hurdy-gurdy girl" romping on a brass bed with a bewhiskered client, she in a negligee, he wearing his cowboy hat. During our stroll up and down Main Street, we had been constantly reminded that the city had been as famous for its brothels as its gold mines. For example, we had been momentarily fooled by the sight of four young women in their underwear, who were apparently beckoning to us from an upper floor. Above them a neon sign identified the place as "Miss P. J.'s Parlour," and it took us a moment to recognize that they were plastic mannequins, a memento of Deadwood's other historic industry that used to thrive in Upper Main Street, a couple of blocks that formed the town's "badlands." This mock brothel was housed in one of the prettiest buildings in Deadwood with four oriel windows and green paintwork: the Bullock-Clark Building, 616–618 Main Street, built in 1894 on the site of what had been the Bella Union Theatre and the IXL Hotel.

Yet, for all its efforts to re-create the wickedness of 1876, the Deadwood of 1992 seemed a strangely sexless place. The dance-hall girl with her net stockings, button boots, feathers, and cleavage was to be seen more in pictures than the flesh, for the personnel at work in the gambling halls were demurely dressed and no more provocative than bank clerks. The only women we saw dressed in period costume were in the Midnight Star, then the newest gambling saloon in town (and owned by the Costner brothers), which had been designed with an unusually heavy stress on its turn-of-the-century fittings. These women looked ill at ease in their feathers and fishnets, but then it was only 11:30 on a cold March morning.

We learned the reason for this unexpected modesty from our matronly waitress. It was simple. In order to keep their priceless gambling licenses, Deadwood's casino owners had to run legally immaculate establishments. And so, by a strange commercial irony, while these owners were busy hanging up their nooses, arranging their brothel tableau, and displaying photographs of Deadwood's treasured "characters"—prostitutes, homicides, swindlers, and sharpshooters—they were in fact straining every sinew to keep their dens of iniquity as pure as convents. Deadwood had always been a whore with a heart of real gold, and she was still turning tricks, but this version of 1876 was a refined affair, and no whiff of vice could be allowed to contaminate it: no under-age drinking or gambling, no unruly behavior, no bad language, no ogling of show girls (unless they were made of plastic). Deadwood had been cleaned up at last, and by its own hand. There were even cowboy-style saloons that didn't have a license to sell hard liquor. Imagine that: a saloon that only sold beer. There should have been a law against it!

Deadwood gulch was largely unexplored by white people until the autumn of 1875, when a handful of illegal miners started panning for gold. By January 1876, the whole gulch had been divided into claims, and a city of tents had sprung up, every other one a bar or a brothel if legend is to be believed—a moment graphically captured by HBO's *Deadwood*. On 26 April, the city of Deadwood was laid out, and the tents began to give way to log cabins and frame buildings. In May, the gold rush began, and the population went from hundreds to thousands overnight. When news of the Deadwood gold strikes reached the nearby city of Custer, its population decamped en masse, while Hill City, fourteen miles to the north of Custer, was reduced to a single citizen and a dog. Tremendous wealth poured into Deadwood, and a building boom took place. By September 1876, when General George Crook brought his soldiers to town after fighting the Sioux in the aftermath of the Battle of the Little Big Horn, Deadwood was able to entertain him for a grand lunch at one of its three hotels, the Grand Central, and take him in the evening to one of its five theaters. History does not have to record how the town amused his troops. The number of people, most of them men, attracted to Deadwood and its surrounding area may have been as great as twenty thousand by the end of the year.

Of course, the boom could not last. The fire of 1879 caused many miners to leave, and by the turn of the century almost all the placer-gold hunters had disappeared, leaving only the Homestake Mine in Lead and one or two other deep mines in business. In 1880, the population was 3,777 and a year later the morale of its board of trade was still sufficiently high for it to brag that the city had "the prettiest women, the bravest men, the laziest dogs, the meekest hackmen, the homeliest newspaper reporters, and the toniest bar-tenders in the world."[2]

There was a later mining boom, in the 1930s, from which Deadwood benefited, but for most of the twentieth century, until 1989, the city experienced a slow, inexorable decline, relying on its brothels and Wild West past to bring in dwindling numbers of tourists. Its gambling tradition persisted in that a few bars offered "amusement only" slot machines and covert card games, while its brothels, according to *Dead-*

2. *The Black Hills of Dakota, 1881* (Deadwood, D.T.: Deadwood Board of Trade, 1881); Watson Parker, *Gold in the Black Hills* (Pierre: South Dakota State Historical Society Press, 2003), pp. 201–2.

wood Magazine, were particularly attractive to hunters and oil men from Wyoming.[3]

In 1961, Deadwood was nominated as a National Historic Landmark on the strength of its many old buildings, but by then its commercial vigor had been undermined by Rapid City, just to the east of the hills, and many of its retail outlets had closed, leaving empty storefronts along Main Street. In 1980, the FBI shut down the city's surviving brothels, five establishments, including Pam's Purple Door and the Cozy Rooms, that used to employ about forty women during the height of the deer-hunting season. It was not a particularly popular move in Deadwood itself, where the "girls" contributed to the local economy and provided "a public service, not a public nuisance."[4] But there was to be no reprieve. Rumors of drugs, white slavery, and Mafia connections ensured that Pam's Purple Door remained closed for ever, her "girls" replaced by ageless, innocent plastic mannequins.

By 1989, Deadwood was on the endangered list of National Historic Landmarks, and its future looked grim. However, in a stroke of genius, a group of local business people had formed themselves into the Deadwood You Bet Committee with the ambition of legalizing limited-stake betting in the city. From the beginning, the committee wanted to keep the gambling on a small scale, and their idea was that every casino operator would also be required to run a non-gambling venture. These plans had acquired real urgency in December 1987 when a fire destroyed two nineteenth-century buildings, a catastrophe that might not have been as severe if the city's infrastructure, notably its water system, had been in better shape.

For gambling to be legalized in Deadwood, several obstacles had to be overcome. The constitution of South Dakota had to be amended to permit gambling, and Deadwood's citizens had to approve of legalized gambling in their city by a majority of at least 60 percent. As it turned out, both measures passed with healthy majorities, though the local-

3. Shawn Werner, "A Fight for Gaming," *Deadwood Magazine* (Dec. 2007), http://www.deadwoodmagazine.com/back_issues/article.php?read_id=181.

4. Dustin D. Floyd, "Girls of the Gulch," ibid. (Aug. 2009), http://www.deadwoodmagazine.com/back_issues/article.php?read_id=242.

option vote carried a stipulation that a proportion of the city's revenues must be used for historic preservation.

It was a unique experiment, for no other small community in the United States had tried such a solution to the problem of regenerating its fortunes. The first bet in the new era of legalized gambling was placed— or probably the first coin was pushed into a slot machine—at "high" noon on 1 November 1989 in one of Deadwood's fourteen so-called gambling halls. (The word "casino" was discouraged, for fear it would detract from the city's "historic" legacy.) Projections for the enterprise had been modest; consultants had forecast that gamblers would wager $2 million in the first year of gambling, but in reality, they bet $13.8 million in the first month alone, and after eight months, the figure was $145.4 million. Deadwood's second gold rush had begun. During that first year, more than eighty new gambling halls opened their doors for business, and in June of the following year, gamblers bet $1.2 million in a single day. By April 1991, the city boasted 1,909 slot machines, 27 poker tables, and 83 blackjack tables, more than one for every man, woman, and child in town. There were eighty-four gaming halls, including the town's only Laundromat (two slot machines) and gas station (also two slots).[5]

In time the boom slackened, and in 1990 a strong-minded candidate was appointed to be Deadwood's first historic preservation officer. The original downtown business owners had made a gentleman's agreement that the exteriors of the gambling halls should reflect the city's western character.[6] The owners had a significant say in requests for building proposals and those that did not respect the collective image were turned down. You might argue that this policy has induced a certain monotony, since there is a limit to how many changes you can ring on the theme of frontier gambling dens, but in its favor, the restriction has saved the city from becoming a kind of mini-Vegas.

The success of Deadwood's gambling experiment was sensational, and the city's fortunes were quickly reversed. Millions of dollars became

5. Ibid.
6. Heidi Bell Gease, "Deadwood gambling spurred change," *Rapid City Journal*, 1 Nov. 2009.

available for improving the appearance and infrastructure of the city. Main Street was lit with street lamps and paved from end to end, and a trolley service was installed to carry tourists. The water and sewage systems were replaced; the steep hillsides surrounding the city were shored up. City hall, the old railroad depot, the Adams House, and Mount Moriah Cemetery all had restoration money spent on them. The local police and fire departments benefited, as did various state institutions, including the South Dakota State Historical Society (money very well spent). In short, Deadwood's gamble hit the jackpot. "What other town of 1,300 people has an income of nearly $7 million per year for historic preservation?" asked one of the original members of the You Bet Committee with understandable satisfaction.[7] By 1992, the National Trust for Historic Preservation had upgraded the city's status, and since 2009, the trust has rated Deadwood's prospects as "favorable" on its watch list.[8]

However, not everyone was pleased. In the rush to stake their claims in the new gold field, local people turned their premises into gambling halls or sold them to outsiders, and soon enough the city had lost more than forty retail businesses. Residents suffered. Agnes Ayres, redoubtable owner of a plumbing and hardware store on Main Street that had been in her family since the earliest days of 1876, summed up the feelings of many residents. "I think most of us thought it [gambling] would be like it was in the 1960s, in the back of four or five saloons. Before you knew it, all the car dealerships [three] in town were gone, the department store was gone, everything was casinos. Now you can't even buy a pair of socks in downtown Deadwood. We didn't think it would take over the whole town."[9] Despite many lucrative offers, she refused to sell her building during the gold rush of 1990. It is an indication of the destructive effect that gambling has had on Deadwood's residential community, as opposed to its business sector, that the city's population has

7. Werner, "A Fight for Gaming."

8. National Trust for Historic Preservation, "11 Most Endangered Historic Places," http://www.preservationnation.org/travel-and-sites/sites/mountains-plains-region/deadwood-historic-district.html.

9. Quoted in Evan Moore, "Deadwood Comes Alive: Gambling Boom Replaces Gloom in Historic S.D. Town," *Houston Chronicle*, 9 Sept. 1990.

steadily dropped since the introduction of gambling: from 1,830 in 1990, to 1,380 in 2000 and 1,272 in 2010.

The Deadwood Chamber of Commerce distributes a glossy brochure for the benefit of tourists. It bears the title "The West Doesn't Get Any Wilder Than Deadwood," and it shows a picture of four men in western clothes, one of them dressed to impersonate Wild Bill Hickok, as they stand beneath a sign saying, "Saloon No. 10, the site of Hickok's murder." Below them is a hand of cards and pictures of smiling young women, who appear to be having a good time at the slots and tables. In case the point about wildness is lost on the reader, a couple of bullets are incorporated into the design.

Inside there are several spreads devoted to Deadwood's early history, including one that shows pictures of Wild Bill Hickok, his so-called death chair, and a miner's pan containing a couple of handfuls of gold nuggets. Printed in an old-style font, the strap line invites you to "Sit Where Wild Bill Sat and Live To Tell About It." Below is a short text that opens with the words, "The Dakota Territory was a *fairly uninhabited* [emphasis added] place until gold was discovered in 1874 by Colonel George Armstrong Custer's expedition." This statement was so astonishing I had to read it to my wife before I could be certain that I had not mistaken its meaning.

To say that Dakota Territory (i.e., today's South *and* North Dakota) was "fairly uninhabited" in 1874 understates the number of American Indians then legitimately occupying what was the Great Sioux Reservation. It also has the effect of making the Custer Expedition of 1874 appear to be an innocuous venture of exploration. What is really meant, I suppose, is that the territory was largely uninhabited by white folks.

It is not easy to know precisely how many American Indians lived in the territory in 1874, but accepted estimates indicate that approximately 16,000 Sioux lived on the Great Sioux Reservation, a huge area lying west of the Missouri River that had been guaranteed to them by the Fort Laramie Treaty of 1868.[10] One of the treaty's provisions stipulated that

10. Robert M. Utley, *The Last Days of the Sioux Nation* (New Haven, Conn.: Yale University Press, 1963), p. 20.

white men without authority were forbidden from entering the reservation, an exclusion that the army was ordered to maintain.

The treaty was probably unworkable from the start, not least because there was continual pressure on the government to allow gold hunting in the Black Hills, where it was rumored to lie in fabulous quantities. Under the "peace policy" launched by President Ulysses S. Grant, American Indians were being confined wherever possible on reservations, and those who resisted were to be treated severely. In order to contain the southern part of Dakota Territory and protect the planned route of the Northern Pacific Railroad, the Unites States government decided that it needed a military post in the Black Hills. Lieutenant Colonel George Armstrong Custer was given orders to reconnoiter a suitable location.

Custer's expedition set out from Fort Lincoln (near present-day Bismarck, North Dakota) on 2 July 1874 to the tune of a sixteen-piece brass band. The exploration force comprised ten companies of the Seventh Cavalry, two infantry companies, three Gatling guns, an artillery piece, one hundred Indian scouts, together with a train of one hundred and ten wagons and the usual civilian auxiliaries; it also included an osteologist (bone expert), a stereoscope photographer, Custer's personal cook, and four newspaper reporters in case this little jaunt should be overlooked by the public. The whole force amounted to more than a thousand men. Colonel Fred Grant, the president's son, accompanied the expedition and is said to have been drunk much of the time.[11] Custer amused himself en route with his hunting dogs. Any doubts that Custer's expedition had a secondary purpose of gold prospecting were settled by the presence of two miners and a geologist.

If, as the Deadwood brochure asserts, Dakota Territory was "fairly uninhabited," why did a simple reconnaissance expedition require the protection of a thousand soldiers, three Gatling guns, and a cannon? From whom were Custer and his men protecting themselves in this empty wilderness?

I know that I'm applying a sledgehammer to a nut, but while I'm happy to scoff at this silly line in the brochure, my real point lies elsewhere. Deadwood has staked its prestige, to say nothing of its commer-

11. Parker, *Gold in the Black Hills*, p. 24.

cial life, on its history. Its Main Street has been dubbed "Historic" Main Street, and that sobriquet appears in all its literature. The brochure itself invites you take a vacation "back in time" and "see how the West was really won." The reader is assured that the city's ongoing restoration is transforming Deadwood "back into the frontier town that once drew legends and legions in search of their fortune." It refers to itself as "Historic Deadwood" and to its "historic attractions." In other words, tourists are encouraged to believe that they are doing something far more adventurous than simply gambling in a kind of Vegas in a cowboy costume; they are visiting history.

However, it is Deadwood's conception of its history that is problematic. The city's idea of its own past is neatly encapsulated by a monument that greets visitors as they approach on U.S. Highway 385 from the south. Standing by the road at the entrance to the city is a large construction made of pink and cream sandstone blocks, an elaborate affair with recessed pillars and decorative brickwork, enclosing an area resembling the side of a small truck. This serves as the frame for a bas-relief bust, cleverly sculpted in pink brick, of a man with flowing locks, droopy moustache, bow tie, and ten gallon hat. "Welcome to Deadwood," the sign reads, and below, as if anybody could doubt the identity of its subject, are the words, "Resting Place of Wild Bill Hickok." To one side is a hand of cards, the famous "dead-man's hand," which Hickok was allegedly holding when he died—aces, eights, and another card whose value is obliterated by a couple of bullet holes.[12]

If Deadwood has a patron saint, it is surely James Butler Hickok, who came to town in July 1876 and did the place the inestimable kindness of getting himself shot in the back of the head while playing poker. Facts concerning Hickok are hard to grasp with certainty, but it seems that by the time he rode into Deadwood his life was at a low ebb. In the previ-

12. The information included here about Wild Bill, Calamity Jane, and early Deadwood is taken from three excellent sources: Parker, *Gold in the Black Hills*; James D. McLaird, *Wild Bill Hickok & Calamity Jane: Deadwood Legends*, South Dakota Biography Series, no. 2 (Pierre: South Dakota State Historical Society Press, 2008); and Joseph G. Rosa, *They Called Him Wild Bill: The Life and Adventures of James Butler Hickok*, 2d ed. (Norman: University of Oklahoma Press, 1974).

ous March, Hickok had married Agnes Thatcher Lake, one-time high wire artiste, equestrienne, and lion-tamer, whom he had first met when she brought her "Hippo-Olympiad and Mammoth Circus" to Abilene, Texas, where he was briefly and bloodily employed as the city marshal. However, he chose not to bring his bride to Deadwood, traveling instead in the dubious company of "Colorado Charlie" Utter and his brother. At Fort Laramie, the twenty-year old "dance-hall girl" Martha Canary, by then known as Calamity Jane, joined the party. It seems that the "big-hearted" woman did not endear herself to Wild Bill, perhaps, because she made extravagant demands on his keg of whiskey, calling out to him "Mr. Hickok, I'm dry again."[13]

Once in Deadwood, Hickok hoped to strike it rich like everyone else, but he mostly confined his gold-hunting to the poker table. Although only thirty-nine, the "prince of the pistoleers" must have cut a less-striking figure than he did in his Abilene days when he favored boiled white shirts, scarlet jackets, black-velvet trousers, calf-skin boots, sombreros, and perfume for his long, wavy hair, which he parted down the middle of his head. Alcohol (he liked a drink before breakfast), failing eyesight, and plain poverty had since taken their toll, and, like all true heroes, he seems to have been haunted by a sense of his imminent doom. The day before he died, he wrote to his wife, telling her, "If such should be we never meet again, while firing my last shot, I will gently breathe the name of my wife—Agnes."[14]

One historian insists that whenever Hickok took his gun out of its holster, the fight could be attributed to one of the same trio of causes: poker, politics, and prostitutes. Another describes him as "a gambler, part-time gunman, and full-time liar."[15] But whether these judgements are fair or not, it is certain that by the fateful year of 1876, Hickok, the man, had long since become detached from "Wild Bill," the legend, and the two of them led almost separate existences. Henry M. Stanley, destined to be a legend himself as the explorer who found David Livingstone, was one of the journalists responsible for manufacturing the fantasy Hickok. In

13. McLaird, *Wild Bill Hickok*, p. 49.
14. Rosa, *They Called Him Wild Bill*, p. 213.
15. Parker, *Gold in the Black Hills*, p. 164.

1867, he asked Hickok how many white men he had killed to his certain knowledge and got the reply, "considerably over a hundred," but none without "good cause."[16] Greatly impressed, Stanley asserted that Hickok was "one of the finest examples of that peculiar class known as frontiersman, ranger, hunter, and Indian scout."[17]

In fact, Hickok was a classic example, along with "Buffalo Bill" Cody, of a western hero confected by journalists and writers of dime novels. Both Bills were made famous for deeds they had never accomplished, and could not possibly have done, by appearances in dozens of dime novels, which were published in huge quantities. We have many modern ways of turning people into "celebs," famous for being famous, but there is no contemporary equivalent of the dime novel, in which the hero carries the name of a "real" person but performs dauntless adventures that are entirely imaginary. Despite leading a life signally lacking in glamour or achievement, Calamity Jane received the same treatment in her lifetime, though in a convoluted form, because she was represented in innumerable dime novels as a real person paired with the fictional Deadwood Dick. I suppose it could be said that the dime tradition is being perpetuated in Deadwood, which is a kind of novel translated into a tourist destination, with the legendary Hickok as its immortal hero, ceaselessly undergoing death and resurrection (with Calamity Jane as his Mary Magdalene?).

There is nothing so potent in myth-making as sudden, violent death at a relatively young age. Take, for instance, Custer, who at thirty-eight was a year younger than Hickok when he made his last stand on 25 June 1876. The scene of Hickok's murder was Nuttall & Mann's No. 10 Saloon on Main Street, where, on 2 August 1876, he had come to play poker. His murderer was a certain Jack McCall, for whom history does not seem to have a kind word. Hickok presented him with a defenseless target that day; in a fatal gesture of weakness, such as all tragic heroes must succumb to, he broke with his usual custom and sat with his back to the door, allowing McCall to shoot him through the back of the head. As he slumped over the table, he held the "dead man's hand," a motif

16. Quoted in McLaird, *Wild Bill Hickok*, p. 26.
17. Quoted ibid., p. 25.

now seen everywhere in Deadwood, together with the crossed six guns, which have virtually become Hickok's coat of arms.

McCall was immediately captured and tried the next day by a miner's court convened in the Gem Theatre (since burnt down). He argued in his defense that Hickok had killed his brother in Abilene, but the presiding judge noted later in his memoirs that McCall had been prompted by nothing more than a desire for celebrity inflamed by whiskey.[18] Perhaps he can be credited as the perpetrator of the first modern homicide, committed on what you might call the Andy Warhol principle: McCall, an unknown murderer, murdered a famous murderer because he wanted to be famous himself, as a murderer. (He was given the same motive in Cecil DeMille's 1937 film *The Plainsman*, starring Gary Cooper as Hickok.) In true Deadwood style, the jury found him not guilty—guilty verdicts for murders alleged to be justified were rare. McCall then went to Fort Laramie, Wyoming Territory, where he could not resist boasting about his coup. He was arrested again and tried in Yankton, Dakota Territory, in front of a less indulgent jury, which found him guilty; he was hanged for murder.

Deadwood, however, cannot let McCall or his victim rest in peace. During the summer season, the whole episode is re-enacted six days a week (no shows on Mondays). McCall is captured promptly at 7:30 P.M. in front of the Saloon No. 10 and tried at 8:00 P.M. Families welcome! For those families whose taste is more bloodthirsty than legalistic, there are three shoot-outs every afternoon on Main Street when gunslingers "play out key moments in Deadwood's past," to quote the brochure. Wild Bill himself is shot inside the Saloon No. 10 no less than four times a day.[19]

On the face of it, Hickok is a curious figure for the town to have adopted as its hero, since he did little more than get himself shot here. But then, it is his death that is the key to his significance: whatever his record elsewhere, he died an innocent in Deadwood. A newly married

18. Parker, *Gold in the Black Hills*, p. 166.

19. The spot where the original saloon stood is marked by a sign on Main Street, but the establishment has since been moved to its current location. The original business was called Nuttall & Mann's No. 10 Saloon, but the modern version is known as Saloon No. 10.

man, he had come to town with the honorable ambition of getting rich quick but fell foul of Jack McCall. It is not Hickok the gunslinger that Deadwood celebrates, but Hickok the blameless victim; not his life, but the moment of his death that is re-enacted and fetishized. By making himself vulnerable to his fate, he elevated himself above the sordid story of his life. It is McCall, the motiveless drunk, who is the psychopath, while Hickok, "slayer of a hundred men," is canonized as the saint of Deadwood. His defenselessness at the moment of death washes clean the rest of his murderous life and, by extension, absolves the violence in which the town was steeped. Hickok's martyrdom has been exploited to lift Deadwood, whose early history was as dissolute as his, into the never-never land of "legend," where there is no right or wrong, only tall tales and colorful characters.

Deadwood was a city founded in 1876 on a particularly naked version of greed. As its publicity triumphantly proclaims, it was lawless, licentious, and alcoholic, and its first principle was the chance of making money for nothing, whether with gold or cards. Here was the American Dream at its crudest, for anyone with a dollar or a spade could get rich. (According to reports of the Custer expedition in 1874, there was gold from the grass roots down.[20]) Deadwood's second gold rush is a virtuous one, exploiting the mythology of the first while indulging in none of its depravities, except greed—the effortless shortcut to riches. After all, a gold rush without greed would be like an orgy without lust.

Deadwood has played the cards it had inherited with considerable finesse. To persist for a moment with this occupational metaphor, it held two aces in its hand: Main Street's buildings and its reputation for lawlessness. The city skillfully exploited the latter as its unique selling point, evoked in every bar, saloon, and gambling hall, and on every brochure and website. At the same time, the city marketed itself as a place of harmless fun, suitable for all the family. "Plenty of fun for the whole family," the chamber of commerce brochure says. "You can see Wild Bill's six shooter or visit his gravesite." Thus gambling was made to seem innocuous; it wasn't really gambling, it was just reliving the wild and woolly days of '76. You weren't really losing money, you were just play-

20. Quoted in Parker, *Gold in the Black Hills*, p. 65.

acting; to quote the brochure again, you were releasing "your inner out-law in a town that's still wild at heart."

Under these circumstances, it is not surprising that Deadwood's pre-sentation of history is selective and self-serving. But then why should it have any responsibility to truth? It's a gambling town and a tourist desti-nation, not a university. Nor is it the job of Deadwood's brochure writers to record the sorry story of the 1868 treaty and the illegal expropriation of the Black Hills from the Lakotas. Yes, they made a mistake in describ-ing the territory as "fairly uninhabited," but otherwise weren't they re-ferring, admittedly in their own purple language, to events that really did happen? Gold was found in the Gulch, Hickok was murdered at No. 10 Saloon, the West was indeed at its wildest in Deadwood in 1876.

Tourism does strange things with history. It eliminates the time be-tween the present and its particular moment, in Deadwood's case, 1876. The brochure says, "When you stand on Historic Main Street you're transported back to a wilder time when whiskey ruled and gamblers took a chance just walking down the street." Actually, when you stand on Historic Main Street, you're transported back to 1900 or thereabouts, when most of the buildings were constructed, and the reign of whiskey and gamblers had come to an end. But that's not the point; tourism has no time, to coin a phrase, for the truth offered by spoilsports and pedan-tic historians. Tourism projects a truth of the imagination, a truth that tells a popular story that everyone can grasp, young and old, a truth that translates history into legend and replaces shades of gray with bright colors. This imaginative world can only exist in a certain dimension of time, where a few mythic events endlessly repeat themselves without a past or a future: Wild Bill is shot every day, and every day he is resur-rected. And, of course, tourism is bound to construct time into a form that can be sold. That is its genius: it finds a way of turning an abstract—time—into a commercial commodity, and nowhere is this genius more apparent than in Deadwood.

The trick that every casino must pull is to prevent gamblers from re-minding themselves that they are bound to lose—in the long run. Who else paid for Deadwood's lovely Victorian street lamps? True, you would have to work hard to lose your shirt in Deadwood, even though the cap on stakes is now $100. The stake limit was raised from the original $5 when other states began to permit gambling and it became clear that Deadwood's modest limit was putting its casinos at a disadvantage. Nonetheless, the city must continue in its artful way to distract the gamblers from their true function, losing money. In this context Hickok is indispensable, for he is a redemptive figure. He is at once the incarnation of the Wild West and its sacrificial victim. He died to save Deadwood's sins, and his agony can be witnessed every day, except on Monday. The "dead man's hand" is both a holy relic and a talisman that serves to exculpate those who come after him. He is the town's favorite son, who had to be killed that others might gamble; he played and lost, in the largest sense, that they might win. He casts his charisma over each gambler with her dwindling pot of quarters or his dud poker hand and makes them feel they are not losing in vain. They're not losers, they're wild, like Bill.

Seventeen years were to go by before I set foot once again on Historic Main Street. On a sunny morning in May 2011, I parked my car in the lot behind the Bullock Hotel, paid my fee at the desk ($5), and walked through the hotel lobby. Three stories high, built in 1896 of pink and white sandstone with sixty steam-heated rooms, this hotel was financed by Seth Bullock, Deadwood's first sheriff, now immortalized in HBO's *Deadwood*.[21] Gambling money paid for an extensive renovation in 1992, designed to re-create the original nineteenth-century atmosphere and décor, but as with the Franklin Hotel, the intrusive presence of slot machines ruined the effect. I picked my way past these jingling sirens; nothing seemed to have changed. I relished the old vulgarity and felt a pang of nostalgia for my old infatuation, as if I had glimpsed a familiar face in an upstairs window.

But then I stepped onto the street, and my sense of familiarity evaporated. True, the season was not really under way, but that did not explain a certain eerie something that I couldn't immediately identify. The explanation was simple. I realized that the music that used to explode from every doorway had fallen silent, and the street was quiet, except

---

21. For more information on Bullock, *see* David A. Wolff, *Seth Bullock: Black Hills Lawman*, South Dakota Biography Series, no. 3 (Pierre: South Dakota State Historical Society Press, 2009).

for the soft sound of piped music. And what was playing? Nat King Cole. Yes, the velvet voice of Nat King Cole was serenading Deadwood with "Let There Be Love."

It was a sunny morning and Main Street was busy without being crowded. I visited some familiar places and some that had opened for business since my last visit. I got the impression that Deadwood had turned respectable; it had scrubbed off its make-up and exchanged its high heels for sensible shoes. For example, the Adams Museum still displayed the noose that had hanged Charles Brown, but the explanatory card had gone and so had the invitation to the execution of Two Sticks. I was glad to see that Mr. Poe's 107 carved wooden figures were still to be seen, along with the two-headed calf.

The city seemed to have toned down its old emphasis on murder, hanging, and prostitution; at any rate there were fewer nooses and brothel tableaux to be seen. Murder was still a source of entertainment, for once the season was under way Wild Bill was due to be shot four times daily as usual, but there was no question that the town's atmosphere was more in keeping with its clientele (no more oil men from Wyoming in search of upstairs girls, but families, honeymooners, and innocuous oldsters). I was sorry to see that Durty Nelly's had closed its doors, following a change of ownership for the Franklin Hotel. Saloon No. 10 still exhibited Hickok's so-called death chair, but instead of being in a position of inescapable prominence, as it had been in 1992, it was now encased more discreetly in a niche above the door. The saloon itself retained its old flavor, thanks largely to its magnificent bar, a mighty edifice of polished rosewood built in what had to be called the Richardsonian Romanesque style—a truly fitting backdrop for a hero's assassination. (Not that Hickok actually died on this spot; the site of the original Nuttall & Mann's No. 10 Saloon was across the street, but who cares?) The plastic girls were still flaunting themselves in the Bullock-Clark Building, but there was a notice on the door that the building was under new ownership, and I was willing to bet the girls would disappear when renovations got under way.

In previous years, eating in Deadwood had been an instrumental affair, a matter of necessary refueling not to be lingered over, but one undeniable boon of the new respectability was the appearance of several good restaurants. The Midnight Star, for example, owned by Kevin Costner, had dedicated its third floor to Jakes ("finest dining in South Dakota"), where you could eat lamb or duck or salmon, as well as the inevitable steaks, and pay $50 for your food and $30 for a bottle of wine. My memory of the old Deadwood was that you couldn't have found somewhere to spend $50 on a meal if you had wanted to. I chose to have a less-expensive lunch at the Deadwood Social Club, an excellent Italian restaurant, improbably located on the floor above Saloon No. 10. I lingered.

After lunch, sobered by Deadwood's unexpected probity, I drove my car through Deadwood's southern district, which took me past Harrison Street, named no doubt after President Benjamin Harrison, and up the steep hill to the Mount Moriah Cemetery. This spacious institution occupies several acres at the edge of the bluff and overlooks Deadwood Canyon, giving you a view of the city laid out like a map. From here you can study the topography of the gulch, and it is easy to see how it functioned as a perfect trap for the gold particles washed down by the various streams that flowed into its narrow, sinuous ravine.

The cemetery is well maintained, and an index of the people buried in its more than 3,400 plots is available at the entrance. I found the name Harrison registered twice: James who died in 1910 at eighty years old and John E. who died in 1879. (As it happens James is a common name in my spindly family tree, but I am sure I have no genetic connection with these two men.) The register helpfully provided their plot numbers, so I bought a "walking tour guide" and went in search of my namesakes.

The graves are laid out in concentric rings, making an ellipse reminiscent of a classical hippodrome. These rings are divided by paths that carry names such as Jabez, Hiram, Jachim, Boaz, Darius, and so forth, which apparently reflect the influence of the Masons, as does the name Moriah, and the bodies of various Masons lie in the spacious central section of the design shaded by a scattering of pines. The rest of the necropolis is divided into numerous little neighborhoods radiating from the Masonic downtown area. A large section with a spectacular outlook onto the Black Hills to the north of the town once catered to the Chinese population, but their bodies have mostly been exhumed and repatriated. The Jewish section (how often do Jewish characters feature in westerns?) is filled with tombstones inscribed in Hebrew. There are three Potter's Fields, the final resting place of prostitutes and other "early-day indigents," as the cemetery guide tactfully describes those who failed to dig their dream out of the gulch.

Wandering among these orderly dispositions made for a soothing contrast with the hurly-burly of the city. Deadwood has done its best to turn Mount Moriah into a tourist attraction by encouraging people to visit the graves of Hickok and Calamity Jane, as well as those of other "characters" from the golden era of 1876, but the place has clung to its dignity, and the atmosphere is suitably reflective. It is a tribute to the good sense of the two million tourists who visit Deadwood every year that eighty thousand to one hundred thousand of them are willing to make the journey, some on foot, to a site where nothing is sold, where no gambling takes place, where the historic hype is muted.

I took my time in the cemetery, drawing the peculiar comfort that is to be had from strolling among the graves of strangers, especially those that were dug many years ago. The style of memorial favored by the wealthy citizens of late-nineteenth-century Deadwood was severely monumental with no sign of emotional extravagance (winged skulls, weeping angels) or western kitsch; in fact, there was nothing in Mount Moriah to connect it with the lawless, debauched spirit of Deadwood conjured up by the city's publicists. It was as if, by ascending in their coffins from the Sodom below to the redemptive heights of Mount Moriah, the corpses, if not the souls, of its citizens were purified and saved for a reputable end.

In the central areas of the cemetery, where the bodies of the wealthiest citizens lay, the gravestones were mostly granite slabs with plain lettering and a tendency to the monolithic, but scattered among them were a few columns and obelisks and the occasional urn balanced on a pillar, decorated with sculpted drapery. In the outer rings these imposing tombs gave way to modest headstones made of granite and marble, and among them I searched for the Harrison graves, but despite following the map closely, I was unsuccessful. Like many graves of that era in the distant suburbs of the cemetery, theirs were no longer dignified by any kind of marker, and I couldn't even be certain that I was looking in the right place. I had to be satisfied with taking dutiful photographs of a bare patch of grass.

Finally, I took the path to the cemetery's most celebrated graves. Hickok occupies an appropriately fashionable address on a block between Darius and Boaz streets, which he has been obliged to share with Calamity Jane since her death in 1903. Hickok's grave was originally marked by a wooden headboard supplied by his friend Charlie Utter, but it was whittled to bits by souvenir hunters. It was replaced by a bust in 1891, of which a photograph exists taken by local photographer John C. H. Grabill. Its epitaph, carved in a scroll on the plinth supporting the bust, is worth reading:

J B HICKOK

DIED aug 2 1876

BY PISTOL SHOT

AGED 39 years

CUSTER

WAS LONELY

WITHOUT HIM

ERECTED BY

J H RIORDAN

OF N.Y. 1891

Despite its tear-jerking reference to the reunion of these two heroes (Hickok had briefly scouted for the army in 1867), this marker was also chipped away. And so was its replacement. Seth Bullock and other leading citizens subscribed to a new bust carved in sandstone and paid for the cost of a protective fence, but even that was defaced by determined relic collectors. For its protection, the bust was enclosed in a cage, but in the 1950s, relic hunters cut through the wire and stole it. The city was finally forced to erect a not very convincing imitation of Utter's first headboard made of indestructible material and bearing the immortal words, "Wild Bill, August 2nd, 1876. Pard, we will meet again in the happy hunting ground to part no more. Goodbye. Colorado Charlie. C. H. Utter."

If Wild Bill's *mise en scène* in Deadwood is the poker table, Calamity Jane's is her grave. Though lucky with Hickok, Deadwood has not had the same good fortune with its few historic women. For example, "Poker" Alice Tubbs, a ferocious-looking, cigar-chomping brothel keeper from Sturgis, won her place in Deadwood's tawdry hall of fame by bringing her considerable profits to town and gambling them on the poker tables. But even Deadwood's mythology does not like to play fast and loose with sacred notions of womanhood, and the likes of Tubbs are doomed to remain forever at the lower rank of "character," with no chance of promotion to heroine.

The only serious candidate is Calamity Jane, though she too is a problematic figure. Doris Day notwithstanding, the real Martha Canary is not easily reconstituted as a folk heroine suitable for family consumption. (Nor would Hickok have been, of course, had he not been exalted by his death.) The few surviving photographs of Canary reveal an unprepossessing, defiant figure. According to one acquaintance who met her in 1876, she was "built like a busted bale of hay" and "was about the roughest looking human being" the miners had ever seen, which presumably made her very rough indeed.[22] She habitually wore buckskins and men's clothing, was reputedly lousy, and was certainly foul-mouthed, in every sense. On the other hand, there are reports that suggest she was kindhearted, courageous, and something of a raconteur. The most commercial thing about her is her name, though its origins, like Hickok's, are probably irretrievable. One theory maintains that it alludes to venereal disease in that contact with her would prove calamitous. If so, it seems unlikely that she would have been able to pursue what was her lifelong source of employment, for the blunt truth is that she was a prostitute.

Deadwood has always been a little nervous of Calamity Jane, not knowing quite how to place her in the pantheon of '76, and she tends to feature mostly as the inamorata of Hickok. Though she acquired remarkable fame in her short lifetime, no particular episode lent itself to legend, and her death in 1903, unlike Hickok's, was merely sad—dead at forty-six of "inflammation of the bowels," probably brought on by her incurable alcoholism.

22. Parker, *Gold in the Black Hills*, p. 168.

The real difficulty posed by Calamity Jane is that she was likely more representative of women in Deadwood than the city fathers are now happy to acknowledge. In one respect she was not typical; the suicide rate among women gulled or driven into prostitution during the gold rush was shockingly high, and survival in a mining town with an over-whelmingly male population must have required many of the qualities that now render Calamity Jane so unglamorous, so unfitting for beatifi-cation as a folk heroine.

Just as Robin had his Marion, Clyde his Bonnie, and Johnnie his Frankie, so Wild Bill has his Jane, though he died without knowing that mythology had partnered him up with the woman he probably thought the least desirable in Deadwood. Not a scrap of evidence has been found to link him emotionally or sexually to Calamity Jane—indeed, one of his friends confirmed that "he surely did not have any use for her"—but from the moment he died, she declared they had been lovers, and she never relinquished her claim on his memory.[23] It proved to be her ticket to immortality. At his funeral, an event well attended by both miners and prostitutes, no one was as deeply affected as Calamity Jane, "whose grief for a time seemed uncontrollable."[24] When she died twenty-seven years later, she allegedly made a deathbed request to be buried next to him, a wish that local officials granted, though their motive may well have been more commercial than romantic. "Now Deadwood will have a double attraction to exhibit to visitors from the east" was the cynical comment offered by a local paper, the *Belle Fourche Bee*.[25] Its cynicism was vindicated when the date of her death was changed from 1 August to 2 August to coincide with the date of Hickok's assassination.

When I visited Deadwood in 1993, a wire fence surrounded Hickok's grave and its plastic marker, while Calamity Jane's was cordoned off by a chain. The two plots were so close they were like twin beds, a pairing that must have delighted her shade and infuriated his. Although Hickok's grave was unapproachable, the needs of his fans had been respected by the city, which had provided a set of benches where one could sit in

23. McLaird, *Wild Bill Hickok*, p. 49.
24. Ibid., p. 55.
25. Ibid., p. 108.

comfort among the pines and contemplate the downfall of great men. I was therefore shocked to discover in 2011 that the last resting place of this ill-starred couple had undergone radical rearrangements. Hickok's grave was now immured behind a forbidding cast-iron and mesh fence, which resembled a jail cell and placed an impassable division between his plot and hers. He had at last been granted his divorce from Calamity Jane. As if to keep him locked up tight, a massive bronze bust had been erected on the grave; displayed on its pillar were the crossed six-guns that Deadwood has adopted as its logo.

Calamity Jane's grave was marked with a simple plaque giving her married name (Martha Jane Burke), but was otherwise undecorated. Someone had placed a pot of plastic tulips inside Hickok's cage, but the wind—the last romantic—had blown a couple of blooms over to her side. I wiped away a tear.

6 Wounded Knee

I have visited the site of the Wounded Knee massacre several times, and it has always been a distressing experience; however, at the risk of sounding sententious, I believe it is a place that everyone should visit. I shall attempt to explain why.

If a state can be said to have had formative experiences while it was a territory, akin to those childhood experiences that shape an adult's character, South Dakota's would surely be its wars with the indigenous population, its gold rush, and its agricultural expansion. What has been the outcome of these shaping events?

By the time this book is published, 144 years will have passed since the signing of the Fort Laramie Treaty of 1868 and the creation of the Great Sioux Reservation and 136 years since the 1876 gold rush and the invasion of the Black Hills. In that relatively short period, gold mining has come and gone; indeed, the industry was virtually finished by the close of the nineteenth century, and for a long time, the Homestake Mine in Lead was the sole surviving mine capable of producing commercially significant quantities of gold. It finally closed in 2002, and nowadays most of the mining done in the Black Hills is performed for the amusement of tourists. Balanced on my desk, next to my dollar chip from Deadwood's Franklin Hotel, is a small column of gold-bearing rock from the Homestake Mine, but no day will ever be rainy enough for me to cash it in because the ratio of gold to rock contained within this slate-gray slug is one ounce to six tons of crushed ore.

The fate of agriculture since 1876 can be gauged from the

state's population statistics. The population of South Dakota has grown a little during the most recent decade, from 754,880 in 2000 to 814,180 in 2010, an improvement—if more people can be regarded as an improvement—on previous decades when the figures were either stagnant or diminishing. But these numbers do not reveal a more significant factor. In common with other Great Plains states, South Dakota has been suffering a steadily falling population in many rural areas, a phenomenon known as "rural flight." This decrease in population is partly the product of increased mechanical efficiency, but it also reflects the gradual decline of small family farming, the activity on which the state was founded. Thirty of South Dakota's counties lost population between the 1990 and the 2000 census, and the trend continued in the most recent decade. For example, Douglas County, which has the honor to have Harrison among its small towns, lost 13.2 percent of its people.

The fact is that since the Dust Bowl years (most of the 1930s), when it became clear to even the most self-deluding homesteader that farming would be a continual struggle interrupted by periods of disaster, rural populations have been shrinking irrecoverably. At the moment, agriculture is still the state's biggest business, but it cannot be long before it is overtaken by its rival, now lying in second place: tourism. In 2010, visitors to South Dakota spent an astonishing $1.059 billion, an increase of 10 percent over the previous year and a sum that represented 20 percent of all state and local tax revenue. Or, to express these figures in a formula no one can fail to grasp, the South Dakota Department of Tourism calculated that without tourism every South Dakotan household would have paid roughly $828 more in taxes.[1]

Thus, the territory over which the Indian Wars were fought in order that its indigenous people should make way for miners and farmers looks as if it will be metamorphosed into that most phantasmagoric of places, the tourist destination. The tourist industry has several resources at its disposal, such as the state's landscape and sports opportunities, including pheasant hunting on which the Department of Tourism has

1. South Dakota, Department of Tourism, "Fast Facts about the South Dakota Tourism Industry," http://www.sdvisit.com/tools/facts/index.asp.

been laying special emphasis in its "Rooster Rush" campaign. A more abstract resource, and one that has the potential to be extremely profitable, is South Dakota's nineteenth-century history, but the tourist industry is notoriously selective and fallacious when it comes to the marketing of history, and it can make surprising choices. In Deadwood, as we have seen, the squalid, cut-throat competition of 1876, so graphically captured by the HBO television series, has made top-quality grist for the tourist mill, precipitating a second gold strike that is as respectable as it is lucrative. By the same token, Borglum's defacement of the mountain to create his peculiar vision of democracy has produced a shrine where patriots come to cry and an emblem that has given the state its slogan for purposes of tourism—*Great Faces, Great Places*. However, two of the foundational experiences I mentioned earlier—the Dust Bowl and the Indian Wars—have not as yet provided tourism with much suitable material, except in the latter case for a brief period when Kevin Costner's *Dances with Wolves* was fashionable.

A brief diversion: in 1992 my friend Alvin and I were privileged to meet "Cisco," the handsome quarter horse that performed so wittily and movingly as Costner's mount in *Dances with Wolves*. The film, which was mostly shot in South Dakota near Pierre, had been released two years earlier, and by the time we paid our respects to the equine star, whose real name was Buck, he was earning his keep as an attraction in Murdo's dubiously named "Original 1880 Town." His dignity had been respected to the extent of a private paddock and a tent bearing the insignia of the United States Cavalry. He received us graciously, and we took his photograph. The 1880 Town museum also displayed some bits and pieces salvaged from the film, including a sod house, a tent, and the Timmons Freight wagon that brought Dunbar (Costner) to his post on the prairie. I subsequently discovered that Buck was in fact the stand-in for the real star, a buckskin gelding known as "Justin" to his friends and living in Texas. Buck continued to receive his fans until 2008 when he died, aged thirty-three. A memorial marks his burial place in the 1880 Town.

At the beginning of this book, I described the childhood origins of my interest in the Wild West, and I am sure that my continuing desire to return to South Dakota is inspired by the classic landscape to be found in the great grasslands west of the Missouri River, where the Sioux and the buffalo used to flourish. But that landscape, for all its beauty, is now tainted by my knowledge of what took place there and the price the Sioux paid for its surrender.

Wounded Knee is the quintessential locus of the Sioux's subjugation, and like the rest of the Pine Ridge reservation, it does not make an obvious target for mainstream (white) tourist development. Nonetheless, people of all nationalities persist in going there, even though the place is remote and lacks facilities or concessions. I assume they are drawn, as I was, by a mixture of historical awareness and morbid curiosity, a powerful emotion when roused by scenes of atrocity.

Despite its lack of development, Wounded Knee is a place that should be visited; it represents a symbol, not only of the Sioux's final, conclusive defeat, but of the last perceived challenge to the white population's acquisition of the Sioux's traditional lands. The latter aspect of its symbolism is not often acknowledged, though it was thoroughly understood at the time of the massacre. South Dakota was wrested from its American Indian occupants, a fact that does not deserve to be erased by tourism's need for an inoffensive account of history. Among other things, Wounded Knee is a monument to the country's completed transition to white authority, and it is therefore worth seeing because it quantifies the price of that transition and shows who paid it.

I am not suggesting that Wounded Knee should be turned into a tourist attraction—that is a decision for the Lakotas themselves; however, I do think that when visitors come to the massacre site they should be able to comprehend what they are looking at. As things stand, visitors are likely to leave as ignorant as they were before they arrived.

From 1877 onwards, the United States government drove the Sioux into a life of enforced dependency, confining them to reservations. No longer able to hunt for buffalo, which had been exterminated, and humiliated by their impotence, the Sioux were often at the mercy of incompetent and more or less venal agents, who dealt corruptly with the tribe's rations and supplies. And these men, even when they attempted to treat their charges honorably, had in their turn to contend with unscrupulous traders and bureaucrats, who saw rich pickings in the federal resources allocated to the Indians.[2]

In 1889, the worst drought on record caused many white farmers to abandon the land the Sioux had recently been forced to leave, and it also put an end to the Indians' own half-hearted efforts at farming the poor land they had been granted. The government saw fit to choose this moment to cut their beef ration, causing a state of semi-starvation among the Sioux that left many of their children too weak to withstand the measles epidemic that struck during the winter, coming on the heels of previous epidemics of influenza and whooping cough. In February 1890, President Benjamin Harrison completed their misery when he announced that their reservations were to be further diminished, leaving the so-called ceded land open to white settlement. The Great Sioux Reservation was dismantled and formally replaced by the six reservations that exist today. The Oglala band was given the dry, rolling hill country now known as the Pine Ridge reservation to the southeast of the Black Hills.

By the summer of 1890 the Sioux were, in the words of historian Robert M. Utley, "depressed, despairing, and drained of hope for improvement."[3] Under these circumstances, it was not surprising that they responded with fervent credulity to the preaching of Wovoka, a Paiute in Nevada, who promulgated a revelation heavily influenced by Christianity that foresaw the return of the Messiah as an American Indian. Wovoka promised a second coming that would usher in a kind of paradise in which Indians would once again inhabit a land without

2. For my account of the Wounded Knee massacre, I have relied on Robert M. Utley, *The Last Days of the Sioux Nation* (New Haven, Conn.: Yale University Press, 1963); Utley, *The Indian Frontier of the American West, 1846–1890* (Albuquerque: University of New Mexico Press, 1984); James H. McGregor, *The Wounded Knee Massacre from the Viewpoint of the Sioux* (Baltimore, Md.: Wirth Bros., 1940); Ralph K. Andrist, *The Long Death: The Last Days of the Plains Indian* (New York: Macmillan, 1964); and Jack Utter, *Wounded Knee & the Ghost Dance Tragedy: A Chronicle of Events Leading to and Including the Incident at Wounded Knee, South Dakota, on December 29, 1890* (Lake Ann, Mich.: National Woodlands Publishing Co., 1991).

3. Utley, *Indian Frontier*, p. 251.

white people, who would be driven into the sea. In this paradise there would be no sickness or hunger; they would be free to pursue their old way of life; and they would live in peace reunited with the ghosts of their dead relatives and friends, who would all reappear in their youthful vigor and beauty. The Nevada holy man preached that this idyll could be invoked by performing a Ghost Dance, for which a special shirt was required.

Wovoka's vision was peaceful, but the desperate Sioux gave it a distinctively war-like interpretation. A number of influential chiefs became convinced that direct action might hasten the longed-for second coming, and some Ghost Dancers came to believe that their shirts would turn aside bullets and preserve their lives. They began to perform the dance ceremony in large numbers and with menacing intensity, while turning increasingly defiant on their reservations. The agent at Pine Ridge, Daniel F. Royer, a man whom the Oglalas contemptuously nicknamed "Young-man-afraid-of-the Sioux," panicked and called for military support. Fearing a resurgence of Indian militancy, the authorities ordered Major General Nelson Miles to put a stop to the Ghost Dance movement and suppress any threatened outbreaks of hostilities. A list of Indian leaders thought to be fomenters of trouble was drawn up, which included both Sitting Bull and Spotted Elk, known to non-Indians as Big Foot, a man in his late sixties who was the leader of a band of Minneconjou Sioux attached to the Cheyenne River Agency.

A botched attempt to arrest Sitting Bull, then residing on the Standing Rock reservation, resulted in his death on 15 December 1890. When Big Foot heard the news, he feared arrest and even assassination himself, and during the night of 23 December, he set off with his people in the direction of Pine Ridge, hoping to be united with Red Cloud and his much more numerous group. Miles deployed several units to search for Big Foot, and he was finally located on 28 December by a squadron of the Seventh United States Cavalry, an unfortunate stroke of fate since this was Custer's old regiment, which had been comprehensively defeated by the Sioux at the Battle of the Little Big Horn.

Big Foot surrendered immediately and unconditionally. Dragged by his family in a travois, he was by then almost too weak to travel at all, for he had contracted pneumonia over Christmas. He was coughing up blood, and blood dripped from his nose, freezing where it fell on the boards of the wagon in which the soldiers placed him. In any case, his people were in no state to resist. Anyone who has experienced a winter on the prairie in South Dakota will be able to imagine the condition of his followers, many of them women and children, some of them on foot (they had been forced to eat some of their ponies), after two weeks of crossing the prairie in the bitter cold, under-dressed, under-fed, and in constant fear of attack.

The soldiers escorted Big Foot and his exhausted people to their camp near a place called Wounded Knee, which was no more than a post office and a few houses on a creek where the trail that connected the Pine Ridge and Rosebud agencies was crossed by a small bridge. Big Foot was transferred in his blankets to an ambulance vehicle in the hope that it would give him a more comfortable ride. At the camp, the Indians put up their tipis, and a message was sent by courier to Pine Ridge, informing headquarters that Big Foot and his band had been intercepted and that his people numbered 120 men and 230 women and children. Towards nightfall the soldiers were joined by four more troops of the Seventh Cavalry, a company of scouts, and a battery of Hotchkiss guns, all under the command of Colonel James Forsyth, who took charge of the camp. This brought the total of armed men thought necessary for containing Big Foot's band to just over five hundred.[4]

Forsyth gave instructions for a cordon of soldiers to be placed round the Indian tipis and had the four Hotchkiss guns hauled to the top of a small knoll overlooking the camp. He arranged for Big Foot to be moved into a tent with a stove and asked the army physician to do what he could for the critically sick chief. Rations were distributed, but the Indians were kept under tight security. The night passed without incident, though the officers celebrated their triumphant capture with a keg of whiskey. Alice Ghost Horse, a survivor, recalled that some soldiers got drunk and made insulting comments about the Lakota women.[5]

On the morning of 29 December, Forsyth set about fulfilling his

4. Utley, *Last Days*, pp. 196, 201.

5. Mario Gonzalez and Elizabeth Cook-Lynn, *The Politics of Hallowed Ground* (Urbana: University of Illinois Press, 1999), p. 17.

orders, which had been relayed to him by heliograph from the army's headquarters at Pine Ridge. His orders directed him to disarm the Indians, taking every precaution to prevent their escape. If they choose to fight, Forsyth was to destroy them. At this point, it is important to understand the topography of Wounded Knee and the disposition of the Seventh Cavalry. The creek runs more or less north, and to its west, at right angles, is a dry ravine. The Indian camp had been set up on a flat piece of ground just to the north of the ravine, and dismounted soldiers had been stationed in a tight ring around their tipis. At the same time two troops of mounted men and their officers had been deployed on the far side of the ravine in a line running parallel with it. Another mounted troop had been positioned to the east of the camp, close to the creek. The four Hotchkiss guns on the hill to the north were trained directly on the camp site. Thus, the soldiers formed a kind of box that enclosed their prisoners on every side. For their part, the Indians had raised a white flag in the middle of their lodges.

At 8:00 A.M., Forsyth ordered the Indian men and older boys to assemble in front of Big Foot's tent in a semi-circle. The chief himself was brought out, but he was too weak to stand and had to be propped up on the ground. The Indians were told that they were safe and would continue to receive rations, but they would be obliged to hand over their weapons, of which they almost certainly had a good many. A few old rifles were reluctantly given up. Forsyth ordered the tipis to be searched, an operation performed by soldiers who made bullies of themselves, scattering belongings on the ground. More weapons were found, but Forsyth was still not satisfied. He ordered that the Indian men should file past for inspection.

The atmosphere, already extremely tense, was made more so by Yellow Bird, a Ghost Dance fanatic, who is said to have begun a dance, throwing dust in the air to symbolize the coming destruction of the old world and the white man. A scuffle broke out involving an Indian who was probably deaf, and a gun went off. The troopers immediately fired a volley into the semi-circle of Indian men, killing most of them, including Big Foot, and inadvertently hitting some of their fellow soldiers in the crossfire. The soldiers disengaged, and the Hotchkiss guns on the hill above opened fire, aiming their shells at the Indian camp, where the women and children were gathered. The outer cordons of troops below the ravine and close to the creek also began shooting.

Subsequent events are not easy to piece together; however, the words of historian Ralph K. Andrist will serve to sum things up: "The 7th Cavalry," he wrote, "had a splendid record, but all witnesses agree that from the moment it opened fire, it ceased to be a military unit and became a mass of infuriated men intent only on butchery."[6]

The few Indian men who survived the initial onslaught scattered, only to be hunted down and shot. Some tried to escape to the seeming safety of the dry ravine to the south of the camp but found it crammed with terrified women and children. They died under the fire of the Hotchkiss battery, which had been moved so it could sweep the ravine. Some made a run for it, but they, too, were hunted down and killed; the line of bodies discovered later stretched for two miles beyond the camp—all women and children.[7]

The Oglala holy man Black Elk, reported: "Dead and wounded women and children and little babies were scattered all along where they had been trying to run away. The soldiers had followed along the gulch, as they ran, and murdered them in there. Sometimes they were in heaps because they had huddled together, and some were scattered all along. Sometimes bunches of them had been killed and torn to pieces where the wagon guns hit them. I saw a little baby trying to suck its mother, but she was bloody and dead."[8]

Colonel Forsyth finally brought the carnage to an end by screaming, "For God's sake! Stop shooting them!"[9] It was noon. By the end of this terrible morning, the army had lost twenty-five dead, with thirty-nine wounded. It is not known precisely how many members of Big Foot's band were killed, and the figures have been disputed ever since, but it was certainly the majority, including many women and children. Later

---

6. Andrist, *Long Death*, p. 351. *See also* Utley, *Last Days*, pp. 200–230, for a detailed account of the actions that fateful day.

7. Andrist, *Long Death*, p. 351.

8. John G. Neihardt, ed., *Black Elk Speaks: Being the Life Story of a Holy Man of the Oglala Sioux* (1932; reprint ed., Lincoln: University of Nebraska Press, 2000), p. 259.

9. Utter, *Wounded Knee*, p. 24.

that day nature intervened, unleashing a blizzard that forced the soldiers to withdraw from the site, transporting their dead and the wounded of both sides to Pine Ridge. They left the Indian dead on the field. Three days were to elapse before the weather relented sufficiently for a burial party to be sent from Pine Ridge. On New Year's Day 1891, the bodies that lay frozen on the massacre site—adults and children—were collected and thrown into a long trench dug into the crown of the hill where the Hotchkiss guns had stood.

In May 2011, I drove west on U.S. Highway 18 through the Rosebud reservation into Bennett County and then into Shannon County until I reached the turning on to B.I.A. Highway 27, which runs due north into the Pine Ridge reservation towards Wounded Knee. From previous visits, I remembered a neglected secondary road that came to an end just beyond the reservation boundary at Scenic (a misnomer if ever there was one) and carried little traffic apart from battered local vehicles on their way to and from Porcupine. I remembered a road that took its lonely route through an empty prairie landscape with encroaching horizons that left no need to explain the name of Pine Ridge. I was therefore surprised to find myself on a newly resurfaced highway. After six miles I was forced to stop at a set of traffic lights filtering cars and trucks through a one-way system so that work on the road could continue. Earth movers and tractors were grinding their way up and down the stretch under construction. A sign said, "No Through Traffic," the first to offer this helpful message. I asked for advice and was told that, as luck would have it, I was only a few hundred yards short of Wounded Knee.

Once the lights had changed, I left the highway and took the dirt road that brings you to the massacre site and probably follows the old wagon track that led to the creek crossing used by Forsyth and his troops when they brought in Big Foot's band. I parked my car a few yards from the bottom of the high ground where the burial trench was dug, which is now called Cemetery Hill. As I walked the last few yards to the summit, I was accosted by two young women and a little girl. They offered me a selection of what they called "art works," which they said they had made themselves, and for $20 I bought a bone-and-bead necklace with a pendant in the shape of an arrow. It is hanging from my desk lamp as I type this. One of the women acted as a self-appointed guide to the place, though I got the impression that beyond knowing that Indians had suffered something dreadful at the hands of the army she was pretty vague about the actual details. She talked scathingly about the ignorance of the average American tourist, who would ask if her people still lived in tipis and rode horses. In fact, so far from riding horses, she didn't even own a car and had to hire a taxi for $15 if she wanted to go shopping in Porcupine, though she liked visiting Crawford, Nebraska, because Crazy Horse was buried nearby. I told her that the following day I planned to visit Fort Robinson near Crawford, where Crazy Horse had been arrested and killed, and she looked pleased that I was taking an interest in her people's history.

My guide told me that most Americans confessed to her that they were shocked by conditions on Pine Ridge and offered to send Christmas presents. In her experience, German tourists were much better informed than Americans. I told her I was from England, and she immediately asked if I had been at "the wedding" (Prince William and Kate Middleton had been married two weeks earlier). I had to disappoint her.

We stood together at the top of the hill on a sunny, blustery afternoon, the graveyard behind us, the massacre site laid out below us, as legible as a map: there was the creek, there the dry ravine, there the piece of flat ground on which Big Foot's band had camped and where the first shots were fired. She pointed to the upper slopes of the valley and told me that about three hundred people lived in cabins scattered around; none of them had jobs. Their only source of income was making and selling art works such as I had just purchased. In the summer as many as a hundred visitors stopped here every day, but that made the competition much tougher, and many other locals gathered along the road to sell their stuff. The websites describing Wounded Knee are full of complaints by tourists who have been "pestered" by trinket sellers, a commonplace of travel in any relatively poor country but unexpected in the United States, especially when those doing the pestering are themselves American citizens.

My amiable guide said that her family owned eighty acres of land— she pointed to a particular ridge—but that tribal red tape was so obstructive they could never get to use it. What would she do with the land if she did get permission, I asked. She shrugged. She didn't know.

"God bless Obama," she said, adding that she blessed him every day because he had signed the United Nations Declaration of the Rights of Indigenous Peoples. The United States was the last member-state to do so. What did the declaration mean, I asked her. What was the president going to do now? Once again she shrugged.

Since my last trip in 1994, a visitors' center had been built not far from the creek, but it was closed. I asked her when it would open, but she couldn't say, though she added that her father had helped to construct it.

"Grandpa built it," the little girl chimed in, the first time she had spoken since I'd arrived. She said it again, louder, and I told her I was happy to hear her speaking up for grandpas. She nodded unsmilingly. I told them I was a writer there to do some research and pointed to my maps and notebook. They seemed glad that someone had come so far to take an interest in their history and showed no sign of resentment when I left them and began to survey the site.

I stood at the point where Forsyth had commanded the Hotchkiss guns to be positioned. What is a Hotchkiss gun? To the unprofessional eye, it is a small cannon mounted on large wheels, though its technical name is a breech-loading steel mountain rifle, which indicates the purpose for which it was intended. The 1.65-inch gun and its accessories could be packed on two mules with the ammunition mule carrying seventy-two rounds (at more than two pounds each). The first gun of its type was purchased by the United States military from the French arms firm of Hotchkiss and employed against the Nez Perces in 1877. It was popular with soldiers because it was light, well built, and simple to operate. With an effective range of 4,200 yards, it could fire rapidly and accurately, even at distance. As a weapon, its true value lay in its ability to deliver shells that were designed to explode on contact and shower the enemy with jagged fragments, causing gruesome injuries. Some Indian witnesses claimed that many of those killed could not be buried because their bodies were insufficiently intact and could not be assembled from the parts strewn across the ground. It seems incredible, but one of these weapons in working order complete with shells—"ready to fire"—was recently for sale on a website, aptly named cannonsuperstore.com.

Looking down to the valley, I had no difficulty in putting myself in the shoes of the soldiers who formed the battery that fired on the camp below and then maneuvered their cannon to rake the dry ravine. All the surviving witnesses refer to the smoke that soon enveloped the massacre, but from this small altitude, the targets were no doubt more easily picked out. The real difficulty confronting the artillery men was how to avoid inflicting harm on their own comrades.

As it happens, a photograph exists of one of these batteries. It shows fifteen uniformed men lined up to the rear of three Hotchkiss guns, with a man kneeling and pretending to take aim behind each gun. The photograph was taken by John C. H. Grabill, a local man with studios in Sturgis, Hot Springs, Lead, and Deadwood. Its caption, as it was printed, reads:

> Famous Battery "E" of 1st Artillery.
> These brave men and the Hotchkiss guns that
> Big Foot's Indians thought were toys,
> Together with the fighting 7th what's
> Left of Gen. Custer's boys,
> Sent 200 Indians to that
> Heaven which the ghost dancer enjoys.
> This checked the Indian noise
> And Gen. Miles with staff
> Retnrned [*sic*] to Illinois.[10]

Presumably Grabill added this versified caption himself—perhaps he also composed it—to make the photograph more commercial, and presumably prints of this photograph and the others he took at Wounded Knee and Pine Ridge, including those of dead Lakotas, were for sale in his Deadwood studio.

There is another photograph, also by Grabill, that shows Corporal Paul H. Weinert seated behind the Hotchkiss gun that he fired at the

---

10. The photographs taken by Grabill discussed here can be found in the John C. H. Grabill Collection, State Archives Collection, South Dakota State Historical Society, Pierre, S.Dak.

massacre. Nine other uniformed men are standing with him behind the weapon, at least five of them Indian scouts. A pair of shells has been decoratively arranged on the ground in front of an ammunition box. Weinert later wrote an account of his part in the massacre. It includes the following: "Looking around, I saw [Lieutenant Hawthorn] lying on his side, and then I knew he had been hit. . . . I said: 'By God! I'll make 'em pay for that,' and ran the gun fairly into the opening of the ravine and tried to make every shot count. . . . They kept yelling at me to come back, and I kept yelling for a cool gun. . . . Bullets were coming like hail from the Indians' Winchesters."[11] He expected to be court-martialed for his refusal to withdraw, but he was awarded a Congressional Medal of Honor instead.

I walked back to the cemetery, which occupies the flat top of the hill. Its entrance is marked by a pair of stout, four-sided pillars made of red brick and white stone that form an open gateway and stand about ten feet high and ten feet apart. If gates ever hung from them, they have long since disappeared. When originally built in 1954, the pillars must have been designed to support some decorative feature—balls, urns, or tablets perhaps—but they too have been removed, leaving no clue to their identity. Nowadays they carry nothing weightier than a skeletal metal arch topped with a flimsy cross.

These decapitated pillars have become the symbol of Wounded Knee. They are certainly the most photogenic aspect of the cemetery, and when pictured against a flawless prairie sky, the shot that every visitor takes, their foreshortened torsos do convey a little of the eerie atmosphere of the place. As if to make things grislier, their front surfaces, the ones that greet visitors as they walk up the hill, have been gouged out, exposing the pillars' hollow interiors. Headless and disemboweled, they appear to have been the victims of some awful carnage, the effect enhanced by the fleshy red of the lacerated bricks. They stand like empty niches that have lost their saints.

The mutilated gates also stand, in another sense, for poverty, and they are shocking for that reason, too. We are used to seeing war graves—

11. Quoted in Utley, *Last Days*, p. 221.

and what is Wounded Knee if not a war grave?—maintained in immaculate condition. They are institutions on which nations do not hesitate to spend lavishly, ensuring that their heroic dead are "laid to rest" with suitable reverence befitting their sacrifice to their country and their country's debt to them. Statues, cenotaphs, and memorials are commissioned without regard to expense in order that honor should be done to the fallen, and these sites are preserved and managed so that the memory of those who gave their lives should never be allowed to fade. For example, in the 2007–2008 financial year, grants made by the relevant governments to the Commonwealth War Graves Commission (United Kingdom, Canada, Australia, New Zealand, South Africa, and India) for the upkeep of graves of soldiers who died in the two World Wars exceeded £42 million. No crime is thought more despicable than vandalizing war memorials, and the authorities concerned invariably take steps to repair the damage—imagine paint thrown on the Vietnam Veterans Memorial Wall in Washington, D.C.,—but as long as I have known them (two decades), these pillars at Wounded Knee have been in a state of ruin, a symbol, I assume, of Pine Ridge's chronic lack of funds.

Immediately behind the pillars is the grave itself, the same pit that was dug on New Year's Day 1891 by a civilian detail, which was dispatched to Wounded Knee under the protection of a military escort. One group was sent to the top of the hill to excavate this communal grave for the Indian dead, a trench fifty feet long, six feet wide, and six feet deep. Meanwhile, another group was dispersed to gather up the frozen corpses that were scattered over the entire area. Many of them were found in grotesque positions, as if they had been frozen the instant they had been killed.

James H. McGregor, writing many years later after interviewing some of the survivors, provided a moving summary of what they told him about this activity. "Another detail," he wrote, "accompanied the mule teams [and] went in search of the dead and when found the frozen corps [sic] were thrown into the big freight wagon like so much cord wood and when the wagon box was full, it was driven to the trench and the bodies were tossed in with no more feeling than if they were unloading sacks of grain. There were no caskets, no ceremony, no tears, no prayers; but jocular remarks were made as the Indians were thrown in the pit. Off they would go for another load, singing and jigging as though they were not in the presence of death."[12]

A member of the burial party remarked that it was "a thing to melt the heart of a man, if it was of stone, to see those little children, with their bodies shot to pieces, thrown naked into the pit," but he appears to have been exceptional.[13] George ("Gus") Trager, who had come to the United States from Germany in 1876, was working as a photographer in Chadron, Nebraska, at the time of the massacre. One of his pictures, captioned "Gathering up the Dead at the Battle Field at Wounded Knee S. D.," shows three men, civilians, standing in front of a wagon pulled by four mules, its wheels crusted with snow. There must be twenty or so frozen bodies in the wagon, and because they are so rigid, they look like a heap of awkwardly shaped branches. The arms of one corpse are thrown above his head as if fixed at the moment of fruitless surrender. Filling the wagon with bodies has evidently been warm work. The man in the foreground has taken off his coat, which lies on the snow at his feet. A second man looks at the camera, his eyes all but covered by the peak of his cap. It is hard to tell, but he looks as if he is smiling, as one does when being photographed.

Viewed purely as a composition, the photograph is a sophisticated piece of work. It is designed in a crescent shape, with the wagon and mules forming the front horn, the rim of a bank against which the snow has gathered forming the inner curve, and a row of cavalrymen and a second wagon silhouetted on the horizon against a gray sky, twenty or thirty yards away, making the other horn. The effect of this design is to showcase the mangled, twisted limbs of the Indians within a semi-circle of seemingly unblemished snow.

All war photographs must be more or less pitiless; otherwise, they shirk their subject. This picture, perhaps because of its clever design, seems especially pitiless: the ring is drawn tight round the Indian

12. McGregor, *Wounded Knee Massacre*, p. 80.

13. Quoted in James Mooney, *The Ghost Dance Religion and Wounded Knee* (New York: Dover Publications, 1973), pp. 878–79.

corpses, which are consigned to disappear into a kind of a white empti-ness, not just a symbolic grave but a void from which history will not rescue them. I doubt that Trager was concerned with such abstrac-tions, but it is hard not to infer from this carefully arranged photograph a sense of finality. This, says the photograph, is the end of Indian re-sistance. The last battle has been fought and they have lost. The burial party may or may not be exulting in its work—the men appear to show no regret for the way they have piled up their wagon—but what the photograph clearly articulates is that the Sioux have been denied their claim to common decencies. These corpses have no right to dignity or ceremony; they are so much human debris that needs to be disposed of. And, by implication, so are their surviving relatives. There were several missionaries in the area, as well as an army chaplain, who might have given the occasion a touch of religious solemnity, especially since many Lakotas had by then converted to a form of Christianity, but for some reason neither the missionaries nor the chaplain were invited to offici-ate at the burial.[14]

The corpse of Big Foot was not given special treatment but was tossed like the others into the trench. Before the chief was buried, Trager took a famous picture of his corpse. It shows Big Foot, a tall man, on his back, frozen in the snow. His head is covered with a scarf, and he is wearing what looks like a heavy overcoat. Snow is lying on his legs, which are bent. He lies in a curious position, seemingly struggling to rise by push-ing himself off the ground with his elbows while lifting up his head. His fingers appear to be long but badly bent, suggesting he was suffering from arthritis. His eyes are closed, and his mouth is set in a grim line. As if not yet dead, he looks old, exhausted, and ill. In the background, sev-eral yards away, are a horse and a pair of soldiers bundled up in coats against the cold. The chief is surrounded by an expanse of unblemished snow. Ralph K. Andrist reproduced the photograph in *The Long Death*, noting that the scene had evidently been tidied before the picture was taken because Big Foot had died sitting on the ground in the area of greatest slaughter and the surrounding earth must have been horribly

14. McGregor, *Wounded Knee Massacre*, p. 82.

bloody.[15] Perhaps his body was moved to a clean patch of snow for the photograph; his position certainly looks strange, as if it has been manipulated like a clay model to suggest he is falling back, having failed in his last effort to rise—a symbolically apt pose.

There are other photographs by Trager that show the desolation of the snowbound massacre site and its scattering of frozen corpses. Captioned "Birds Eeye [sic] View of Battle Field . . . Looking North," one photograph shows some bodies in the foreground that appear to be women, though they have been partially covered by a carpet or piece of heavy material. Behind the bodies can be seen some bare poles and sapling trunks, the skeletons of tipis burnt and destroyed by the Hotchkiss shells; a soldier stands inside one of these ruins, looking towards the camera. Nearby is a shattered wagon, its broken wheels sticking out of the snow, and as one's eye ranges over the prairie in the background, it begins to pick out a dozen, then a score, then perhaps as many as fifty bodies lying about in the mud and snow. It is as if these corpses were overlooked by the photographer as he concentrated on the women, forcing him to compose a suitable caption after he had developed the scene he had inadvertently captured.

In some ways Trager's most disturbing picture, the one that gives the game away, so to speak, shows two civilian men standing in the trench where the dead Lakotas are being buried. The photograph gives the impression they have been interrupted in the middle of their work, for they are in shirtsleeves. A large group of soldiers and a couple of civilians with spades stand behind the grave, looking at the camera; the soldiers are well protected from the weather in their bulky overcoats, and many of them are wearing fur hats. Beside them, also at the grave's edge, is a pile of corpses waiting to be interred. The trench is as deep as the men are tall (think of the effort it took to dig it out of the frozen earth), and in front of them can be seen a heap of misshapen corpses, lying laterally across the width of the hole. The winter sun light is strong; the black shadows are well defined.

Some things are not visible. Recent writers have claimed that men jumped on the piles of bodies to pack them down in the trench and that

15. Andrist, *Long Death*, p. 183.

at least one Indian was buried alive, with the knowledge of the over-seers of the burial party.[16] Many of the bodies were buried naked be-cause the burial details stripped them, looking for souvenirs, and fol-lowing the massacre, a busy trade in Ghost Dance relics sprang up, with ghost shirts fetching a particularly good price. Trager's picture has none of the artfulness of the "crescent" photo; it has the crude feel of a team photograph, though the moment has been selected for its informative content: the soldiers in their uniforms holding their rifles; the civilians holding their spades; the pile of bodies waiting to be dumped in the grave; and, at the bottom of the trench, the layered and stiffened bodies of those already deposited. The message could not be clearer: we win, they lose; the Indians are where they belong, and there they will stay.

The precise number of dead remains controversial, but what can be stated with certainty is that the burial detail later interred 146 bodies collected from the battlefield: 84 men and boys, 44 women, and 18 chil-dren. Of the 51 wounded who were taken to the hospital at Pine Ridge, 7 later died, bringing the total of indisputable deaths to 153.[17] It is impos-sible to know how many bodies were removed from the area by rela-tives from Pine Ridge before the government burial party arrived or how many people managed to flee the battlefield, only to die later. On 25 October 1990, the United States Congress passed Concurrent Resolu-tion # 153, which marked the hundredth anniversary of Wounded Knee and acknowledged the "tragic death and injury of approximately 350–375 Indian men, women, and children of Chief Big Foot's band." This figure must include both the dead from Big Foot's group, which prob-ably amounted to the majority of his followers, and some Oglalas from the Pine Ridge agency, who came to the assistance of their fellow Indi-ans during the massacre and were killed for their pains.[18]

It is often said that a photograph "freezes" a moment in time, but, unlike most clichés, this one doesn't really grasp the truth, which is

16. Gonzalez and Cook-Lynn, *Politics of Hallowed Ground*, p. 255.

17. Utley, *Last Days*, pp. 227–28.

18. U.S., Congress, House of Representatives, *Acknowledging the 100th Anniver-sary of the Tragedy at Wounded Knee Creek, SD*, S. Con. Res 153, 101st Cong., 2d sess., 1990, H. 13640, http://thomas.loc.gov/cgi-bin/query/z?r101:H25OCo-B307.

that photographs necessarily depict the past—there is no such thing as a contemporary photograph—and, so far from freezing the moment, they show something that is forever receding in time. Photographs grow old just like us, but by a different process. The medium of photography is time as much as light, and photographs cannot be looked at without raising questions, often troubling and unanswerable ones, about the nature of time, especially if the subject of the picture is someone known to you. No sooner is the picture taken than the person—the subject—is whisked away, disappearing, as it were, into the future from which we continually re-emerge, while the image in the photograph has become a specter. Irretrievable time is the subject of photography, just as irrecoverable youth is the story of every life.

However, in the case of pictures of the dead, the effect of photography is different; what we see are not corpses but people who are dead. For most of us, the process of decomposition takes place out of sight and is beyond our experience. The dead, unlike the living, never change; they simply disappear. This is one of the definitions of death, and one of the reasons why pictures of the dead are shocking: they exist in a permanent, immutable present.

From William Brady onwards, the photography of war, which became highly developed during the Civil War, was always limited by the fact that the technology required its subjects to remain still. Photography was ideal for individual portraits, posed gatherings, and set pieces but defective when it came to recording action. However, photography came into its own in the aftermath of a battle, when of necessity many of its subjects were immobilized. The pictures taken at Wounded Knee by Grabill and Trager have often been reproduced, but they bear studying again. Reminders of their historical period are unavoidable—the clothes and uniforms, the mules and wagons, soldiers on horseback—but there are other elements that represent constants in our experience, and it is these that give the pictures their never-failing immediacy. We cannot look at the snow, the soldiers wrapped in their big coats to protect them from the unforgiving, relentless wind, and the semi-nakedness of the Indian corpses without feeling the effects of that Dakota winter ourselves. In common humanity, we cannot help but feel for these wretched bodies, even though they are lifeless and no longer in need of comfort. Their wounds cannot be discerned, and the black-and-white photography makes it impossible to distinguish between the blood and the mud that stain the snow, but when we look at those bare arms and legs, we shiver.

Perhaps because of their callousness, these photographs have the paradoxical virtue of giving us an authentic sense of that scene a few days after the massacre, of its physical quality, and of the mentality of those involved. Regret, compassion, respect for the dead, none of these feelings appear to be registered among the soldiers and grave diggers or the photographers. We are looking at pictures that probably would not have been taken and posed for and subsequently marketed if their subjects—"the fallen"—had not been Indians. The photographs were souvenirs of victory. And yet, by a satisfactory irony, these images have left a different legacy than the one intended, for surely no one can look at them today without feeling both pity and horror.

The American public's reaction to news of the so-called battle was generally favorable. Many whites living near the reservations interpreted Wounded Knee as the defeat of a murderous cult; others confused Ghost Dancers with Indians in general; either way, the white population in the recently created states of North and South Dakota was by and large relieved that the incident seemed to bring an end to the long and vexing conflict with the Sioux. Two years later, as if to give scholastic blessing to the new era of peacefulness, the historian Frederick Jackson Turner declared in a famous essay that the frontier no longer existed. "The frontier has gone," he wrote, "and with its going has closed the first period of American history."[19]

The United States Army honored its dead in 1893 by raising a Wounded Knee Monument at Fort Riley, Kansas, which can be seen to this day. The massacre received a still more august warrant of approval when President Benjamin Harrison presented twenty Medals of Honor, the highest military award for bravery in the United States, to soldiers who had taken part in the massacre. The tally was a record in its day, exceeding the number of medals awarded, for example, after the Battle

---

19. Frederick Jackson Turner, *The Significance of the Frontier in American History* (New York: Henry Holt & Co., 1920), p. 38.

of the Little Big Horn, and it remains a record, since no other military action since has collected so many medals, including the Normandy landing, the Battle of the Bulge, and Iwo Jima in World War II. It seems an excessive gesture for President Harrison to have made, but he had been under pressure from reformists to improve conditions for Indians, and the circumstances of Wounded Knee threatened to make him even more vulnerable on this score; giving the event the appearance of a desperate and heroic engagement forestalled criticism of ill-treatment. By the same token, he could also appear resolute in the eyes of those who demanded harsh treatment for the Indians.

The Medals of Honor have been a source of great bitterness to the Lakotas ever since their award. In recent years the term "battle" when applied to the incident has been seen as increasingly offensive, for obvious reasons, and these days most literature that tourists are likely to come across uses instead the word "massacre." In its Concurrent Resolution #153, marking the centenary of Wounded Knee, Congress itself applied the word "massacre" to the slaughter, but the word has not yet achieved universal institutional usage.

In 1999, the controversy took a new turn when Bob Smith, an Oneida Indian veteran, wrote to Al Gore, then vice-president, asking for his help to have the Wounded Knee Medals of Honour rescinded. He had been attending a state ceremony in Washington, D.C., when the United States Army flag was paraded and had noticed that among the battle streamers attached to it was one commemorating the Pine Ridge campaign of 1890–1891, which also honored those soldiers who took part in the Wounded Knee battle. The army flag is displayed and paraded as part of the multi-service Color Guard on state visits and other ceremonial events that pay respect to the history of the United States Army. At that time, 170 streamers, including the Pine Ridge streamer (red with two parallel black stripes), were on permanent display with the army flag at the Pentagon, White House, West Point, and army bases round the world.

While asking for the Medals of Honor and the battle streamer to be withdrawn, Smith also requested that the army no longer classify Wounded Knee as a battle. However justified, this request was never likely to meet with success, not least because, apart from the small matter of the army's pride, battle streamers cannot be removed from the army flag without both congressional and presidential action. The National Congress of American Indians took up the matter, and the army was obliged to make a response in defense of both the medals and the term battle. Needless to say, the army did not yield an inch, and it explicitly repudiated the description of Wounded Knee as a massacre. On this subject its memorandum read as follows: "To characterize Wounded Knee as a massacre—the killing of considerable numbers of human beings under circumstances of atrocity or cruelty, or mercilessly— overlooks the absence of premeditation [on the part of the army], efforts to peacefully pacify the encampment, attempts to spare women and children once the melee began, and the army's sincere efforts to investigate charges of wanton killing of noncombatants after the incident."[20] Thus, the army and Congress see the event in diametrically different terms. I leave the reader to choose the term that seems most apposite.

I walked around the perimeter of the hilltop and realized that I was on my own. There were no other tourists to be seen, no other cars parked on the dirt road, and my new acquaintances had disappeared; they would make no more money today. Finally, I walked through the gates to study the grave itself.

In *Wounded Knee Massacre*, McGregor wondered why the burial detail, with the help of the Indian scouts who were present, could not have dug individual graves, with names where possible, for the benefit of relatives. It is a good question, and his answer, that it was another proof of revenge, strikes me as plausible. The dimensions of the trench that served as the mass grave are marked by a little cement curb, and the whole thing is protected by a chain-link fence on steel poles, a construction of striking ugliness. The grave is covered by a long strip of grass and marked by a single monument: a four-sided, gray granite pillar standing ten or twelve feet high, which supports a large urn. The monument was raised in 1903 by the descendents of some of those who had died in the massacre, and the text they inscribed in the stone reads as follows:

20. "US Army Responses to NCAI Statement," http://www.dickshovel.com/smith 4.html.

This monument was erected by
surviving relatives and other
Ogallala and Cheyenne River Sioux
Indians in memory of
the Chief Big Foot Massacre
Dec. 29. 1890
Col Forsyth in command of
U.S. troops.
Big Foot was a great chief of the
Sioux Indians. He often said, "I will
stand in peace till my last day
comes." He did many good and brave
deeds for the white man and the
red man. Many innocent women and
children who knew no wrong
died here.

On another side there is a tribute to the Horn Cloud family, who lost a relative in the massacre and was largely responsible for the monument. The names of forty-four of those who died on 29 December 1890 are also carved into the stone.

At first sight, it struck me as curious that Colonel Forsyth's name should be recorded on a monument dedicated to the memory of his victims, but then on reflection, it seemed just and satisfying that as long as the massacre was remembered his responsibility for it would be remembered too. The monument stands as a kind of everlasting indictment of his leadership. Major General Miles was appalled by the large number of troops killed and wounded as well as the massacre of Indians; he held Forsyth culpable, but despite his best efforts, charges against the colonel were dismissed and his career in the army was unimpaired. By 1897, Forsyth had risen to be a major general.

Despite its grim origin, the graveyard continues to be used, and scattered immediately outside the fenced enclosure are dozens of graves, some marked with nothing more than little wooden crosses, some with permanent monuments, especially those of military personnel. These are Christian graves, for there have been Christian missionaries in the area since the 1870s, but a Lakota touch was provided by the little colored pennants made of plastic that flutter in the constant wind. A recent grave still had white earth piled above the coffin, and the mound was loaded with a dozen or more big pots of plastic flowers (natural flowers wouldn't last ten minutes in the heat), though many of them had fallen over, and the flowers had scattered.

I left the site with a heavy heart, as usual. I hoped my guides might have reappeared because I wanted to talk to them again, if only for the sake of having a conversation, but there was still no sign of them. The place was deserted, though in the distance I could see the tractors and earth movers still at work, and the sound of their engines was just audible, carried by the wind that never ceases to blow across the grasslands.

In his book about the memorials that commemorate those who died in World War I, Geoff Dyer described his feelings as he walked through a small cemetery in Beaumont-Hammel, France, where 154 soldiers are buried. "I have never felt so peaceful," he wrote. "I would be happy never to leave." He went on to say, "So strong are these feelings that I wonder if there is not some compensatory quality in nature, some equilibrium . . . which means that where terrible violence has taken place the earth will sometimes generate an equal and opposite sense of peace."[21] I, too, have felt that "compensatory" sense of peace in cemeteries and on battlefields, as I expect many people do, but I have never felt it when visiting Wounded Knee, where a spirit of grief and rage still seems to hang in the air.

Wounded Knee remains controversial both as a symbol and as a memorial. The visitor center, a strange circular building that has been likened, not unfairly, to a chocolate cake, provides the visitor (when it is open) with scant information about the massacre. More of its exhibits are concerned with the siege of Wounded Knee in 1973, when the church near the graveyard was occupied by members of the American Indian Movement in protest over conditions on Pine Ridge. It took the combined might of the United States Marshals and the FBI to dislodge them,

21. Geoff Dyer, *The Missing of the Somme* (London: Hamish Hamilton, 1994), p. 130.

and the memory of that incident is no doubt sharper in the minds of those who installed the exhibition than the events of 1890. At the moment the best account of the massacre can be found on a large metal information sign, designed in the style of a skin stretched over a frame, which stands close to the dirt road below the cemetery hill. In a few lines it gives an unflinching account of Big Foot's fatal last journey, though its most eloquent element is symbolic rather than textual. The sign bears the title "Massacre of Wounded Knee," at first sight a slightly odd locution that is explained by the fact that the word "Massacre" is printed on a special plate that has been screwed on to conceal and replace the now proscribed word "Battle."

No map accompanies the sign, and a sign, however well written, cannot be expected to interpret the topography of this extensive site for the benefit of visitors. Wounded Knee has been a historic landmark since 1968, but in 1990 the Wounded Knee Survivors Association called for Congress to offer reparation for the massacre by making an apology, establishing a national monument, and providing compensation to the descendants of victims. The result was Concurrent Resolution #153, which acknowledged the massacre but fell short of an apology by restricting itself to an expression of "deep regret" on behalf of the United States. Compensation was not mentioned, or seriously considered, but the second clause of the resolution did express the support of Congress for "the establishment of a suitable and appropriate Memorial to those who were so tragically slain at Wounded Knee which could inform the American public of the historic significance of events at Wounded Knee."[22] Various problems, not least an argument over the ownership of the massacre site, have ensured that no such memorial has materialized; nor is it likely that one will do so in the near future.[23]

For what it is worth, my own feeling is that the existing monument should be preserved and, indeed, honored. On no account should it be replaced. It was raised in good faith all those years ago, and in its modest way, it has stood witness ever since, alone and unassisted, to the events

22. *Acknowledging the 100ᵗʰ Anniversary of the Tragedy at Wounded Knee Creek.*

23. An account of the tangled politics surrounding this proposal can be found in Gonzalez and Cook-Lynn, *Politics of Hallowed Ground*, pp. 23–78.

of 1890. What is required is educational support on the site so that the words of the resolution can be turned from rhetoric into a presentation of the facts that will, as Congress recommended, "accurately portray the heroic and courageous campaign waged by the Sioux people to preserve and protect their lands and their way of life."[24] In addition, the burial area should be improved and maintained in such a way that the natural respect owing to those who died in the massacre will adequately protect the grave and permit the removal of the hideous chain-link fence and its poles.

I would like to know the origin of the name Wounded Knee, but whatever it is, the place has come to symbolize a wound that will not heal, and cannot heal until conditions on the Pine Ridge reservation improve. The statistics concerning the reservation are scandalous: more than 80 percent unemployment, infant mortality rate at three times the national average, dependency on alcohol, and a diet so poor that half the population over the age of forty is diabetic, life expectancy of about only fifty years, per-capita income less than one-sixth of the national average, and so forth.[25] It is impossible for visitors to contemplate Pine Ridge without feeling they are witnessing an injustice that is in urgent need of repair. Surely, one thinks, a spirit of reparation, no less than ethical compunction, would have impelled the white community to see that the Lakotas, once defeated, should have been excused from further suffering and deprivation? Surely it was not necessary to strip them of everything and leave them in a perpetual state of destitution?

Nicholas Black Elk famously declared in old age that the dream of his people had died in the bloody mud of Wounded Knee and was buried in the blizzard. "The nation's hoop is broken and scattered," he said. "There is no center any longer, and the sacred tree is dead."[26] His words were recorded in 1931; yet, the fact is that the Oglala and the other Sioux tribes have survived with something of their culture intact, a remarkable triumph over appalling circumstances made possible in part by the in-

24. *Acknowledging the 100th Anniversary of the Tragedy at Wounded Knee Creek.*

25. Chris McGreal, "Obama's Indian Problem," *The Guardian* (London), 11 Jan. 2010.

26. Neihardt, *Black Elk Speaks*, pp. 196–201, 270.

spiration of visionaries such as Black Elk. If the Sioux are to flourish in the future, rather than simply survive, a great effort will be required of their leaders, as well as the state and federal authorities, but tourists can make their own small contribution towards mending the hoop. They can visit such places as Wounded Knee and see for themselves how the history of South Dakota and the United States was made.

Back in my car, driving out of the reservation towards the Nebraska border, I switched on my recorder and with a sigh began to put my impressions of Wounded Knee in order. The time was 4:00 P.M., and the sun already lay low on the horizon. I found it easy to recall my guide's tone of voice as I reconstructed our conversation—her scorn for the ignorance of tourists, her pleasure at Obama's gesture. The longer I spoke into my machine, the more my melancholy seemed out of place, and in any case, by the time I finished, it had dispersed. The facts were the facts and nothing could alter the ghastly story they told, but if the legacy of Wounded Knee, for all its many difficulties, could embrace this young woman's defiance, her exasperation, and her good humor, then the "battlefield" was not all blood and mud.

7 Sketches

While traveling for the sake of this book, I drove more than 3,000 miles in South Dakota, a positive odyssey by British standards; however, I can't claim that my trip was packed with adventure. I rarely drove on anything but a blacktop road, and never exceeded the speed limit; indeed, with the magic of cruise control and roads so straight that a mild curve was an event, I could well have got into the back seat and snoozed for much of the way. I never picked up a hitchhiker, colorful or otherwise. And, despite the torrential rain that fell during May 2011, I never encountered any hazards, apart from a couple of miles of road east of Mobridge that lay under nine inches of water but were easily fordable. In a word, I did not so much travel as drive, and for that reason I thought I would make this a travel book from which I would excise, as far as possible, any account of actual traveling. What interested me were the destinations that form the subjects of these essays; the journeys between them were a matter of necessity.

This book is exceptional in one respect. With Marco Polo setting the precedent by journeying from Venice to China and describing his experiences when he returned home, the travel book as a genre has mostly been an account of foreign places written for the benefit and entertainment of the traveler's compatriots. I have reversed the model by addressing myself, not primarily to readers in Britain, but to the people who inhabit the exotic land through which I journeyed. It might be argued that as a result of my unadventurous approach I missed the "real" South Dakota, which is only to be found in farmhouses at the end of remote dirt roads or cabins on reservations or in the bars of small towns with dwindling populations. Leaving aside the question of defining "real," I would counter that, with the exception of the town of Harrison, I was interested in destinations that attracted tourists. As a tourist myself, I wanted to see how they were presented to the outsider. My plan was to describe the face that South Dakota showed to the tourist, but with this twist: that I would also be describing the face to its owner.

Despite what I said about eliminating the travel from my travel book, I encountered many things en route between my main destinations that had me scrabbling for my recorder or camera or notebook, and I have put them together in this last chapter. I have called it "Sketches," using the word in the sense I tried to define when writing about the Badlands. Incidents or scenes that caused me to look closely and think hard, if only for the passing moment, are collected here, and they were as much a part of my trip as the big subjects that have since preoccupied me.

The order in which they appear below is dictated by my itinerary, which took me from Yankton to Harrison, where I heard my pastor friend deliver his Sunday sermon, then westwards to the Badlands and Pine Ridge, with an excursion into Nebraska, then to the Black Hills, then east to Pierre, and finally northwards to Mobridge, my last stop in the state.

Yankton

U.S. Highway 81 leads due south through Yankton County, crosses the Missouri River in Yankton by way of the new Discovery Bridge, and continues its southerly run into the heart of Nebraska. On its last couple of miles, as it approaches the river, the highway assumes the name Broadway Avenue and under this new alias turns into a characterless strip lined with the usual gas stations, fast food outlets, motels, malls. My guidebook had promised a "gem-like historic town," but any such claims could only be justified by the few blocks squeezed into the small business area close to the riverbank.[1] Certainly some fine old buildings made of sandstone and brick stood on either side of the wide streets,

---

1. Samantha Cook et al., *USA The Rough Guide* (London: Rough Guides, 2000), p. 714.

ornamented with handsome cast-iron lamp posts, but they had a for-
lorn and abandoned air. Sweeping down towards the Missouri River,
Walnut Street would have made a fine civic vista if it had not reached
an aimless termination at the blocked entrance of the old, now disused
Meridian Bridge. I wondered why there was no sign of café tables on the
sidewalks, which might have given them a little *joie de vivre*, but then
the wind blew dust in my eye, and my question was answered. A relentless, unforgiving wind sweeps across the Great Plains and is the enemy
of farmer and *boulevardier* alike, ensuring that any café culture must
stay indoors.

On my way out of town, I passed an institution, which I realized
was the prison, whose proximity had been offered by my first choice of
hotel as such a selling point. Located in Douglas Street, close to Broadway Avenue, the Yankton Federal Prison Camp is housed in dignified
brick and stone buildings that had been built in 1881 for Yankton College, the first liberal arts school in Dakota Territory. The college closed
for lack of funds nearly a century later, and the campus was converted
into a prison. Its regime appears to defy South Dakota's reputation for
conservatism, for it can be found on a list of the country's ten cushiest
prisons.[2] The inmates, all men and mostly non-violent drug offenders,
are kept under minimum-security conditions that must represent the
most liberal interpretation of that term. They are confined by a "decorative" fence that does little more than mark the boundaries, placing
them on their honor to remain imprisoned. Few prisoners bother to escape, a matter of simply walking out, partly because recapture brings
severe punishment but also because the prison, reverting to its college
tradition, offers excellent educational opportunities. It is famous for
its horticulture program, but for those less keen on the open air, the
prison offers classes in accounting, business administration, and business management. Not surprisingly, Forbes.com recommends it as one
of the top ten places to go to prison, if that is an unavoidable career
move.

2. As recommended by Forbes.com. "In Pictures: America's 10 Cushiest Prisons," http://www.forbes.com/2009/07/13/best-prisons-cushiest-madoff-personal-
finance-lockups_slide_5.html.

Rosebud Casino

Driving towards Valentine, Nebraska (the "Heart City," of course), I passed the Rosebud Casino, a large, gaudy structure located conspicuously close to the highway at the edge of the border shared by the Rosebud reservation and Nebraska. I noticed that it had hotel facilities, including a restaurant, so I thought I would return there for my evening meal, having checked into my own hotel.

In my room, I did some research on the internet and learned that the casino promised "A Little Bit of Vegas on the Prairie," with the chance to "win big." "Proudly operated" by the Rosebud Sioux Tribe, it drew some of its power from one of the nation's first tribally owned electricity-generating wind turbines. Two-hundred-fifty Vegas-style slot machines awaited the gambler, together with the opportunity to play Bingo, Blackjack, or Poker. The Rosebud Room Restaurant served a prime rib buffet seven days a week, and the whole place was open twenty-four hours a day.

Around 6:00 P.M., I drove onto the reservation and found that, although it was a Monday night, there were plenty of vehicles in the parking lot; business appeared to be good. I parked, entered the building, and was immediately assaulted by cigarette smoke, a miasma so thick and acrid I felt as if someone had thrown a hood over my head.

I write with the prim reproachfulness of an ex-smoker. Indeed, I acknowledge I am the worst kind of ex-smoker because in my smoking days I was what you might call a fundamentalist, someone who had virtually lost faith with fresh air for ordinary breathing purposes, and perhaps this made my disgust with the casino all the more censorious. As a smoker, I was a Don Juan and lusted after every kind of cigarette, a promiscuity I could indulge to the full in those days because I worked in a part of London close to the best-stocked tobacconist in the city, a shop in Old Compton Street, Soho.[3] In its window was a cornucopia of every variety of tobacco, from cigars the size of Zeppelins to a twisted, blackened monstrosity from Italy that looked like a dried bull's pizzle. Here I bought cigarettes imported from all over the smoking world, cigarettes from Russia with gray tobacco and long cardboard tubes that could be pinched into primitive filters; fat, perfumed cigarettes from Egypt; slim

3. A shop whose name I have forgotten and would dearly like to recall.

oval Kyprinos from Cyprus that were so fragrant the[y]
taken for marijuana; a brand that claimed to be ma[de espe-]
cially for James Bond, Du Mauriers (blue or red) that m[y father?]
smoke and were boxed in packets that opened like lit[tle boxes; and]
so on. I tasted them all; I loved them all.

I smoked my last cigarette more than ten years a[go,] [and I take some]
pride in my abstention, for it had nothing to do with will power and was
simply the result of desire gradually and mysteriously withering. By the
time I entered the Rosebud casino, I had become the kind of recovering smoker who recoiled from the odor of tobacco on someone who had
merely been in the company of a smoker; such is the saintly sensitivity
of the reformed nostril.

The word casino may conjure up, at least in the naïve European mind,
suggestions of a Bond film in which chaps in dinner jackets toss chips
worth thousands of pounds across the green baize to impress Russian
beauties, who are secretly employed by SMERSH, but this glamorous
notion was, alas, a far cry from the reality. As I well knew from my Deadwood adventures, in the United States the word casino is really short-
hand for slot machines, and in this case there were dozens and dozens
of them lined up in rows, all flashing and jingling in the fog.

My understanding was that these places, which have been opened
on many reservations across the country, were making large sums for
their tribal owners, a profit that brought the added satisfaction of having
been extracted from the pockets of white gamblers. If so, the plan had
gone sadly wrong, because the great majority of the people slumped in
front of the Rosebud's one-armed bandits were American Indians.

The "restaurant" turned out to be another smoke-filled place, though
most of the gamblers had retreated to the "food hall," which looked like
a school canteen where much cheaper meals were being served. I didn't
stay either to eat or gamble.

Rosebud

Driving though the Rosebud reservation, I stopped in Rosebud (population 1,587; 93.38 percent American Indian) and decided to take pictures
of the poverty and squalor to be seen on every street; however, I lacked
the necessary ruthlessness to make a journalistic photographer.

There was hardly a house to be seen that was not falling apart with a yard full of junk. I did not need to read the statistics—40.8 percent of families and 43.6 percent of the population were below the poverty line—to know that Rosebud was one of the poorest towns in the state, though the situation would presumably have been worse if it had not been the Tribal Headquarters with various agencies providing employment.[4]

As I explored its few streets, I was all too conscious that these houses were not only shocking illustrations of destitution, but, for better or worse, homes as well. In the eyes of a true journalist, the picture presumably improves as the subject matter increases in wretchedness, but I couldn't persuade myself that being a traveler—even an honorable, wonderfully sensitive, well read, historically knowledgeable one—gave me the right to point my camera at these people's misfortune. And yet I did not put it away. Instead, I adopted an ignominious compromise by skulking, my camera hidden in my hand, and whipping it out to snatch a snap when I thought no one was looking. My chagrin was doubled by knowing that I was inhibited as much by embarrassment as ethical scruple. Predictably, the pictures were worthless and often didn't even show the subject I had hastily pointed at.

It was a hot afternoon, and the handful of people on the streets smiled at me in a friendly way and didn't show the slightest curiosity, still less resentment, about what I was doing. Even the dogs, of which there were a great many loose, took no notice of me.

Whiteclay, Nebraska

I knew about Whiteclay, Nebraska, from previous visits, but seeing it again shocked me all the same, especially since only half an hour earlier I had been standing in the cemetery at Wounded Knee. Less than two miles from Pine Ridge, and therefore within walking distance, Whiteclay lies immediately on the Nebraska side of the state line as you leave South Dakota and the reservation on U.S. Highway 87. The border is

4. Wikipedia, "Rosebud, South Dakota," http://en.wikipedia.org/wiki/Rosebud,_South_Dakota.

marked by a sign that announces, "The Good Life," Nebraska's slogan. Never was a slogan more grotesquely misapplied.

The town, if it can be called that, had a population of just fourteen at the 2010 census, and it consisted of a handful of buildings on either side of the highway, four of which were stores that sold beer. One of them was called the Fireside Inn, a name that must have been bestowed on it by someone with a savage sense of irony. Between them, these four liquor businesses were said to have sold 4.6 million 12-ounce cans of beer in 2010, the equivalent of 12,900 cans per day. The great majority of their customers were residents of the Pine Ridge reservation where the sale and possession of alcohol was forbidden under tribal law.[5] Since they had no legal place to consume their purchases, this great river of beer, of necessity, must have flowed from source to outfall within White-clay itself.

It was not difficult to identify the beer stores. Outside each one I could see the bodies of men too drunk to stand, some leaning like dolls against the walls, some simply lying flat on their backs on the sidewalk. Business appeared to be brisk, for there were plenty of customers stepping over these fallen men as they came and went.

This shameful place has not always been part of Nebraska. In 1882, at the urging of the Oglala Lakota leaders and the Indian agent, a buffer zone of fifty square miles was annexed from Nebraska and added to the southern edge of the Pine Ridge Agency precisely to protect the reservation from the incursions of illegal whiskey peddlers. However, in 1904, President Theodore Roosevelt, despite Oglala protests, placed forty-nine of the fifty square miles into the public domain, precipitating a land grab and undermining the original purpose of the buffer zone. Since then Whiteclay has had a sordid and violent history. In the late 1990s a campaign was mounted to have the liquor licenses revoked, but it proved unsuccessful. In 2010, a new state law authorized a grant of $10,000, hardly a fortune, to pay for increased patrols by local sheriffs with the aim of improving law enforcement and reducing violence

5. Paul Hammel, "Grant to Boost Whiteclay Patrols," *Omaha World-Herald*, 22 Dec. 2010.

in Whiteclay.[6] If these measures have been effective, it has gone unreported.

There have been accusations that the beer retailers have violated state liquor laws by selling beer to minors and intoxicated persons, selling beer to bootleggers who resell it on the reservation, allowing beer to be drunk on the premises, and exchanging beer for sexual favors. But even if none of these accusations had any substance—and there have been no prosecutions to date—the beer business in Whiteclay remains horribly and cynically predatory, the free market at its ugliest.

I drove through as quickly as I could.

Harrison, Nebraska

Nebraska is one of the twelve states fortunate enough to boast a Harrison among its towns, and while I was in the vicinity, staying at a bed and breakfast outside Crawford, I could hardly miss the opportunity to make a visit. Compared with Harrison, South Dakota, the Nebraska version is a veritable metropolis, claiming a population of 291 on its town sign. In fact this figure was out of date, because its population was 279 at the 2000 census and had probably dropped since then. However, it could claim without challenge to be Nebraska's "Top Town" by virtue of having the highest elevation of any town in the state at 4,876 feet (or thereabouts, for I have since seen a variety of figures quoted for its elevation).

When I drove into town it was raining heavily, a contingency for which I was foolishly unprepared, lacking even an umbrella. I drove up and down Main Street and admired several handsome buildings, including a substantial courthouse dating from 1930 that seemed to be out of all proportion to the size of the place until I recalled that Harrison was the county seat of Sioux County. Among other larger establishments was the Harrison Hotel, dating from 1888, and painted an arresting shade of green.

The rain cast a sense of gloom over the place, a false impression, perhaps, but one that seemed to be reinforced by the number of stores and businesses that were closed, including Sioux Sundries and its Country

6. "Sheridan County Sheriff's Office Gets $10,000 to Patrol Whiteclay," *Lincoln Journal Star*, 20 Dec. 2010.

Basket Café, famous for its two-pound hamburger, which had been invented to satisfy the appetites of local ranchers. Also closed, to my great disappointment, was the local museum, which looked so neglected I wondered if its doors had been permanently locked up. A young woman walked by and I asked her if it ever opened; she assured me it did, but not until the summer. Seeing that I was downcast, she asked if I would like to look instead at her collection of "skins." I must have registered some bewilderment at this offer because she added that she was the owner of the Longhorn Bar down the street and that was where she kept them. Though none the wiser, I could not resist the offer.

Making our way through the rain, we walked a few doors down to her bar, where she opened the door to reveal a room full of people of all ages, most of them eating. It seemed she had a monopoly on the town's fine dining, or any kind of dining, because I noticed that another café across the street was also closed.

"There they are," she said, pointing upwards, and sure enough, pinned to the wall close to the ceiling was a long line of rattlesnake skins. "I've got antelope heads as well," she said proudly, pointing them out. I asked how she obtained her skins, and she said, "Once I announced it would make kind of a nice decoration people just brought 'em in." She went hunting for them herself as well.

Before I could study the menu, she said, "I'd recommend the burger." I ordered a cheeseburger. What sort of chips would I like: barbecue, plain, or chili? I chose barbecue. Looking round the place while waiting, I noticed that her recommendation was rhetorical since everyone was eating the same thing. A man came in looking as if he had stepped off the set of a western, for he was wearing boots, blue jeans, and a long oilskin slicker. In authentic cowboy style, he tipped his hat to greet the assembled company and rainwater coursed out of the gutter of its brim. This was cattle country.

Fort Robinson, Crawford, Nebraska

After lunch in Harrison I drove to Fort Robinson. I had wanted to visit the place for its own sake and its associations with Crazy Horse, but they were now enhanced by the loyalty to his name shown by my guide at Wounded Knee.

Crazy Horse is the Oglalas' great hero for good reason. He took part in two notable Sioux victories over the United States Army, the Fetterman Massacre of 1866 and the Battle of the Little Big Horn in June 1876, in which he played a leading role. Though never defeated in battle, he was forced to surrender in May 1877, bringing his people to the Red Cloud Agency near Fort Robinson. Four months later, under circumstances that remain confused, he was killed in the fort as soldiers attempted to imprison him. His body was given to his parents, who took it to Camp Sheridan about thirty-five miles to the east and placed it on a burial scaffold. The following month, they moved it to an undisclosed location, and to this day his final resting place remains unknown.

It was still raining heavily when I arrived at the fort, and I was confined to its museum, which was housed in a handsome old building. Before looking at the exhibits, I watched a potted history on video of the fort from the 1870s to the modern period, when it had been used as a dog-training facility and a prisoner-of-war camp, an interlude depicted with footage of jolly Germans mugging for the camera. During the video's account of the 1890s I was surprised to hear the gung-ho commentary refer to Wounded Knee as a "battle."

I then went upstairs to look at the exhibits. Though it was true that the troops at Fort Robinson had played no part in the Battle of the Little Big Horn, I was again surprised to see that the various display boards, arranged in rough chronological order, maintained a chaste silence on the subject of Custer's debacle, in which Crazy Horse had played a decisive part.

The same could not be said of Wounded Knee, in which Fort Robinson's troops also played no direct role, for a whole panel had been devoted to it. Displayed behind glass on a large board was a ghost shirt, with no explanation of its provenance, though it looked suspiciously new, together with a Springfield rifle that had been picked up at the "battleground," and a couple of small items on the contribution of Fort Robinson troops to its aftermath. The exhibit also contained a reproduction of a page from a letter, perhaps written by a soldier stationed at the fort, under the heading "Our Special Reports from Indian Country— Correspondence of the Army and Navy Journal, Pine Ridge Agency." I assumed a soldier stationed on the fort had written it, though there was no caption to say so; nor was a date supplied. In part, the letter read as follows: "Troops should not be concentrated at our expense without some action, and the cost should be taken out [of] the allowance for the Indians." Another section read, "The ghost shirts now being brought in are spectural [*sic*] things. Some old hag has got on to it and is making imitations for sale, and not the original ones worn and hallowed by use." I take this to be sarcastic, and I assume that the "old hag" in question was an Indian woman. "These Indians are children," the letter continued, "and need spanking, but the Great Father in Washington is treating them like men—which they cannot appreciate and never could."

I searched the surrounding exhibits for an account of the massacre or a broader narrative to explain these items, which were both baffling and insulting, and put them in their historical context—this was, after all, a museum—but I could see nothing of the sort. The display could have been assembled in 1891. If this was what an educational establishment had to offer students and tourists, it was not surprising that American Indians were, at best, misunderstood and, at worst, despised.

Crawford, Nebraska

That night I ate dinner at The Ranch House in Crawford, whose neon sign promised, "Steaks and Spirits. It Sizzles." I ordered a New York Strip, and the waitress asked me if I would like it cooked medium or well done; I asked for it to be cooked rare, and she look apprehensive. When she brought my plate, she didn't put it down on the table but told me anxiously that if I wanted my steak cooked more she'd take it straight back. I told her it looked fine. Before I could take a mouthful, the cook herself appeared and offered to give it a few more minutes in the pan. I persuaded them to let me have a taste. It was excellent and I said so, though I don't think I was believed.

The restaurant was located in a barn of a building that also accommodated a separate bar. I noticed it had a tin ceiling that appeared to be in good condition, and I asked the waitress about its history. Among many monographs I will not be writing, but wish someone would, is a history of the tin ceiling, an American phenomenon that brought grandeur to buildings all over the West. My waitress told me that the place had originally been built as two stores, one of them a hardware store, while its basement had served as a mortuary and crematorium. The ovens, she said darkly, were still there. A previous owner, who had lived in the apartment above, had been regularly bothered by ghosts. "She just used to tell them to hush down," the waitress said, but after a while they became too intrusive and the lady had sold the building.

Rapid City

Now and again the best planned trip hits a slack stretch, and the toughest-minded traveler suffers a touch of homesickness. So it was with me when one morning I found myself in downtown Rapid City, feeling downcast and purposeless. Not even the sight of a bronze, life-size version of President Benjamin Harrison, looking wise and caring and by no means regretful about his profligate awarding of Medals of Honor, was enough to restore my morale. He was sitting on a bronze bench, feeding birdseed to a trio of bronze house sparrows, at the corner of Main and Fourth Street. Four blocks away, his ancestor, William Henry Harrison (ninth President, 1841), could be seen perched on a pedestal and costumed in a flowing cape; a general's cocked hat, decorated with feathers, was on his lap and a sword at his side.

These great men, together with their presidential colleagues, now populate the center of Rapid City, which calls itself, with some justification, the City of the Presidents. The area is rich in presidents: not only do Borglum's four heads keep their noble vigil on the mountain top, but there is a Presidents Park near Lead, where the free-standing heads of all forty-three presidents, molded from white Portland cement and standing sixteen or twenty feet tall, are distributed around the park. From the park's website ("Where History Meets Art, And Art Makes History"), it would appear that these monoliths owe something to the Rushmore tradition, insofar as they are super-sized busts. Unfortunately, the park was temporarily closed, so I was unable to pay my respects and study them face to face, as it were.

Rapid City has committed itself to an ambitious project, with forty-two presidents (Barack Obama is yet to be installed) disposed on nearly all the corners of the Streets from Fourth to Ninth that intersect Main Street and St. Joseph Street. The styles vary; a few are cast in heroic postures, but most are presented in casual and homely scenarios. Among the moderns, Richard Nixon is exceptional, for he sits, statesmanlike, on a Chinese chair, but Warren Harding is shown with his dog. Harry Truman holds up the newspaper that wrongly reported him the loser in his 1948 election; William McKinley has a telephone to his ear; Ronald Reagan grins in cowboy clothes; Jimmy Carter waves genially to someone in the distance; John Kennedy holds the hand of his son John, and so on. In other words, by contrast with Mount Rushmore, this is a collective vision of democracy that makes power approachable. Rapid City's bronze presidents, so far from demanding veneration, loiter on the sidewalk with the rest of us. As the city's website puts it, with a sly dig at Mount Rushmore, "Whether you're enjoying downtown shopping, dining, or other attractions, you can enjoy these sculptures free."

Enjoying my own chance of gratis democratic comradeship, I sat for a moment with President Harrison and his sparrows, but then the rain began to fall, driving me to seek more sensual consolation for my low spirits in the shape of lunch. One of the curiosities, at least in my mind, of Manifest Destiny is that so many immigrants to the West seemed to forget their culinary traditions and resign themselves to the lowest common denominator of the frying pan or griddle, with a meaty menu restricted to chicken, burger, and steak. It is true that if an atlas of cooking was designed according to a projection that gave prominence to the great culinary countries, those of northern Europe would be dwarfishly diminished compared with France and Italy, to say nothing of their north African neighbors on the other side of the Mediterranean. However, that does not mean that such countries as Germany, Denmark, Ireland, Holland, and—dare I say it—Britain, from which so many immigrants came, did not have their own modest cooking customs, which they might have transported with them when they made their homes on the prairies. But it seems not to have been the case. Just as my acquaintances in Harrison, South Dakota, had no real interest in their Dutch ancestors, they had none in their culinary heritage either. In 1992, Sally and I visited a dairy factory in Wisconsin where we observed a master cheese maker proudly demonstrate his skills by methodically extracting every last trace of flavor from something that was marketed as Edam. "Cheese," he declared, "doesn't get any milder than this." I have been lucky enough to eat in many of these northern countries and have always been wonderfully surprised by their national and local dishes, especially in Germany. But in the course of emigration, what became of the fifteen hundred different types of sausage for which Germany is still famous? On American soil, a mass extinction seems to have taken place, leaving a single survivor, the bratwurst.

I would love to be corrected on this score, but my experience of cooking west of the Missouri River, which, admittedly, has been based on eating out rather than in people's homes, has so far has led me to believe that only the Italians have broken the monopoly of the burger/steak. Thus it was that when I saw the Botticelli Ristorante Italiano on Main Street, shortly after bidding farewell to Benjamin Harrison, I did not hesitate to enter. I ordered a delicious plate of manicotti ($8.95) and a revivifying glass of Chianti.

After lunch, I decided to go in search of a rainproof coat. I sought advice from my waitress in Botticelli's, and she told me to go to Scheels on the outskirts of town near the Rushmore (what else?) Mall. The name Scheels meant nothing to me, and I was therefore amazed to find myself in an enormous sporting-goods store with a selection of outdoor clothing that would have protected me in any weather condition on the globe, from the Arctic to the Amazon. Captain Scott would have been snug in his tent if he had shopped at Scheels.

But clothing was the least of it, for this place was stocked to cater for the hunter's every need. I looked down the main aisle and saw signs for archery, cycling, footwear, hunting, exercise, fishing, and, of course, guns. In the archery section I noticed that the bow had evolved into something that would be quite unrecognizable to either Robin Hood or Crazy Horse. There was no sign of stout old English yew, for these bows were made of steel, and their design bore no resemblance to the longbow that proved so lethal at Agincourt. They were more machines than weapons, complex killing contraptions incorporating wires and wheels, and one look at them would have left the wicked sheriff of Nottingham begging for mercy.

For some reason, explicable only in terms of the lunacy that overcomes helpless consumers in skillfully designed stores, I was entranced by the so-called cutlery section, where a dozen racks of glittering blades were displayed, as well as some fancy samurai swords and axes secured in a locked cabinet. For $49.99, I could have bought a Scorpion Stinger, which I took to be a kind of homicidal Frisbee made of shiny metal and equipped with pincer-shaped blades—the "stingers." There were knives for every possible function, from skinning a moose or butchering a bear to gutting a fish, from whittling a stick "just like your old grandpappy" (not mine) to chopping down small trees.

Before I could decide which of these utterly essential tools to purchase, I strayed into the gun department. It occupied a good quarter of the store's considerable floor space, and I found myself in a world for which there was no parallel in English culture. Pheasants are shot in England, and in Scotland grouse and deer are shot ("stalked"), but British and American approaches to hunting are quite different.

For many years, I lived on a shooting estate where pheasants were hand-fed by a gamekeeper during spring and summer and then shot in autumn as "game." But these birds were not hunted in the midwestern style. They were driven by "beaters" out of the woods (their cozy home for the last six months) into open ground, where the "guns" stood in a line across a field waiting to shoot them as they took to the air, often for the first time in their lives.

If I sound cynical, it is because I know just how tame these creatures can grow during the spring and summer, when they are virtual pets. A cock pheasant, a magnificent popinjay in his finest mating colors, wandered from our landlord's wood into our garden one April and was soon persuaded to eat from my hand. By mid-summer the stupid creature was so domesticated that he would perch clumsily on my knee to peck from my palm. Clearly, when the time came, it would not require much sporting skill to bag him.[7] In those days I used to write occasionally for *The Times* (of London), and when in October this inevitable slaughter occurred, I persuaded the obituary-page editor to carry a respectful tribute to my bird's doomed career—a journalistic first, I believe.

In England most shooting for "game" (pheasant, partridge, grouse, ptarmigan) is conducted on private land; it is an amusement for the

---

7. I believe that modern, hand-reared pheasants in Britain are now so well fed and so well protected by their zealous gamekeepers that they are losing the ability to fly, a skill for which they have no need, except on their last bloody day.

rich, confined to big estates where the birds are reared at considerable expense by gamekeepers, and the land is specially prepared for the autumn "drives." If you wanted to become a member ("gun") of a syndicate that shot on an estate in Norfolk, for instance, where some of the best shooting is to be had, you could expect to pay $1,000 a day, and that would only buy you the chance to stand in a field beside a dozen other guns, with perhaps a free glass of sloe gin inside you.

Thus, a distinction can be made between shooting, as described above, and hunting, which does not take place in England, at least legally, in any sense comparable to its American counterpart. We have no tradition of hunting (old-fashioned country poaching by the poor is a different matter), and it is one of the great unnoticed differences between our two countries, or at any rate between Britain and those parts of the United States where hunting is a passion for so many people.

American attitudes toward gun ownership are a form of madness in the eyes of the British, among whom guns—rifles and shotguns—are only possessed by so-called sportsmen and criminals. Owning a handgun for personal protection, apart from being illegal, is unthinkable in Britain, and for that matter in most of Europe. We do not even share with Italy and France the tradition of shooting wild birds, apart from pigeons, which hardly count, and although our countryside abounds with deer of various species, they are not hunted, despite the damage they do to farms and gardens. Hunting is simply not in our blood. Indeed, the term carries a different meaning in Britain, where "to go hunting" would be understood by most people as riding a horse in a scarlet coat while pursuing a fox with a pack of hounds—an activity that has recently been made illegal.

In Britain, hunting (deer) and shooting (game birds) have always been associated with privilege and private land. There could hardly be a greater contrast with the American tradition, which derives from the days when people hunted out of necessity and had at their disposal a wilderness rich in game where the notion of trespassing and poaching were meaningless. The frontier may have closed long ago, but what I saw in the gun department of Scheels was the outcome of a history very different from the one that produced my tame and foolish cock pheasant.

Pointing to a particularly gross gun, a kind of modern blunderbuss,

I said to an assistant, "you could shoot an elephant with that thing." She said, quite seriously, "Are you interested in big game weaponry? We fit out many hunters who go to Africa." I broke it to her that I wasn't planning a safari, at least not this year, and then asked her what the regulations were for buying a weapon in South Dakota. She said, a little apologetically, that they were obliged to check your identity—your social security number, driver's license—but assuming they checked out, you could leave the store with your weapon under your arm.

Hill City

Hill City, for those of us who remembered it from the 1990s, was a different kind of town in 2011, a fact I realized the moment I opened my car door after parking on Main Street. As in Deadwood, my ears were bewitched by piped music playing up and down the street—Bach, no less.

On Main Street, I went looking for a new and used bookstore of which I had fond memories. It was housed in a building that claimed to be the oldest hand-hewn log commercial building in South Dakota. The owner, a bearded, bespectacled old man in bib and braces, was knowledgeable about his large stock, which comprehended most aspects of western history. His store was a civilized spot in an unlikely location, a little oasis of culture in what was in those days uncivilized territory. It came as a shock, therefore, to find that its shop sign took the form of a hanging man a life-size effigy of a cowboy dangling at the end of a creaking noose.

I discovered that the hanging man had been laid to rest and the bookshop replaced by a restaurant, Desperados, which promised "Real Fine Western Food." Standing on its roof, where the gallows had previously been installed, was a life-size plaster model of a large bay horse, which presided benignly over the premises, symbolizing the town's newfound gentility.

I walked a few doors down the street to the Black Hills Institute of Geological Research, where I had arranged to meet its president, Peter Larson. Since 1974, the institute has been digging up all sorts of fossil bones in South Dakota and elsewhere, most famously a Tyrannosaurus rex, nicknamed Stan after the person who made the discovery. Dating from the Late Cretaceous period, it was excavated in Harding County,

201

South Dakota, and proved to be the most complete example of its species yet found. Thanks to the circumstances in which it had been buried 65 million years ago, the skull was discovered in a state of near perfect preservation.

Larson kindly escorted me round his museum, which contained Stan's original remains, now reconstructed in a classic upright pose, its mouth gaping open to show its formidable teeth. Larson took me to his workshop where his staff was at work on a reconstruction of another T. rex, this one bound for a museum in China. Its tail had been severed, probably by disease, giving it an oddly top-heavy look. Larson encouraged me to touch its thigh bone. He said, "You can tell your friends that you've touched a real T. rex." I did as he suggested, and informed my friends at the first opportunity.

He then took me to another building, his warehouse, a large place that contained hundreds of wooden cases loaded with bones and labeled "femurs," "skulls," "vertebrae," "teeth," and so forth. Shelves stacked with more fragile bones wrapped in foil and plaster cast lined the walls. These bones were his stock, from which he drew whenever a museum placed an order, and I was astounded by the sheer quantity of his collection.

Since visiting Harrison, I had been eager to visit the institute and look at its fossils, for they were the ones I had mentioned to Steve, my pastor friend, over our lunch, the bones that surely could not be reconciled with "God's infallible written Word . . . the supreme and final authority in all matters on which it speaks."[8] I asked Larson if the implications of his work were ever challenged by visiting Christians, but he brushed my question aside, saying that it happened occasionally but argument was impossible with such people. Standing in his fossil warehouse, surrounded by fossilized material piled from floor to ceiling, I could see that discussion between two positions so distant from each other was out of the question. It was not as if the institute had dug up the odd bone that might give a biblical fundamentalist pause for thought; these paleontologists were digging up fossils from a huge span of geological time—or the sixth day, as Genesis would have it.

8. "The Church at Harrison," http://harrisonsd.com/southchurch.htm.

I thanked Larson for his time. After we'd said goodbye, I looked round the gift shop attached to the museum, and bought his *Fossil Replica Catalog*, which I took with me to study when I went for dinner that evening at Desperados. The owner, Dan Dickey, a dapper, silver-haired man in jeans, boots, and a leather waistcoat, who was an émigré from Minnesota, showed me the menu. He and his wife had completely renovated the place in a style that could only be called cowboy chic. For example, the shades on the lamps overhanging the tables were in the shape of Stetson hats, but these were Stetsons made of pottery, each one individually molded at great expense. I asked him if he'd ever seen his premises in the days of the bookstore and its hanging man. Not only had he never seen the effigy, he'd never heard of it, and I don't think he entirely believed me, so I promised to send him a photograph.

Despite some disconcerting items on the menu—for instance, "Desperados Own Spaghetti Western, $10.99, Served over pasta but not Italian!"—the food was indeed "real fine," especially the sweet potato fries, which were a novelty to me. While eating my BBQ Bunkhouse Pork Ribs, I turned to the fossils catalog and discovered that for a trifling $100,000 I could purchase my own full size T. rex replica. It seemed cheap to me, especially with a waiting time of only six months. In the spirit of romance, I could purchase a mate for him by spending $90,000 on Bucky, a female T. rex, with an extraordinarily complete gastralia basket (belly ribs) and the third most complete tail of any T. rex known. Those with more modest budgets could place an order for the foot of Stan, the T. rex, for a mere $1,750. And this was just the T. rex section. To grace your home, you could have a Gorgosaurus, Velociraptor, Oviraptor, Triceratops, Stegosaurus, or Brachylophosaurus, to say nothing of reptiles, sloths, saber-toothed cats, and mollusks, all at reasonable prices, mounted and displayed in poses of your choice. If you simply couldn't make up your mind, you could opt for the "Rent-A-Rex" Lease Program.[9]

Crazy Horse Memorial

For those who have never seen it, or even a picture of it, the Crazy Horse Memorial is a mountain carving planned on a scale that leaves the

9. *BHI Fossil Replica Catalog 2011* (Hill City, S.Dak.: Black Hills Institute, 2011).

Mount Rushmore presidential heads, twenty miles away, looking like pygmies. When finished, the monument will depict the Oglala Lakota leader seated bare-chested on his horse with his arm outstretched and finger pointing; the head, neck, and a galloping leg of his horse will also be hewn out of the rock. Furthermore, unlike puny Rushmore's bas relief, it will be carved (dynamited) in the round. To illustrate the sheer scale of this rival to Borglum's more famous work, one statistic will do the job: his four Rushmore heads would together fit into the head of Crazy Horse, a nice metaphorical idea in itself. (Two more statistics: when completed, the statue will be 563 feet high and 641 feet long.)

When I last saw the memorial in 1994, work was proceeding on the head, or rather the face, which was a vast featureless shield of rock. The only parts of the sculpture that had been completed were the upper surface of the outstretched arm and a hole that would ultimately serve as the space beneath the figure's armpit. The arm, which would eventually be 263 feet in length, served as a working platform, and I had the good fortune to stand there while men in hard hats drove up and down in vehicles carrying the explosives and drilling equipment used in "carving" the mountain. As for the rest of the statue, it consisted of no more than a profile of the horse's head marked out in paint on the mountainside. The project got under way in 1947, and on the basis of progress achieved over forty-five years, I prophesied that once the face had been blasted into shape the owners would probably put down their tools and abandon their folly.

How wrong I was! Even before I had driven down the Avenue of the Chiefs to the memorial's main entrance, I could see from the road (another free view) that the carving had been transformed during the last seventeen years: the face was now fully modeled, and even the horse's head was beginning to emerge. Completion of this titanic enterprise no longer seemed a foolish boast.

The genius behind the Crazy Horse carving was the self-taught Korczak Ziolkowski. He was employed briefly on Mount Rushmore in 1939, but sacked by Borglum, who described him as a "pseudo sculptor."[10] None-

---

10. John Taliaferro, *Great White Fathers: The Story of the Obsessive Quest to Create Mount Rushmore* (New York: Public Affairs, 2002), p. 327.

theless, Ziolkowski's stint on the mountain seems to have given him a taste for the gargantuan, to which he applied truly heroic efforts. For more than five years, he climbed 741 steps up a wooden staircase carrying a jackhammer on his back in order to blast bits out of the mountain top. Following his death in 1982, the work has been carried on by his widow, the indomitable Ruth, and their ten children, all of whom seem to have dedicated themselves to the family crusade by slaving on, or for the memorial. The family has proved skillful in running the tourist organization that supports their ongoing labor of Hercules, attracting more than a million visitors a year to stand on the viewing veranda and witness the explosions that are gradually shaping the colossus.

The mountain carving is based on a detailed maquette, several times life-size, that is prominently displayed at the back of the veranda and allows you to compare the projected work with the carving in progress. This maquette, a finished sculpture in its own right, is made of marble and is uncompromisingly and dazzlingly white, which hardly seems appropriate to its subject. Fortunately, the granite now exposed on the mountain by dynamite is turning out to be a subdued grayish-brown.

According to the memorial's publicity, the sculpture is not intended to be a "lineal" likeness—there is, in any case, no authenticated photograph or drawing of Crazy Horse—but more a memorial to his spirit. Visitors are informed that his left hand is thrown out as he answers a derisive question put to him by a white trader after the Battle of the Little Big Horn. "Where are your lands now?" the man asked. Crazy Horse's memorable (and apocryphal?) reply was "My lands are where my dead lie buried."[11] Now he points towards them with what will be his thirty-three-foot-long index finger.

Ziolkowski always claimed that he was invited by the Lakotas to make his sculpture in the Black Hills, despite the fact that the Hills were sacred and excursions into them by miners and gold diggers had been partly responsible for causing the Great Sioux War. The invitation came from Chief Henry Standing Bear, and a copy of his letter is displayed at the visitor center. In a way it represented a compromise because his brother

11. Robb DeWall, *Korczak, Storyteller in Stone: Boston to Crazy Horse, September 6, 1908–October 20, 1982* (Crazy Horse, S.Dak.: Korczak's Heritage, Inc., 1986), p. 26.

Luther Standing Bear had previously approached Borglum. In 1931, writing from California, where he was working as an actor in westerns, Luther Standing Bear thanked Borglum for the supplies he had recently sent to Pine Ridge and then suggested that it "would be most fitting to have the face of Crazy Horse" sculpted on Mount Rushmore as the only Indian "worthy to place by the side of Washington and Lincoln."[12] Borglum never responded, though he did campaign for better conditions on Pine Ridge.

By 1939, Standing Bear's brother Henry had despaired of seeing Crazy Horse's head as a fifth sculpture on Mount Rushmore and decided to approach Ziolkowski, who had just won an award at the New York World's Fair with his outsize bust of Jan Paderewski, the pianist and prime minister of Poland. He wrote a letter, which reads in part, "a number of my fellow chiefs and I are interested in finding some sculptor who can carve a head of an Indian chief who was killed many years ago." (Some head! It will be 87½ feet high, with a 44-foot feather rising vertically from the top of its skull; Washington's head is 60 feet high.) "This is to be entirely an Indian project under my direction," Standing Bear continued. "This is a matter of long standing in my mind which must be brought before the public soon." The visitors' center at the memorial claims that Standing Bear wrote another letter, in which he stated, "My fellow chiefs and I would like the white man to know the red man has heroes too," but the original has been lost. (Or "lost," as John Taliaferro cynically reported it.[13])

It has never been clear exactly who Henry Standing Bear represented when he made his request, or who his "fellow chiefs" were. He may have been speaking for his immediate family, since he was a cousin to Crazy Horse, and his sister, Black Shawl, had been one of Crazy Horse's wives. Nor is it clear that Standing Bear and his chiefs wanted an entire mountain turned into their "head." Ziolkowski always claimed that the enterprise was for the benefit of the Lakotas (no American Indian is ever knowingly charged an entrance fee to the memorial), but it did not meet with their unanimous approval. John Lame Deer, who wrote so scath-

12. Quoted in Taliaferro, *Great White Fathers*, p. 322.
13. Ibid., p. 329.

ingly about Mount Rushmore, was predictably cynical. Of Ziolkowski, he wrote memorably that if a white man "says he wants to do something for us. . . . it's time for us Indians to run," and he was in no doubt that Ziolkowski and his family were interested in making money.[14] Lame Deer likened the feather on the statue's head to an air valve sticking out of a tire, and he said it looked as if the chief's arm was pointing the way to the men's room. "The whole idea of making a beautiful wild mountain into a statue of [Crazy Horse] is a pollution of the landscape. It is against the spirit of Crazy Horse," wrote Lame Deer.[15]

John Taliaferro shared Lame Deer's cynicism, writing that the Ziolkowski family is "not so much *erecting* a monument as they are digging a hole in the sky in which to bury Crazy Horse. When and if the Ziolkowskis ever finish their gargantuan excavation, that's when we'll know that Crazy Horse is actually dead. . . . Ruth Ziolkowski and her children are already mining a mother lode of tourists, the precious metal of the new Black Hills."[16] What John Lame Deer might also have written is that, if the maquette is faithfully reproduced, the final work will be a pollution in both the environmental and the aesthetic sense, for it will be horribly ugly. This was not an opinion I would have voiced as I stood on the Viewing Veranda and watched the dynamite gouge yet another lump of flesh out of the mountainside because, to my surprise, the majority of people standing with me were American Indians, large numbers of them, and they appeared to be treating the memorial as patriots treat Mount Rushmore—with reverence. They were judging the sculpture, not so much as a work of art, as a shrine to one of the great figures in their history. Their numbers suggested that they were not troubled by its intrusiveness, still less by its promise of a hideous and vulgar outcome.

Out in the parking lot, I searched in vain for my car. I had forgotten where I had parked it, but, worse, I couldn't remember anything about it, except its color—maroon. Although there were a great many maroon

---

14. John Lame Deer and Richard Erdoes, *Seeker of Visions: The Life of a Sioux Medicine Man* (New York: Washington Square Press, 1976), p. 95.

15. Ibid., p. 96.

16. Taliaferro, *Great White Fathers*, p. 410.

cars to choose from, I had no memory of the make of the vehicle I had rented (actually a Nissan), for the sad fact is that I am car blind. Losing my car was hardly a new experience, and I knew that my only chance of locating it was to whistle it up like a dog by activating the key. Running up and down the rows of cars in a state of increasing hysteria, I finally heard my faithful steed neighing to me as its locking system released itself. I could have kissed its steely flank.

All solo travel, even the least intrepid, involves an act of defiance, an assumption of power over your own destiny, and these sensations are wonderfully enhanced by the use of the automobile, which becomes a kind of destination in itself. To cover my 3,000 miles required many hours of unavoidably tedious driving, and in the process my car assumed a significance considerably in excess of its function. While it remained a constant in an ever-shifting universe, it also acquired a magically protean capacity for assuming different forms. It was not only my trusty charger and beast of burden—my Rocinante—but it also became my mobile headquarters, base camp, supplies wagon, and security compound.[17] It was my partner, companion, and servant, my source of entertainment and information, my unfailing collaborator. It was the Nautilus in which I wandered the world like Captain Nemo, stateless and autarkic, observing the strange depths of a foreign sea through the glass windows of my craft.

Spearfish Canyon

I stayed in the Spearfish Canyon Lodge in the northern Black Hills, which gave me a chance to walk to Roughlock Falls and take innumerable photographs of bark peeling off the birch trees that lined the hiking trail. I also persuaded myself that I saw a golden eagle circling the sheer cliffs that frame the canyon, but it may well have been an unusually solitary turkey vulture passing itself off as a different species to mock

---

17. John Steinbeck called his camper truck "Rocinante" when he set off on the journey that gave him the material for his marvelous *Travels with Charley* (1962). The fate of the truck itself is recorded at http://www.campingandrving.com/roci nante_travels_with_charley.htm.

the ignorant tourist. The hotel quite rightly boasts about its surrounding scenery by quoting Frank Lloyd Wright on its brochure; visiting the place for the first time, the great man is alleged to have said, "How is it that I've heard so much about the Grand Canyon, when this is even more miraculous?" This may have been hyperbole, but the place is certainly beautiful.

I never approach a new hotel or lodging without experiencing a little pang of excitement, but as I unpacked my suitcase and set up my makeshift office for the seventh time on my trip, I also felt a touch of impatience with the whole business of traveling. My mood had not improved when I went downstairs to eat in the dining room and was made still worse by what I conceived as the dawdling manner of my waitress. I decided to time her to see how long it took her to carry my order from table to kitchen. It was 7:20 P.M. With mounting annoyance, I watched her stroll, not to the kitchen, but to the cash register where she served a guest who, after prolonged deliberation and several changes of mind, bought a postcard. At this moment another guest presented himself at the desk with his bill in his hand. She took his money, and the pair of them engaged in flirtatious banter, to the tune of my grinding teeth, as she hunted in the till for his change. My order still in her apron pocket, she then sauntered back across the dining room but paused at a table to clear a couple of plates. Finally, she took a last few leisurely paces and disappeared through the kitchen door. With the triumphant satisfaction of one who had a legitimate complaint, I looked at my watch. It was 7:23 P.M.

Spearfish

The town of Spearfish (population 10,494) was not looking its best because Main Street was undergoing major repairs. However, I was pleased to explore the so-called antique store in the Mathews Opera House block. I say "so-called" because in Britain the term "antique shop" generally indicates a place selling old things with pretensions to value at high prices, whereas the American antique store equates more to our idea of the old-fashioned junk shop. The term may sound insulting, but in fact it refers to a sorely missed feature of our high streets and villages.

When my wife and I first moved to Suffolk in the 1970s, several villages in our area had junk shops, whose stock was largely derived from what were known as house clearances, a phrase often painted on the livery of ancient vans that trundled round the countryside collecting the goods and chattels of people who had recently died. Having few possessions of our own, we were devotees of these places, where the stock had the great allure of being both cheap and stylish, at least in our eyes. We lived in a Victorian house, and though we could not afford expensive antiques of the period, we could fill it with objects that dated from an earlier age and seemed to have the virtue of superior design or eccentric character. These junk shops were repositories of rubbish, which like worthless gravel concealed rare nuggets of gold that could be uncovered by dint of determined mining.

We were fond of a particular shop owned by a Dickensian character who moldered in a back room of his broken-down house, struggling to keep warm in front of a coal fire, while allowing his customers to wander and rummage in his other rooms. Outside in the garden was a shanty town of sheds that had been erected to accommodate larger pieces of furniture—immovable pianos, vast sideboards, cupboards voluminous enough to live in, sofas that resembled small boats—all destined to rot and fall apart in the rain that fell through the leaking roofs. Most of his goods were unpriced, and you were required to take them to the great man's sanctum, where he would shrewdly nominate a figure according to his estimation of your prosperity. This ritual was never painful since he was not greedy and loved to make a sale. We practically furnished our home from this graveyard of junk, and even today, many homes later, the light bulbs that hang from our ceilings are softened by Edwardian shades made of pearly glass that we bought from our friend.

Everything in his ramshackle house was for sale with one exception, and that was a pair of handsome Victorian rocking horses, which stood in a window facing the street and acted as a kind of shop sign. These he would not sell at any price. People who did not know him would assume his refusal was a bargaining technique, and I have witnessed smooth-talking dealers offer him more and more money, going far beyond the most extravagant valuation in their desire to force a deal on this obdurate yokel, but for some reason that remained forever mysterious, he would not yield. In the end he was parted from his precious horses, but only after someone took the brutal expedient of smashing his window and stealing them.

As the years went by, these junk shops gradually disappeared. Now they are almost extinct, at any rate in the countryside, having been replaced by car-boot sales (the British equivalent of yard or garage sales), outdoor events that resemble fairs where people gather to sell their unwanted bits and pieces, and where collectors and dealers circle like vultures. I find them uncongenial, and perhaps out of nostalgia for the junk-hunting days of our early married life, I find myself much more at home in small-town American antique stores, which in some ways are respectable versions of those vanished junk shops.

Like so many of its kind, the antique store in Spearfish occupied extensive premises and overflowed with stock. The owner was seated at a desk near the door, and I asked her permission to look around. "Help yourself," she said, and I set off on an expedition that was in effect a survey of the midwestern house in the 1960s or 1970s, with a scattering of older items. The place was divided into sections that were rough equivalents of rooms in a typical home, kitchen, dining room, bedroom, and so on, and it might have served as a museum of domestic life if its goods had not been heaped up on every surface and tucked away in every corner and hung from every wall and stacked from floor to ceiling. While some prices took me by surprise, by and large they seemed to be reasonable—not cheap, but not exorbitant either. In my time I have been a keen collector of inexpensive glass, and I was particularly interested in a selection of what is known as depression glass, the pressed glass that was first manufactured before World War II in all sorts of fancy designs and colors. If I had an American home I would fill it with pale green and cobalt blue glass, and I could have made a start right there in Spearfish by purchasing as many plates, water glasses, jugs, and so forth as I needed, for there were shelves and shelves of the stuff to choose from.

When I had finished my tour of her wares, a good half hour later, I approached the owner once again and offered to go into partnership with her. She looked somewhat surprised but heard me out. I explained that shops like hers no longer existed in the United Kingdom, and if we shipped her stock to my home town and opened a store selling antique Americana, we would make our fortunes. I don't think she took me seriously, but she graciously chose to turn down my offer by thanking me and saying she was too old for an upheaval of that kind. Instead of the colonial-style dinner set in fluted jadeite glass that I had picked out to grace my imaginary residence, I was forced to leave her store with a small souvenir Coca-Cola glass ($5).

Sturgis

Famous for its motorcycle rally in August, Sturgis in May seemed to be twiddling its thumbs while waiting for the bikers to ride into town. Though the Dungeon Bar was open, a couple of restaurants on Main Street were closed along with several other stores, including Big Bad Bertha's Biker Bar; nor could I see a tattoo parlor that was open for business. I bought a T-shirt with a motorbike motif for my grandson and asked the storekeeper how long it would take me to drive to Pierre; she told me "a couple of hours, easy." I asked again at a gas station as I was filling up and was given much the same answer.

My journey east on South Dakota Highway 34 took me through Meade County and then for a few miles through Ziebach County, which makes up part of the Cheyenne River Indian Reservation and had the distinction in early 2011 of being the poorest county in the country. I crossed the Cheyenne River, and *three* hours after leaving Sturgis drove into Pierre, having traveled 175 miles across the most remote and underpopulated part of the state I had yet encountered.

Why had both my advisors underestimated the length of the journey by so much? They seemed law-abiding citizens and not the kind who were tacitly recommending that I exceed the sixty-five-miles-per-hour limit, which I had in fact slavishly respected with the use of cruise control. I could only conclude that they had both followed a natural inclination to foreshorten a journey that crossed so desolate a piece of land. Perhaps, by unconsciously contracting the gap between Sturgis and Pierre and eliding its controversial parts, they made their own position seem less isolated, less exposed to difficulties they could not solve.

Selby

On my way to Mobridge on U.S. Highway 83, I approached the town of Selby, whose sign declared it was "Home of the Lions" and claimed a population of 736 (though in fact the 2010 census recorded only 642 people). It suddenly appeared on the horizon of the otherwise empty prairie as a conglomeration of enormous silos and grain bins, a sure sign that the railway passed through, for there could be no other reason for its scale, or even existence. The map confirmed my guess, and the line was identified as part of the Burlington Northern Santa Fe Railroad.

I turned off the highway and found a small town with the usual cluster of residential streets and a single, wide main street representing the business district. The two sets of silos that I had seen from the road stood on either side of the rail track, dwarfing the rest of the town. These enormous installations did not seem to have brought much prosperity to the town, for many of the businesses and stores on Main Street were closed or empty.

It was a surprise to see that one of these buildings, a handsome red-brick, two-story edifice with a grand doorway, bore a painted sign saying "Opera House." A smaller sign below it said "Built 1908." I was taking a photograph of this incongruous institution when an old man, getting out of his car, asked me why I was doing so. Before I could answer, he said, "You're not going to put up our taxes, are you?" I reassured him and said I was interested in the building. "Do you want to see it? I'm not doing anything." He took me across the street, said hello to a woman working in an office, and opened the door to the auditorium, which he told me now served as a community hall. It was empty, apart from a small stage and a kind of platform over the door, on which two old movie projectors were displayed. It was a bleak, empty space, but the floor looked new, and I wondered if the building also served as a sports hall.

My new acquaintance told me it had once been the town's movie house, and he showed me a little booth with a glass window where tickets had been sold. He couldn't remember when a movie had last been shown there; it must have been a long time ago. Nor had he ever seen a theatrical production there, operatic or otherwise. The town had raised

213

a lot of money to fix the place up and make it waterproof, but it was still not used much, and the front of the building had been turned into offices for the mayor and council. My guide left me, and I stood alone for a moment in this abandoned palace of entertainment. No echoes of Verdi, Puccini, or Rossini could be heard, even by the most wishful visitor. Nor was it easy, despite the ticket booth and projectors, to imagine the town gathered here to watch movies. The place was now a shell, devoid of all theatrical ambience.

As I drove away, I wondered about this forsaken cultural outpost. Selby and its outlying community had presumably paid for their grandly named building, but what use had they originally intended to make of its enormous space? Did they stage amateur productions of operas and plays? Did they listen to lectures? Or did the railway bring professional productions to town, complete with props, costumes, scenery, special effects, and posters, to say nothing of divas, orchestra, and chorus? What an extraordinary experience it would have been for these farmers and shopkeepers to attend a performance of, say, *Tosca* or *Rigoletto* at a time when the only other way of hearing such music was through a gramophone or listening to a home-grown singer with an accompanist on an upright piano in someone's home.

By contrast, it only took the press of a button on the dashboard of my rented car to command the voices of Verdi's ill-fated lovers to entertain me with arias from *La Traviata*, my favorite opera. They sang *Un di felice* ("one happy day") as I bowled across the prairie in my private opera house. Where else could I have dueted with Pavarotti?

Mobridge

Having checked into my hotel room, I found this note on the table: "FOR YOUR CONVENIENCE We have place [*sic*] these clean, useable rags in your room to be used for cleaning your guns, drying your dogs, polishing your boots, etc. The towels and washcloths in the bathroom are reserved for personal use only. Thank You." The following morning, after breakfast when I met the hunters who were planning their campaign against the prairie dogs, I took the bridge that gave Mobridge its name and drove on U.S. Highway 12 across Lake Oahe, which should more accurately and less romantically be called a reservoir. There was no sign to indicate you had entered the Standing Rock Indian Reservation, but a few hundred yards down the road, the fact was confirmed by the presence of the inevitable casino, in this case the Grand River Casino. Just before the casino a sign directed me down a gravel road to the Sitting Bull Monument, which lay a mile or so away on a site it shared with the Sacagawea obelisk, overlooking the water.

This monument has a curious history. Sitting Bull had been buried in Fort Yates, North Dakota, not far from where he had been killed in 1890, but in 1953, some Mobridge citizens drove to his grave, dug up his remains, and brought them back to South Dakota. They kept the remains overnight in a funeral home while they dug a deep pit in a bluff overlooking the river just across from Mobridge. As soon as the hole was prepared the bones were interred, and to ensure they would never be returned to North Dakota, or removed to any other location, twenty tons of concrete were poured on top of them. Armed guards patrolled the site for several weeks. A month later there was a funeral service, and the vault was further sealed by a monumental bust carved by none other than our old friend Korczak Ziolkowski.[18]

The bust of Sitting Bull stands on a stone plinth and depicts the great chief holding a pipe, with a feather in his hair, and beads around his neck. Though clearly based on a famous photograph of Sitting Bull, it bears little resemblance to the man and is carved in a lumpish, monolithic style. But its position is splendid: the holy man, who was probably born close to the Grand River, looks out over the reservoir, and on a clear day, such as the one when I made my visit, his view extends far beyond the water.

The inscription on the plinth reads "Tatanka Iyotake, Sitting Bull, 1831–1890," and below it, scattered round the base, I found several little tributes that had surely been left by American Indians: some white sea shells, several bundles of herbs tied up with scarlet wool, a bead neck-

---

18. "Mobridge: The First 50 Years," *Mobridge Tribune*, 31 May 2006; Robb DeWall, *The Saga of Sitting Bull's Bones: The Unusual Story Behind Sculptor Korczak Ziolkowski's Memorial to Chief Sitting Bull* (Crazy Horse, S.Dak.: Korczak's Heritage, Inc., 1984); Friends of the Little Bighorn Battlefield, "Sitting Bull's Burials: A History," www.friendslittlebighorn.com/sittingbullsburials.htm.

lace, and an unopened packet of Marlboro cigarettes with an unused book of matches from a Best Western motel.

Despite Ziolkowski's ham-handed rendition of Sitting Bull's face, there was something affecting about this massive, solitary figure as it kept its vigil over territory that had been familiar to the great warrior. He had known what it was to suffer loss. During his lifetime, Sitting Bull saw the Great Sioux Reservation reduced to fragments as treaty after treaty was broken, but if Ziolkowski had been attempting to convey something of this in the expression he carved in 1953, he should have been commissioned to start again later when the Oahe Dam was installed. The stone Sitting Bull was forced to witness yet another deprivation for his people. As a result of flooding caused by the dam, the Cheyenne River and the Standing Rock reservations lost a total of 160,889 acres. These losses included the reservations' most valuable grazing land, most of their gardens and cultivated farm tracts, and nearly all their timber, wild fruit, and wildlife resources. Ninety percent of the timbered areas on both reservations was destroyed. More than 180 families, about 30 percent of the tribal population living on the Cheyenne River reservation, were forced to leave their homes.[19] In later years, a visitor asked why there were so few older Indians on the reservation and was told that the "old people had died of heartache" after the construction of the dam.[20]

After leaving the Sitting Bull Monument I decided to drive north over the border to North Dakota in order to visit Fort Yates, also on the Missouri and headquarters of the Standing Rock reservation. It was here that Sitting Bull had been buried before his bones had been hijacked to South Dakota.

As usual I underestimated the distance and found myself driving for more than an hour, but I didn't resent it, because I passed through some truly beautiful countryside: more rolling prairie with occasional buttes and ponds and creeks splitting the dry ground with their wrig-

19. Michael L. Lawson, *Dammed Indians Revisited: The Continuing History of the Pick Sloan Plan and the Missouri River Sioux* (Pierre: South Dakota State Historical Society Press, 2009).

20. Edward Lazarus, *Black Hills White Justice: The Sioux Nation versus the United States, 1775 to the Present* (New York, Harper Collins, 1991), p. 190.

gling courses—nothing I hadn't seen before, yet all of it seeming more lovely, perhaps because the sun shone, perhaps because it was continually changing in a way that ordinary prairie, whose name is monotony, does not.

The town of Fort Yates appeared to be a little more prosperous than those I'd seen on the Rosebud and Pine Ridge reservations, but then it was the tribal headquarters of the Standing Rock Sioux Tribe and county seat of Sioux County, both of which must have generated employment. My map said its population was 193 in 2000, but that was hard to believe. (Checking later, I found that its population had dropped to 184, according to the 2010 census.)

I found the old Sitting Bull burial place on the edge of the town near a pond. Marked by a large stone and a metal information panel, it contained a tactful, if puzzling reference to the removal of the remains: "He was laid to rest here and may have been disinterred in 1953 at the request of his family." At the bottom of the panel were some words supposedly spoken by Sitting Bull and they made melancholy reading:

> What treaty have the Lakota made with the white man that we have broken? Not one. What treaty have the white men ever made with us that they ever kept? Not one. When I was a boy the Lakota owned the world; they sent ten thousand men to battle; where are the warriors today? Who slew them? Where are our lands? Who owns them? What law have I broken? Is it wrong for me to love my own? Is it wicked for me because my skin is red? Because I am a Lakota; because I was born where my father lived; because I would die for my people and my country?

On the way back to Mobridge, I crossed a small creek that seemed to be shimmering or trembling, an effect caused by hundreds, possibly thousands of cliff swallows flying in and out of the bridge's opening. I stopped and attempted to take a photograph but only obtained a blur, with a few spots. I had seen these little birds under bridges before but never in such numbers. They flew fast, performing extraordinary aerobatics, and never seemed to crash into each other, despite the tight space in which they were congested. If they were catching insects, their prey was too small for me to see, and in any case their behavior seemed to have a social purpose, because they weren't flying to and from their nests—little mud pouches attached to the walls of the bridge—but were continually circling and zigzagging while emitting their high-pitched shrieking calls.

Back on the outskirts of Mobridge, I thought I'd try my luck with lunch in the Grand River Casino. Built in the style of a log cabin, if hugely and lavishly expanded, this casino was more civilized than the Rosebud Casino near Valentine, and although smoking was permitted, the atmosphere was breathable. There also appeared to be a much more even ratio of white to Indian gamblers in front of the slot machines. A sign propped on the bar said, "If you are visibly intoxicated you will not be served." I ordered a buffalo burger with the usual trimmings ($8.95), and it was excellent.

My last visit of the day was to the Klein Museum in Mobridge. The volunteer in charge of selling tickets told me in a schoolmarm's tone that after I'd looked through the main room there were four more buildings to look at. I could hardly believe her since the first room was laid out like a small town. Walking down the central aisle, I passed a doctor's surgery, a dentist's surgery, a lawyer's office, a barber's shop, a trapper's shack, a beauty salon, a telephone exchange, a general store, and an optometrist's shop, as well as a house laid out in its various parts: kitchen, parlor, and bedroom. All these displays were so fully stocked they appeared to be ready for immediate use, and in case they were lacking some vital element, there were additional collections in reserve of typewriters, gramophones, early radios, dolls, glassware, and so on. I was taken with a small collection of hats made of pheasant feathers, especially a cute little beret. Don't ask me why.

The schoolmarm had not exaggerated. Sure enough, outside the main hall, arranged around a garden, was another small town: a school, a post office, and a fully furnished two-story residence with its own privy. I wandered around the house, which was enviably designed and appointed. Upstairs, there were two bedrooms (no bathroom), one for the children, represented by a pair of dolls, and one for the adults, represented by a plastic mannequin dressed in period clothing: white shoes, a white hat reminiscent of a lamp shade, and a black silk frock decorated with white spots that I knew Sally would have coveted. Wearing scarlet lipstick and a dreamy look on her lovely face, Mom was posed with a distinct backward lean, as if about to collapse on the bed after one too many cocktails—and to hell with the kids.

After dinner that night I returned to the river, which was made accessible by a dirt road and cycle path that ran along the bank for a mile or so. There was a residential strip above, but the houses were set well back and separated from the water by the railway track that also followed the bank. By now it was growing dark, and the sky was gathering itself for a fine sunset. I parked my car and walked the length of the road, taking photographs in the dwindling light of the river, the clouds, the little beaches, the trees with their feet in the water, of the bridge in the distance. Finally I came to the end of the road—in more senses than one. My journey was over. And, seeming to make the point, a spur of the railway track eerily crossed the road and ran straight towards the river, as though to plunge into the water, stopped only at the very edge by a buffer. I had begun my trip with the Missouri at Yankton on the southern border of South Dakota, and now I was ending it upstream at Mobridge, close to the northern border.

I was ready to go home.

Envoy

I was ready to go home . . .

veryone—readers and writers alike—enjoys a tidy ending, an ending that conveys a satisfying sense of conclusion and says its farewells gracefully. But the end points of travel, despite appearances (ship's hull edging away from the harbor wall, dwindling coastline, open sea), do not necessarily make for tidy endings or clear-cut finality. Coming home does not mean that you altogether leave the place you've visited, any more than you altogether left home in the first place. I have always suffered badly from jet lag on my returns from the United States, enduring a strange kind of despondency that leaves me stranded in mid-Atlantic, dispossessed of what I've left behind, but unable to reclaim what waits for me at home. But on this occasion I took steps to insure against such feelings; I was determined not to mourn the South Dakota I had just acquired.

I have already described the anxieties that plagued me on the journey about losing my hardware: passport, camera, audio recorder, wallet, binoculars, and especially my notebook. As the travel writer Bruce Chatwin once wrote, "To lose a passport was the least of one's worries: to lose a notebook was a catastrophe."[1] But I was also concerned about losing something intangible, the essence of the places I was visiting, an immanent quality that might be irretrievable. Of course, I had my notes, photographs, and recorded commentary, and I had also taken care to gather as much ephemera as I could along the way, maps, brochures, handbills, local newspapers, hotel information sheets, and even café checks. But I still feared that, despite these aides-

---

1. Bruce Chatwin, *The Songlines* (London: Cape, 1987), p. 161.

memoir, I would not be able to conjure up the unique *flavor* of the place. I was terrified of losing what I had come all that way to obtain.

On my last day in South Dakota, as I was having breakfast in the Grand Oasis restaurant in Mobridge, this fear finally overwhelmed me, and in a desperate attempt to salvage at least one moment from the trip, I wrote down in my notebook the features that seemed distinctive about the restaurant. Before my breakfast arrived—two over-easy eggs, bacon, hash browns, wheat toast, orange juice, and coffee—I had time to list the following: plastic weatherboard attached to the walls to suggest the interior of a log cabin, white Christmas lights draped and flashing over the swing door to the kitchen, pictures of pioneer life designed to imitate oil paintings, fake oil lamps hung from the ceiling on a fake wagon wheel, a sign announcing "Certified Angus Beef Brand," and next to it a picture of a steer with a caption saying "Catch of the Day," mock-leather books on a shelf, piped country music (Patsy Cline, "I Cried All the Way to the Altar"), a gumball machine at the entrance hall, a Stars and Stripes stuck in a flower planter. I also noted that, not for the first time, the baffled waitress failed to understand my English accent when I asked for water, and I had to translate my "worter" into her "watter." At the next table was an old man wearing a cap with a badge that read, "Where the Hell is Trail Town?" Looking out of the window, I could see the river on the far side of the highway, gray as aluminum in the rain, and I knew from notes made the day before that just opposite the restaurant, though now out of sight, was a butcher's store, something of a rarity and another clue that this was cattle country. It advertised itself as a "Wurst und Kase Haus," and outside the premises an illuminated sign offered its wares with these words, or what was left of them:

BUFFALO MEAT

R OAST

STEA   K

SALAM

Relieved, I ate my breakfast; the Grand Oasis would not be lost after all.

As I grow older and more time accumulates "behind" me, so to speak, and the fear of memory failure becomes ever more threatening, I try to preempt oblivion by making a record of what it seems important not to

 221

lose. For example, I keep a diary of my grandchildren's activities and utterances, without which these fleeting moments would certainly be forgotten because they are so rapidly succeeded and cancelled out by others just as poignant and absorbing.

In the same spirit, I feel a strong sympathy with small-town museums, which in their way are the notebooks and photograph albums that communities keep to remember their collective childhood. On the road, my only regret was that I found myself standing outside the locked doors of several museums, such as the one in Harrison, Nebraska, that were closed until Memorial Day. On previous trips I have been luckier with my timing and have spent many happy hours examining clusters of barbed-wire strands decoratively stapled to boards, displays of battered and rusted agricultural implements whose function was no longer discernible, and warehouses crammed with venerable tractors and trucks and automobiles. I have seen a ball of dried gumbo (mud) the size of a large watermelon reverently exhibited in its own glass cabinet, which had been presented by the owner of an oxcart that had been halted when this monster gathered round its axle.[2] With the same pleasure I've looked at countless "rooms" fitted out with the furniture, domestic equipment, ornaments, and bric-a-brac that once stood in farm houses and the homes of people living in small towns.

The antiquarian value of these collections cannot be great, and their educational value is usually dubious since they tend to be thrown together without much regard for period consistency or chronology (which is of course how most homes are furnished), and it is easy to feel that time itself has been driven mad among the dusty chapters of the town's "heritage." But there is something heroic about the modest nature of these exhibitions, because they attribute a deserved and often overlooked importance to the mundane; they acknowledge that the creation of an everyday normality by pioneering farmer families was an achievement. They are also a declaration that such triumphs should not be surrendered to oblivion. These museums are the autobiographies of small towns that may have nothing more significant to memorialize than the effort made by their forebears to establish their commu-

2. To my great annoyance, I've forgotten the location of this museum.

nity. But what better subject to honor? They are both museums and, in their small way, monuments to the perseverance of those early immigrants who survived the atrocious weather that South Dakota threw at them. (However, they should not be regarded as reliable curators of history, especially when it comes to the history of relations between homesteaders and the original residents of the land.)

This book—my homage to South Dakota—is a sort of museum for displaying my souvenirs, to which I've added a long caption. Rather like the Adams Museum in Deadwood, it contains a few freaks and items of questionable taste, and like all museums, its selection and interpretation is subject to an editorial bias, in this case an interest in the past at the expense of other topics that might have been represented. But like the small-town museums that I relish, it is also an attempt to preserve something local and personal: the essence of my particular experience of South Dakota. I have had a kind of infatuation with South Dakota, an attraction not wholly explicable but irresistible, and even as I write these final words, I feel the old enchantment tugging at me, and I begin to lay plans for my next visit.

Here at home, I was greeted on my return by my elder grandson who gleefully shouted my name and said, "We missed you!" After that I could hardly give way to jet lag or travel melancholia for very long. On my journey, I had convinced myself that I would be missing the time when my younger grandson first learned to talk, a loss that seemed a great deprivation. I needn't have worried; his vocabulary had expanded by no more than a single phrase, "Night-night," which he put to indiscriminate use. ("Would you like a biscuit?" "Night-night.") On the other hand, he had learned a new kind of laugh, not the merry, innocent laugh of babyhood, but what could only be called a mirthless chuckle, which he emitted now and again, and always at unexpected moments. Unprompted by anything noticeably funny, it seemed to rise from a deep contemplation of life's incorrigible gift for folly; a philosopher's laugh. Ha-ha!

Its salutary echo rang in my mind as I sat down to write up my travels in South Dakota, the infinite west.

Index